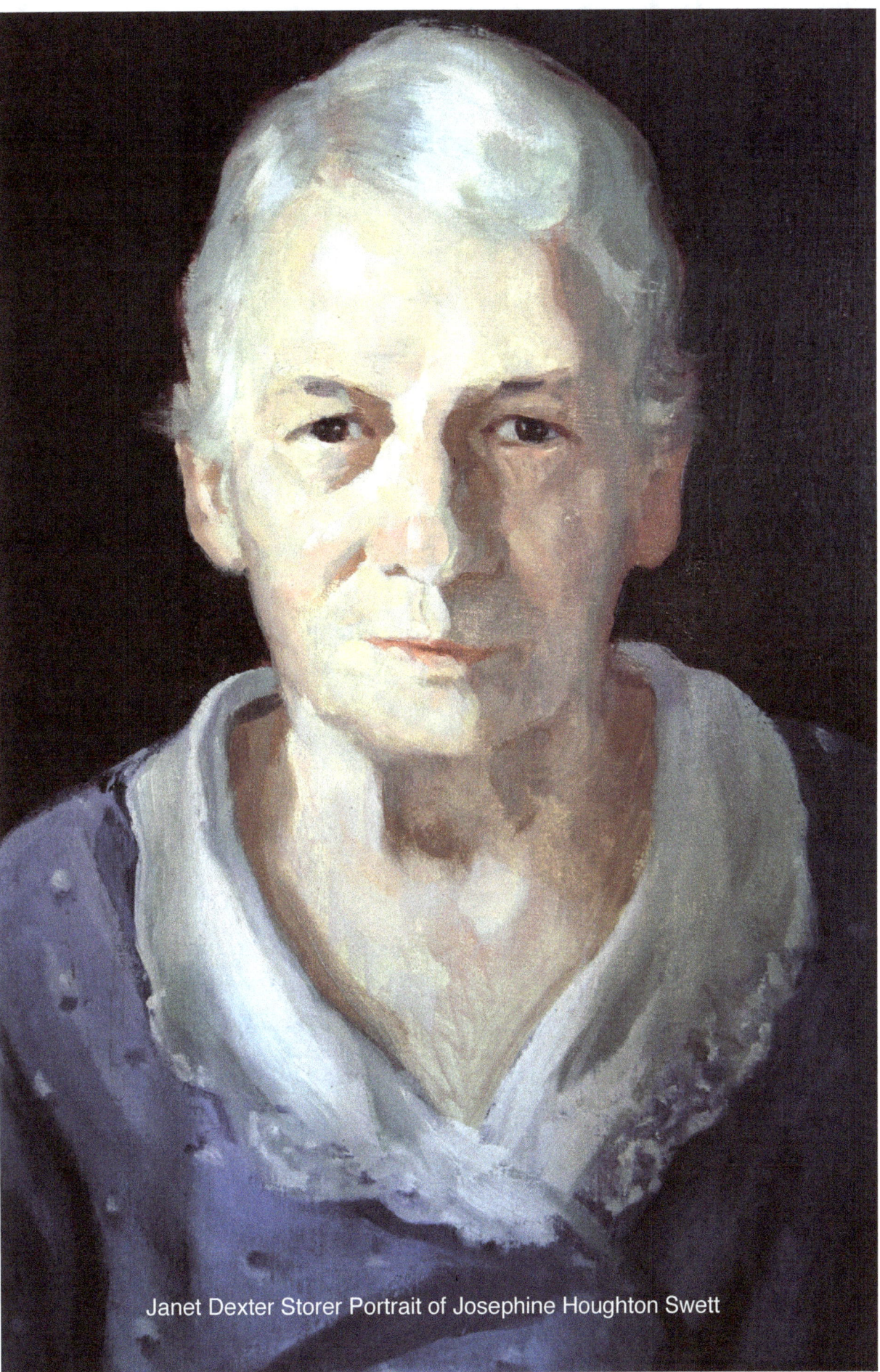

Janet Dexter Storer Portrait of Josephine Houghton Swett

Janet Dexter Storer:
The Consummate Artist
of Broadway Celebrities
and Maine's Rural Life
1895-1980

Published in the United States By Cathedral Art Gallery Records, PO Box 808, Glenwood Landing, New York, USA 11547-0808
cleasby@optonline.net or dennis@denniscleasby.com
©, 2014 Dennis Cleasby

Graphic design and photography by Dennis Cleasby. Additional Photographs: Joanie Hale, and Jim Dexter

All images reproduced with the permission of the owners. A special thanks to the Weld Historic Society, and the Storer and Dexter families for their support in this project.

To learn more about the author visit us at www.denniscleasby.com.

Authors Note: The images in the book have been altered in Photoshop to give the book consistency. Some of the paper works were yellowing due to aging and mold. The writing of the book is very personal to me because of my friendships with the Storer Family that have been ongoing for over fifteen years when I first went to Weld, Maine. I never met Janet Dexter Storer but I feel closely linked to her by these writings and due to my own background in Photographer and Fine Arts. I am eternally grateful to the people of Weld (family and friends) whom have opened their homes to me and allowed me to seek artworks and information. I am sure some parts of her life have been unintentionally omitted while parts included will have varied points of view. It is important her story and talent be shared with the world.

ISBN: 978-0-9817015-5-4

9 780981 701554   90000

FIRST EDITION
(ISBN-13: 978-0-9817015-5-4)
(ISBN-10: 0-9817015-5-8)

Library of Congress Number 2013920953

Chapter One.

The Gifted Child

When a thirteen-year-old child writes a book, it is indeed a rare and precocious undertaking. The world where the young Janet Dexter grew up was one of comfort and extraordinary wealth. Her main character is a wealthy man's daughter, living in that rarefied air of robber barons around the turn of the century. Her heroine eventually shuns class privilege and luxury for true love, and perhaps a premonition of her own life to be. This tiny tome of a mini-morality tale of wealth and life in the America of that era is an extraordinary work to be have been written by a mere child. It is set in yet another time like our own, which exhibits extreme discrepancies in the distribution of wealth and class near the beginning of a brand new era of upheaval.

We know nothing of her early life except for the two, almost prophetic to her latter years, handwritten and self-illustrated books she wrote in a lined notebook. A gifted child who must have stood out among her peers, she was evidently quite sensitive, and displays emotions and awareness to visual detail of the much more mature. This precocious awareness is exquisitely expressed in the small illustrations that fill the borders and pages of her book. For her age she wrote superbly and rendered figures and small faces of the characters with the detail, dexterity and maturity of someone much older. Here in its entirety is the first book a

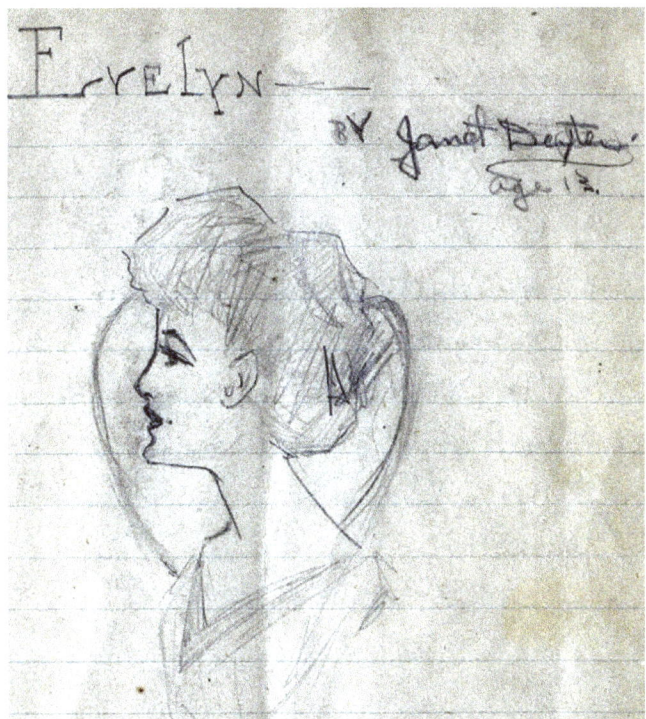

Title Page: Evelyn by Janet Dexter, Age 13

very young Janet Dexter wrote and illustrated.

Janet Dexter was born in Brookline, Massachusetts on June fourth in 1895. At age thirteen she wrote and illustrated the follow novelette; Evelyn.

Evelyn

Written in 1908 by Janet Dexter

Dedicated to Ruth Drew

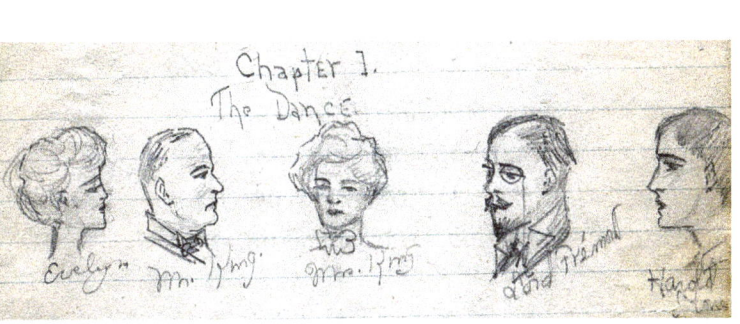

Evelyn

Chapter One:

The Dance

"Evelyn!"

"Yes mother", called the girl from her room.

"Are you dressing for the dance, dear?"

"Yes mother, the best I can. These hooks are almost impossible."

"Oh, I'll call Kate to help you."

"Poor Kate", whispered Evelyn to herself.

"She is always working" I could do it myself nearly as well.

She lay down on the couch to wait for the girl fairly out of breath from fastening her gown.

At last Kate came. She was very modest and seldom spoke unless she was spoken to. The King's owned eight servants. Kate was Evelyn's maid. Mary, Mrs. Kings'. There was also Maggie, the cook, Sara, the second girl, Mareia the laundress. Michael the coachman, John, the chauffeur, Harold, the stableboy.

Harold was at that moment clearing chairs away from the hall and parlor to make room for dancing. He was allowed to do that because the other servants were all very busy and the work could be dome more easily by a man.

At last the gown was all hooked and Evelyn went down stairs to play the piano. She played very daintily with her pink and white fingers, all the newest songs. She also sang and her voice was sweet and low. She had just finished singing, "Love me and the world is mine", when she thought she heard a noise behind her and turning around she beheld Harold looking at her. He had hold of a chair and had stopped to listen. She had not known he was there, and as she looked into his eyes he turned scarlet. "Pardon me", he stammered. "But I – I couldn't help it." Then he took the chair and went into the next room. She watched him until he was out of sight and then took a novel and went to the other end of the room to read.

Before long she heard the door open and in came her father. She ran and throwing her arms around his neck, kissed him. "Oh father isn't really exciting I am really having a dance", she said joyfully. "Why Evelyn you certainly have had enough parties to know that they are not much." "Oh but they are." They're awfully exciting," she said sitting down and placing a chair for her father.

"Evelyn", said her father when seated, "Lord Fremont is stopping in town now." He is a very wealthy young nobleman in England whom I met on my last trip. He is going to stay a while so I told him to come tonight."

Evelyn was silent and in a few minutes Sara came in and announced dinner. After dinner they sat around until "The" guests began to come. Last of all to come in was Lord Fremont. He had a small black "goatee", a very weak face, and was dressed in a grand dress-suit. Mr. King hurried up to him and greeted him with much ceremony. Then he introduced him to his daughter. He had the first dance with her and two more later. They dance until one in the morning and then the quests began making their "adieux".

When they were all gone Evelyn went to her room and no sooner had her head touched the pillow that she was asleep.

Lord Fremont went home to the city and made up his mind that he would try to get her and her money before he went back to England. As for Evelyn she hated him at first sight.

Chapter Two: In the Stable

When Mr. King came home the next evening he talked with his wife a while and then he called Evelyn and no one seemed to know where she was. While he was hunting for, she was in the stable on the hay. She was

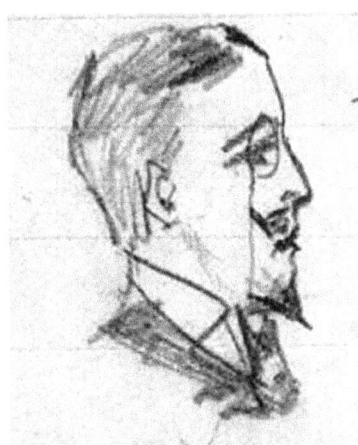

singing all the old and new songs she could remember.

And while she was there Harold came in. He listening and she sang on regardless of his presence. After a while she spoke to him. "Harold", she said "will you come

Lord Fremont

up here with me, I-I should like to talk to you". In a moment he was sitting by her side.

"Ms. Evelyn", he said softly, "you sing better than anyone I ever heard. When you sang yesterday I-I thought I was dreaming it was so beautiful. I longed to hear more now and now you have given me what I wished. You have no idea how I love it."

"Harold. You must remember that you are a servant. You must not talk that way", she said.

"Miss Evelyn" he cried, "You do not know who I am. Let me tell you about myself".

"Tell me! Tell me your whole life," she cried eagerly.

"When I was a young boy," he began, "I lived in England. I was very rich my father was a Lord of England. Lord Clinton. He had an enemy named Lord Fremont and when I was fourteen years old this Lord Fremont came to our house with many friends of his and after killing my father and mother, burned our mansion and I was left to starve in the streets of England. II got passage on a steamer crossing the ocean and changed my name. Here I am a servant with no friends and no money".

"Harold", said Evelyn after she had fully recovered from the shock, "I am your friend if no one else is. Forgive me for saying that you had no right to talk so to me, for you have".

"Then I will tell you this, Evelyn", he said gently his voice trembling, "I love you. I shall always love you. Even if you marry some rich young man I shall love you and dream of you even as I do now."

He took her in his arms and she rested her head upon his shoulder.

"Oh, Harold what would father say", she whispered, "What would he say if he ever knew how-how I love you."

He kissed her tenderly upon her smooth forehead and neither spoke for some time.

At last Evelyn lifted her head and whispered, "I hear my father coming. Good bye Harold". She climbed down the ladder and he followed her.

Then she went out of the stable and walked swiftly towards the house.

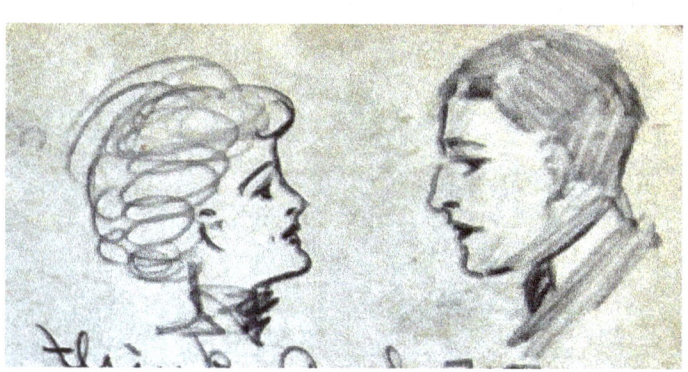

Chapter Three:

Concerning Lord Fremont

Evelyn ran to the garden and was busily picking roses when her father found her. "Evelyn", he said when he reached her, "You are getting old enough to get married and I should like to have you before long. I

have a friend who has asked me for your hand and I told him you would certainly accept such an honorable husband. He is Lord Fremont. He would add a few millions to yours. "

"Ok father", cried Evelyn angrily, "All you ever think of is money which I don't care about, and besides I would not marry Lord Fremont, money or not".

"Why? What objection do you have".

"I have heard this of Lord Fremont, and I believe it", she said sharply, "He has killed a Lord and Lady of England, and burned their mansion. They were innocent I am sure, and he was wicked".

"I was told this by a person I trust and believe".

"I do not believe any such talk", she thundered, "And I will tell Lord Fremont that he may have what he asks for so prepare for a wedding with him, and the sooner the better." He stamped off to the billiard room and Evelyn ran upstairs and flung herself upon the bed.

Chapter Four: The Plan

The days went on slowly and sadly for broken hearted Evelyn. For a week it rained unceasingly- Then at last the sun shone gloriously through the dull gray clouds and the sky regained its tints of azure blue. Evelyn sallied forth one bright morning out to her father's grapevine to sit and embroider.

She heard a rustling in back her and presently from an opening in the vine appeared Harold with a basket in his hand.

She sprang up and fluttered into his encircling grasp. "Oh my dear love I have bad news to tell you," she sobbed.

"What is it dear?" Then she related the decision of her father and how she had attempted to make him understand how wicked Lord Fremont really was but could not.

"What shall we do about it, sweetheart", he murmured fondly.

Her brow clouded and she thought deeply for a few moments. Then she suddenly broke the prolonged silence.

"Oh Harold! Let's elope" she cried. "Alright dearest, when shall we do it?" "Tomorrow", she replied excitedly. "It will be the best thing to do I guess. I will have the horses ready early." "Yes, have then ready at half past four tomorrow morning. Good bye dear."

Chapter Five: O'er hill and dale

The clock struck half past four. Evelyn jumped from bed, slipped on her riding habit, took the bundle and money she had made ready the night before and tiptoed down into the great hall. There she hurriedly wrote as follow: "Good bye, Father. Remember Lord Fremont" Evelyn.

Then she silently closed the door behind her and ran swiftly to the stable where Harold was waiting for her. He had the horses harnessed up. He then bound her bundle to the horses back and they mounted.

Out of the stable door and out across the fields they rode swiftly jumping brooks and fences. Evelyn was an excellent rider and so they got along very well.

"Oh, Harold", Evelyn cried as she looked over the road, "There's our automobile coming". "It can't get over the fence here, so we needn't worry. If we go fast enough", he said smiling. At that moment the automobile crammed up against the fence. He could see Mr. King banging his fist on the side and knew he was mad." Evelyn laughed musically. "And they can't use a carriage because we have both horses", she said.

On they went faster and faster until the town was out of sight.

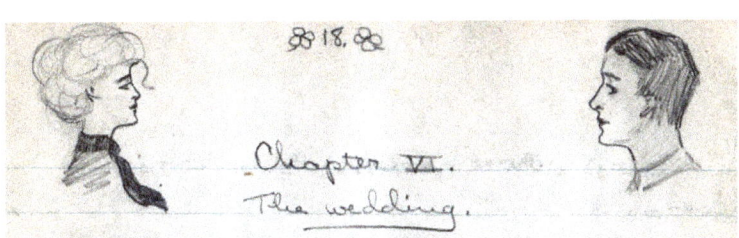

Chapter Six: The Wedding

After a long time they came to a sign saying Weldfield 12 miles.

"Lets go there," said Evelyn. "Alright it isn't far and some farmers will probably give us lodging." "Let's get off and rest now," said Harold jumping from his saddle and helping Evelyn to dismount. They had some lunch which Evelyn had secured and they shared it between them. They rested peacefully for a while and then started off again.

About three o'clock they came to Weldfield. They saw a farmhouse and rode to it. After dismounting they walked together to the front door and knocked. A middle aged woman came to the door and asked what they wanted. They asked her if she wanted a man to tend the horses. She said she would like it but couldn't pay him. "Oh he doesn't want any money. And I will milk the cows Evelyn cried joyfully. And so they went into the house and put their luggage in their room.

The next morning they told the woman that wanted to get married and she said her husband was the town minister. When he came home late in the afternoon he married them. Evelyn put on a little lawn dress she had brought and she had flowers in her hair.

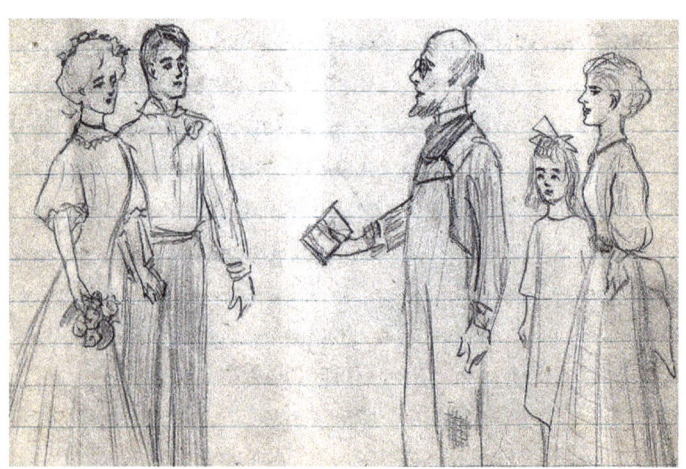

Chapter Seven: Harold Stone Jr.

Three years passed. Harold and Evelyn were living in a little house in Weldfield.

"Mama!" Called a little voice. "Yes deary", answered Evelyn.

"I wants a cracker", said little Harold Jr. toddling into his room. "Oh you little precious, come here and kiss me", she said holding out her arms. "Nice 'ittle mama he cried as he hugged Evelyn as hard as he could.

"Come, lovely, and go out to walk with Mama", said Mrs. Stone. They went out in the fields and found Mr. Stone haying. Little Harry jumped into a mound an got a ride home on a load. Then came the best fun.

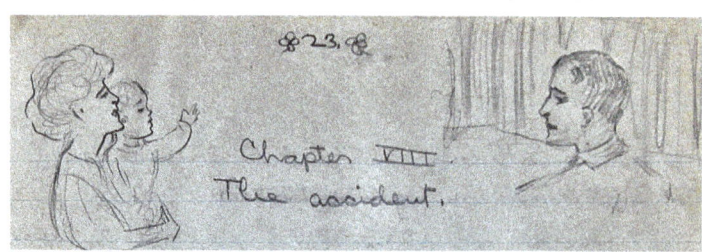

Baby had his bath in the big wash tub.

Chapter Eight: The Accident

It was late in the afternoon. Harold was lumbering. He was just cutting the last tree before going home when his axe slipped and struck him in the knee. He fell to the ground and lay there unconscious.

Meanwhile his wife was putting Harry to be and worrying about him. It came supper time but she left the meal untouched. After a while her anxiety grew so intense that she went over to a friend's house and asked the farmer if he would drive her over to the woods where Harold had gone. He harnessed up the horses and they started out. The farmer's wife took care of the baby. The cold moon shone clearly in the sky. The night air was brisk but Evelyn did not feel the cold. She thought of nothing but Harold- her Harold; what could have become of him. This ran through her mind unceasingly.

At last they reached the place where he had been working. In the bright moon light Evelyn saw the body of a man stretched out on the grass. With a shriek, she ran, knelt down throwing her arms about his neck, drew his head to her lap and cried brokenly, "Harold, oh my beloved." The farmer ran up and together they managed to lift him into the wagon. Late in the night they reached the village.

It was not until morning that Harold recovered. When he opened his eyes he found Evelyn kneeling by the bedside. The village doctor had bandaged his knee. Little Harry was crying for his breakfast but Evelyn was so busy soothing her husband that she didn't have time.

"Evelyn, don't bother about me. I'm alright, the doctor will tend to me dear.", said Harold weakly. Go and give baby his breakfast." By and bye the doctor came down stairs and told Evelyn that it was not so serious as he had thought and Harold would be able to walk in about a week.

Chapter Nine: Matters at the Mansion.

Meanwhile at the mansion there had been trouble. Mr. King and his wife sat one evening talking it over. "Ah, it's all terrible," sighed Mrs. King. "I always thought he was a wicked man and in no way worthy of- of Evelyn." "Oh yes, yes I should have guessed it. I looked over the house and found that he had taken a lot of silver and cut glass besides a lot of jewels. Oh I should have guessed that he meant to ruin me. Evelyn told me, and I wouldn't believe her. Look, dear." He handed her Evelyn's note saying, Good bye father. Remember Lord Fremont. Evelyn. Albert said his wife brokenly," I think we should try to find our daughter and forgive her." "She must forgive me murmured Mr. King resting his

head in his hands. "It was all because of me, my selfishness and love of money".

His wife knelt down and threw her arms around his neck. "Dearest, she whispered, "I will write to different towns around here and try to find out where she is." No my dear, it is my duty to write to her. When she went she was going toward Weldfield. I will write to there and they may forward it if she has gone anywhere else." "Alright. Good night. She went slowly upstairs to bed.

Chapter Ten: Correspondence

"Dearie." "Yes.", said Harold limping to the front door to let in his wife. "I've just been to the village and Uncle Josh in the post office gave me this letter. It's from home and its fathers writing. I haven't opened it yet but I will now."

She opened it and read as follows. Dear Evelyn, You were right in telling me about Lord Fremont. He did steal from us many valuable things. I am sorry I have been so selfish and ask you to forgive and forget. Come home and bring your husband. We will welcome you both heartily. With Much Love, Your Father.

"Oh Harold! Just think. And your knee will get well so much faster and Harry will surprise them so.", she cried running to him and giving him the letter. "It will be fine, dearie", he said happily. "I'm going to write them a letter Harold, and tell them we will come on Wednesday."

So Evelyn went to the table and wrote to her parents. "Dear Mama and Papa," she began, "We'll come Wednesday on the three o'clock train. For certain reasons we can't ride the horses home but we'll have them sent. We have a surprise too. With great love, Evelyn."

Chapter Eleven: "There's no place like home."

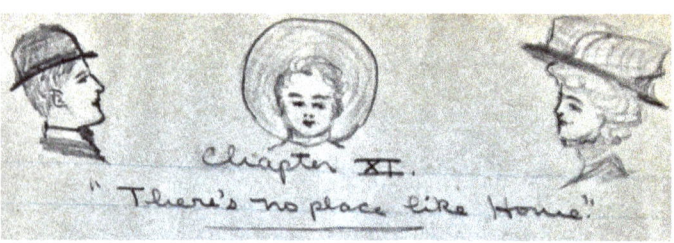

They were all ready and Mr. Stone picked up the dress-suit case and they went to the little station. In a few minutes the train came. They all got in and it started toward home. "O-o see de smoke mama", cried Harry at the top of his lungs.

By and bye the conductor shouted out the name Evelyn had heard so many times. They all descended from the platform and found John waiting for them with the automobile. "I'm glad to see you back Miss- Mrs. Ahem. Well my land whose baby have you got there?", he said. "Ha-ha, why this is Harold Junior, John", laughed Evelyn.

They all got into the automobile and rode swiftly through the well known streets. At last the house came into view. It thrilled Evelyn's heart as she saw her parents on the piazza.

As soon as John had opened the automobile door Evelyn had put Harry on his feet and was in her mother's arms. Harold and Mr. King were shaking hands heartily when Harry came up to Mr. King and said,

"Is- o my gwampa?" And Mr. King simply got on his knees and hugged him saying, "Yes little boy, and I didn't even know I had you." Then Harry was kissed over and over by Mrs. King and all was made happy again.

The End.

Any child of thirteen has their fair share of fantasies and dreams. The town of Weldfield could have been a reference to Weld, Maine where Janet Dexter's family kept a summer cottage on Lake Webb. Her father was a wealthy businessman successful enough to own a property in Maine, a property that was kept in the family for many years. These summer retreats were the

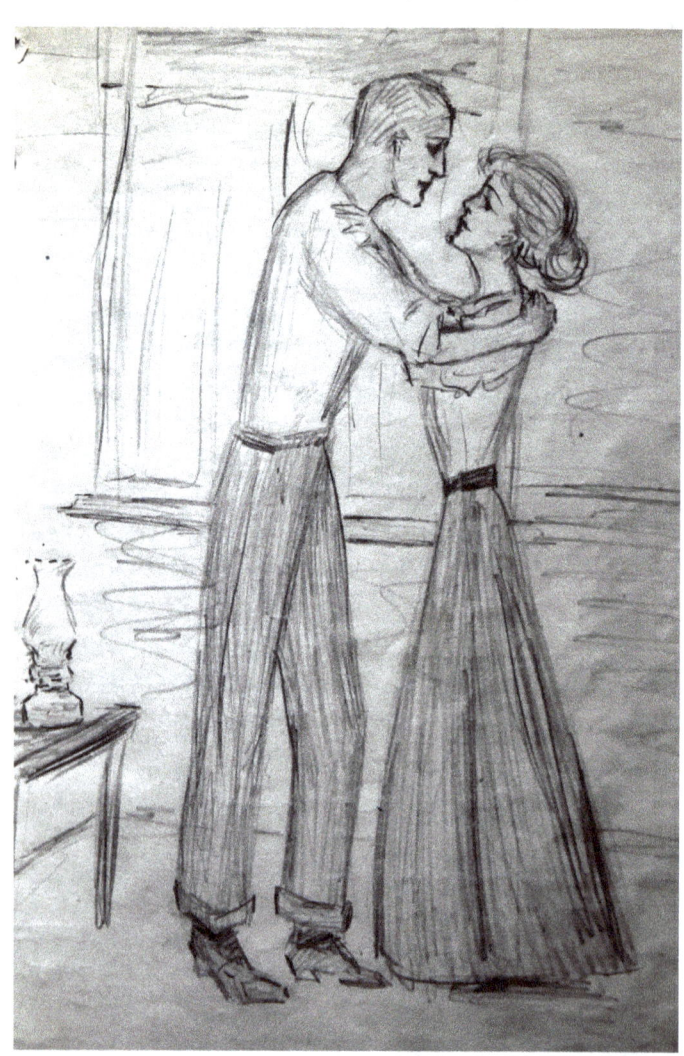

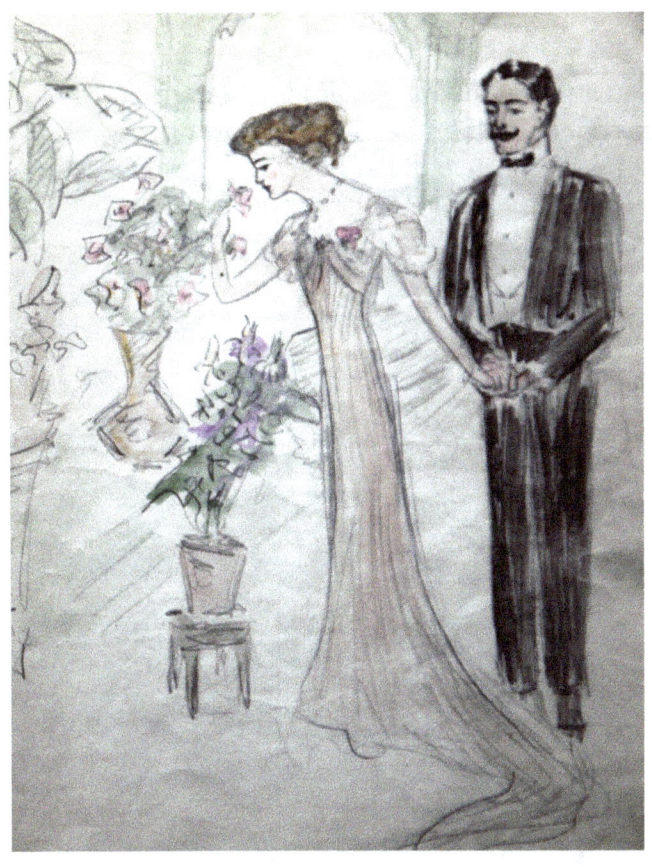

beginnings of a long lasting love for the country life and rural America which became a passion of Janet Dexter. Her work ethic and awareness of the potential corrupting evil of too much money are readily apparent even in her adolescent writing. The romantic tone of the story and recognition of the simple and pure qualities of rural living is a characteristic of many artistic and literature movements throughout history. It is also a romantic point of view of someone whose own wealth is used to nurture and advocate for those that are less fortunate, and most importantly an acknowledgment of one's own good fortune. This is not an arrogant child, but a compassionate and unreasonably mature youngster, willing and happy to care for those less fortunate. The youthful spirit of rebellion for a higher cause is present in this extremely talented child, something she exhibited in the way she lived throughout her life.

Janet's grandfather, George S. Dexter, was said to have amassed millions of dollars in New England in the paint industry. Janet's father, Wallace D. Dexter, unlike his brothers who lived off their inheritances, worked and created a real estate business. Janet was raised in the rarefied, 1% America of stately mansions, many servants, and privileged class like the characters of her novelette.

Years later the mature Janet Dexter would move to Weld, Maine and open a painting studio. Her connection to the dignity of physical labor and those who worked the land is fostered in her early life and writing. The refined drawings of this thirteen year old shows astounding detail. Body proportions, character, body language, facial expressions and consistency of line all add up to an excellent and precise execution of subject matter, a skill not yet fully released which later led her to a career as a portrait artist. The accuracy of her line in such tiny details, where no eraser marks show, where a refined sketch is expert enough to capture facial expression, and clothing details, all appear to be beyond comprehension to our contemporary way of expressing life. Years later she taught her step-grandchildren to "never erase but draw over what you have already done". This learned technique was to stay with her all her life. How could this child of thirteen be so talented?

There are no written records of Janet Dexter's personality. She is said to have a peaceful loving demeanor towards all. We have what family members recall of her mature years, and with some subtle speculation we can imagine an articulate youngster, well educated, experienced in the lifestyle of the wealthy, with a healthy imagination. We know she had been raised upper class from the size of the family home that still stands in Brookline, Massachusetts.

The characters in the novelette are obvious upper class and feed right into the dreams of a young girl finding her way through puberty with the handsome Harold and sinister Lord Fremont. We might speculate a model child that is shy and stays in her room and spends hours writing fictional tales of wealthy male suitors. A lonely wealthy child may find comfort in spending hours by herself writing, drawing and passing the time. Her world of creative isolation was the fertile soil of a future artist willing to spend time in her studio alone.

We know that Janet's mother was stern and said to have less than a warm personality. The product of such a personality type may have been very common for the beginning of the nineteenth century. Life in America produced wealth but that wealth was well protected and guarded, thus a guarded and "proper" personality in Janet's mother. The child of a strict parent may have been rebellious enough to be attracted to a male dominated profession and willing to cast her role as an artist in a time woman were expected to stay in the kitchen and feed babies. Yet the simplicity of her story line and impeccable handwriting and grammar in her novelette suggests some kind of adult supervision. We know that Janet Dexter was close to her mother all her life and lived near her until she died. This closeness found root in the creative output of a young gifted child that later established herself as a successful portrait artist, married three times, traveled to Europe, and studies art in Paris, France at the age of thirty-four.

Throughout her life she continued the highly creative example in these early writings by sending letters to family and friends with illustrations of where she were living and what she was doing. In small, neat hand written letters she illustrated her life with her favorite dog- a beloved Border Collie she

called Stripper. The drawings in her letters were not that different from the drawings of first novelette. Two of her novelettes have survived and have been handed down to family members.

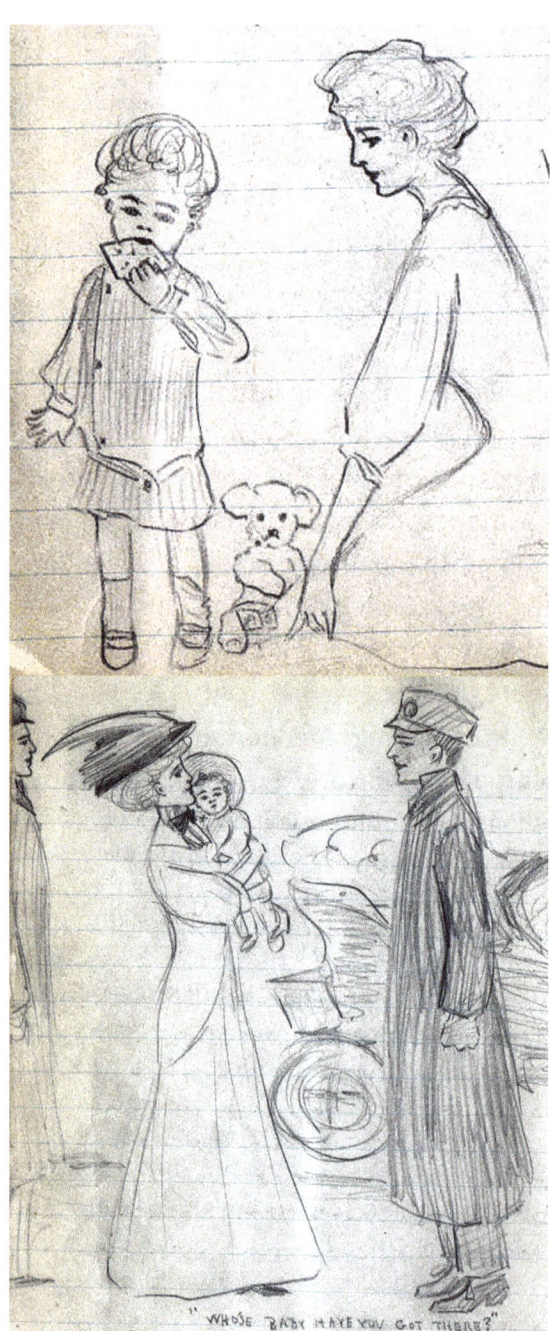

"WHOSE BABY HAVE YOU GOT THERE?"

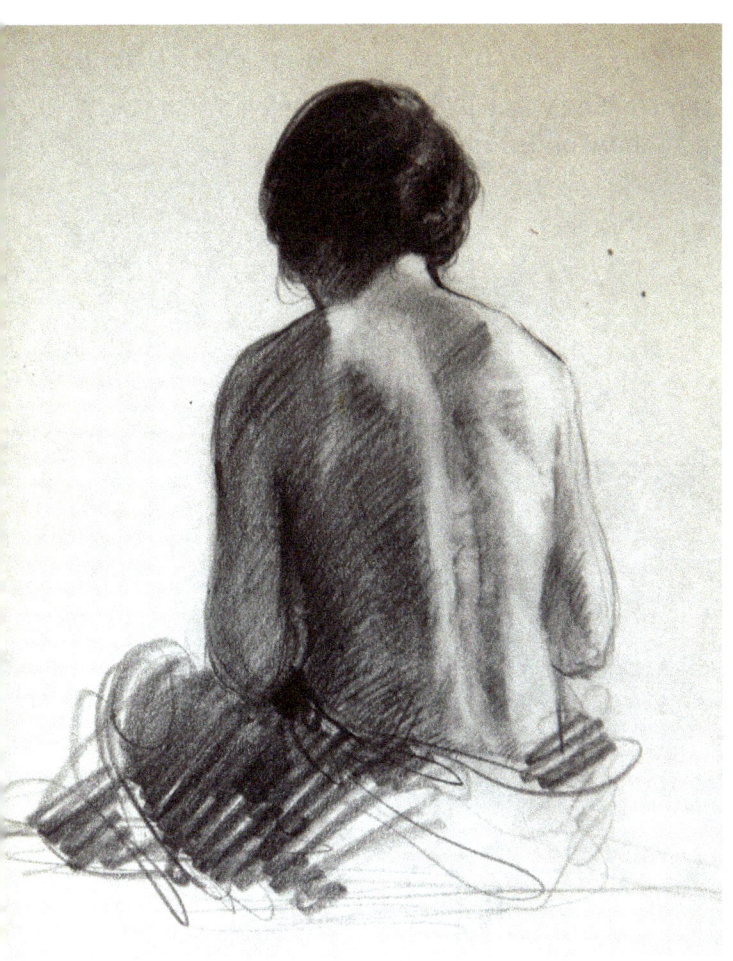

Chapter Two
The Middle Years

We know Janet Dexter was a burgeoning writer and illustrator and at an early age had her sights set beyond the walls of her parent's house in Brookline, Massachusetts. The political climate of the United States at the time was ripe for new ideas. Communism and Socialism were in their infancy. Janet Dexter was surely influenced by the new politics of idealism. Like her first novelette, we know her first husband was a communist and she married him partially out of rebelliousness towards her parents and their social class. Her parents strongly disapproved of this first union. This marriage ended in a divorce. Her second husband died and she was widowed in her late twenties.

Her talent did not go unrecognized and she took on formal art training at the Art Students League in New York City. Janet entered instruction at the early age of nineteen. This in turn led to the exposure she needed to land a prestigious job as a portrait artist for the New York Times and the Boston Globe. Her assignments were to visit the actors backstage and do quick sketches. These drawings were used in the newspapers to illustrate the characters of Broadway and Boston stars of the stage. This gave her the rare advantage of meeting many of the stars of the day and also helped established her as a sought after portrait artist. She too became a star among the young artists of her day. Her teacher was the Russian emigre Dimitri Romanovsky (1887-1971); an academic-realist. Some of these sketches were drawn from photographs, but most of them were drawn within a ten minute period while back stage at the most popular theaters of the time. This body of work is the most concentrated accumulation of her artistic talent. The majority of these sketches remained intact because she never sold them and kept them in her private collection. It wasn't until after her death that these works were donated to the Weld Historical Society of Maine, thus a practically full collection of works from that period of her life exists. Few if any of these works have been lost from this collection, thus in many ways these works are a better collective representation of her work than later illustrations which were sold.

Instead of following the expected path of raising a family and settling down, she was a rebel before her time and established a career in art that gave her independence and financial stability that lasted the rest of her life. We know little of her second husband, only that he died and she was again single at the age of thirty. It is understandable that after her husband expired she turned her attention inward and found comfort in creating art and traveling abroad. Losing her husband remained a strong reason for this free spirit to travel the world and seek intellectual pursuits. America at the time was in its own social upheavals. Unions were beginning to take hold. Communism was considered a new and different point of view rather than a failed system of government. The country was ripe for a social movement that included many people who were discontented with, and disenfranchised from, the power of the wealthy few.

Comparatively, the American Artist Thomas Eakins comes to mind, his realistic-academic style, is a similar style Janet Dexter expressed in her sketches. She was part of an American School of Art that drew it's inspiration from Classical Greek Art, with a primary purpose of duplicating realism, making the human form as real as possible, to seek the natural states of the human body. Janet Dexter was willing to travel the globe as a young, single female. She was willing to put herself into an art school and study when males

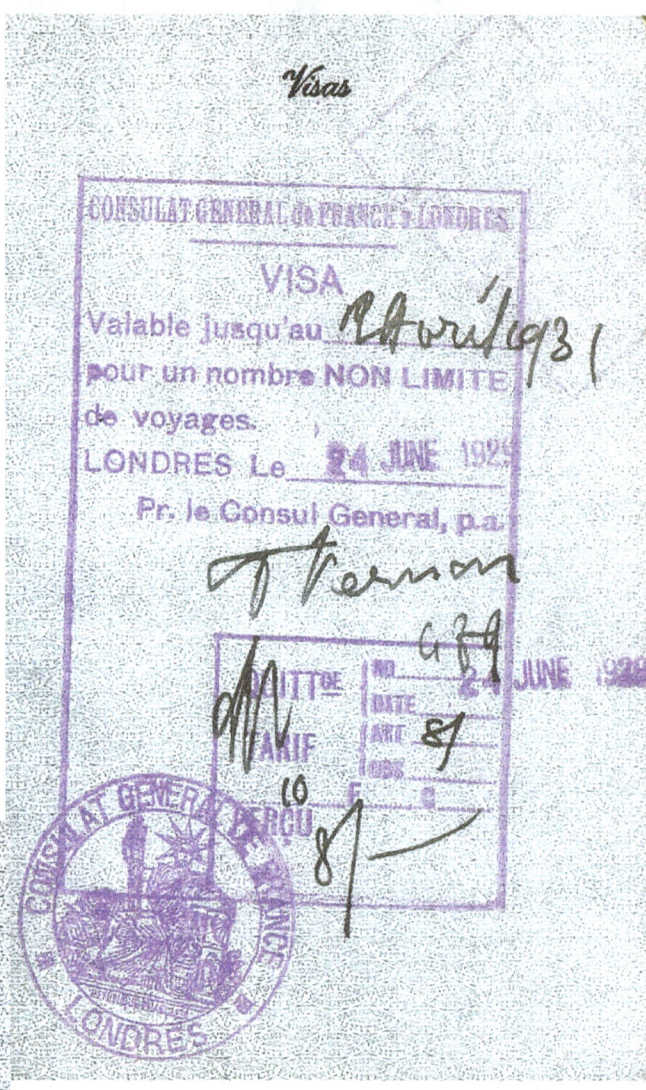

predominated. A young woman virtually alone in the sea of a male dominated art world. She was a rare and brave soul who was not afraid to lead and not merely follow.

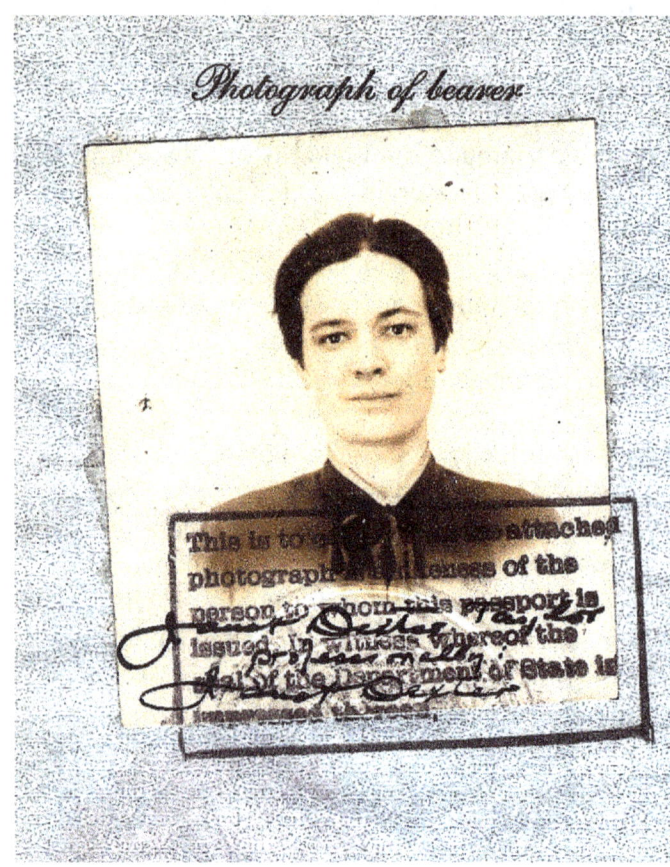

One of her Step-grandchildren recalls her telling stories of those years where she bicycled through England before moving to the lights of Paris. What her exact travel route was we do not know, but what begins to emerge is a personality of independence and self-direction that was influenced by the Suffrage Movement where equal voting rights begin to lead women towards an early form of feminism. A young woman bicycling alone though parts of Europe is likely to be paying more attention to the beauty of nature and evolving an awareness of the human form. She would not then be the dissident, deconstructive approach to creating art by fragmenting reality, like the Cubist, for example, but the more traditional approach of classical studies. She was undoubtedly exposed to modern trends in art through her travels, but she personally favors and develops a talent in drawing the human form realistically. She is closer to Neoclassical Art, more inclined to draw like Louis David than explore line and abstraction of the human form like Picasso.

Consider her family background in the more conservative, wealthy, traditional life, and the young woman now beginning to reject those values and become a young artist who wants to embrace Bohemian values. She expresses herself in realism, not modern trends of Europe but into the universal appeal of Classical Greek and Roman Art. But she begins to break from a traditional view of conservative life of her childhood and finds solace in the view that wealth is more powerful if evenly distributed. She becomes a Socialist. Her art reflects the importance of each individual in the family of humankind. Yet her leanings toward a political art were never expressed. Her art has no pretense of propaganda. She studies the essence of the human character and goes to the root of the human experience by delving into portraiture.

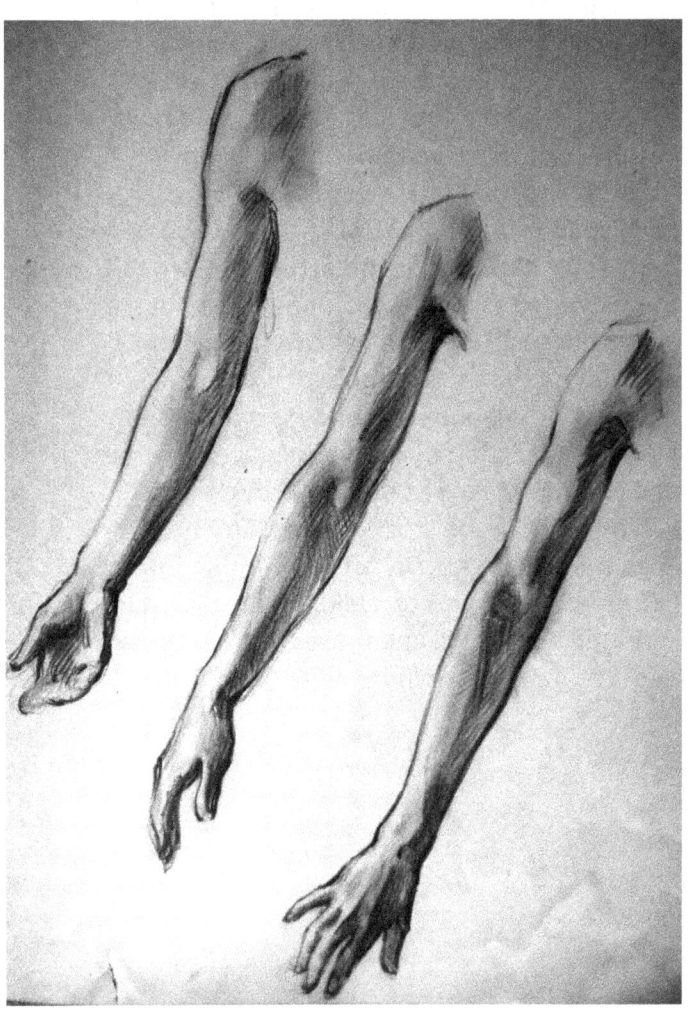

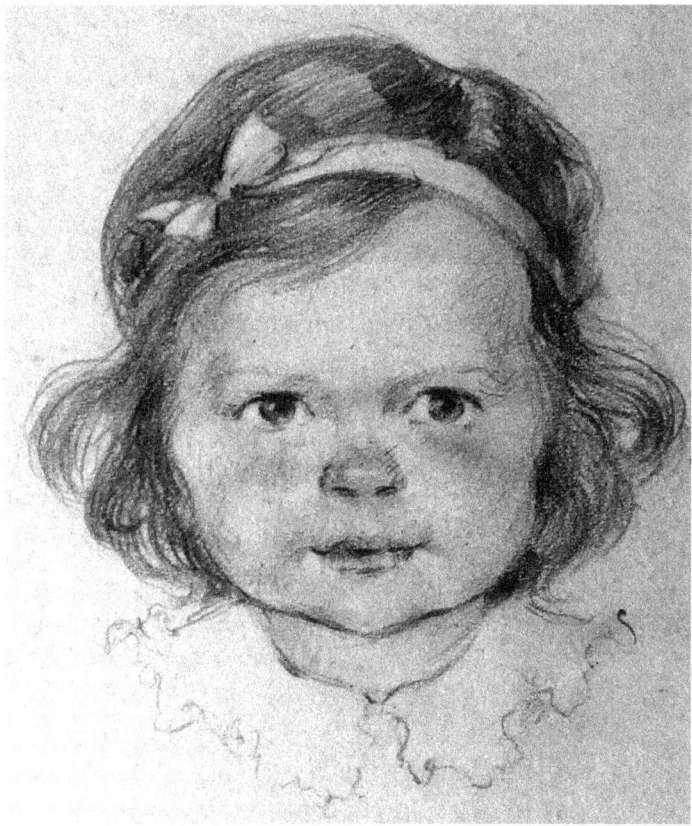

Sadie Storer circa age three.

If Janet Dexter was in Paris in 1929 it is possible to speculate she would have viewed the art works of European Modernists. By putting herself in Paris during this time she was in the epicenter of Western creativity. Paris was the cultural "center" of Western civilization in the early twentieth century while she lived there. Picasso and Matisse would have been defying the accepted traditional view of realism and performing radical departures from those that strove to capture realism in art. In this time period a fledgling artist became a traditional realist or a modernist. Jane Dexter was a Realist. She was more a kindred spirit to Winslow Homer of Maine than Pablo Picasso or Henri Matisse.

Her dedication to the land and her respect for the common laborer was a personal characteristic she held onto well into her grave. At a time she could have lived in a high social class with great comfort she chose to travel the world and seek new horizons. Yet she took advantage of her upper class status and prestige as a popular artist only in that she used her money to further educate herself, and to travel abroad. She was gifted enough to know she needed to be in the artistic center of the world. There is no record of her educators or attending a Parisian art school, but we have the fruits of those endeavors in the sketches she completed in those years and thus left behind for generations to see.

In April and May of 1929 Janet Dexter applied for visas to Ireland and England. She arrived in France on June 29, 1929 and her passport exit from France was stamped April 1931, she was thirty-four years old. For those two years she continued to form her artistic and political identity. By the age of thirty, she had married and become widowed twice, worked for major newspapers, visited Ireland and England, and lived in Paris. She was as well trained in Classical Art and the traditions of realism as she was self-trained and self-directed.

She pursued a career in realism as a portrait artist for newspapers. She lands a job doing sketch portraits of Broadway stars before the glamour of Hollywood movies, when the live stage performance was more popular than the silent movie. Newspapers were not able to use photography yet; because of technical limitations with the printing it was easier to hire a portrait artist than print a photograph. Janet had the talent and ability to capture the personalities of Broadway stars, back stage, in brief sittings. Her work was displayed in such prominent newspapers as the Boston Globe and the New York Times.

In a matter of a few years she goes from studying art to being employed by the top newspapers in the United States. She was no longer the child of a wealthy family but an independent, self-reliant artist with a bright future. But this career was short lived; with the advancement of technology in newspaper printing the portrait artist's image was soon replaced by the actual photograph. However, this job she had entered for future financial security, gave her the savings to pursue further goals in the art world and eventually expand her horizons and career. We she had a family inheritance and she was able to maintain her wealth through investment in the stock market. Around the age thirty-four, shortly after returning from Europe, she moves to Weld, Maine. She has created a nest egg and more or less retires to her country way of life.

Chapter Three
Rural Life and Happiness

In a low-light room, a middle room turned into dining area, in Weld, Maine, a painting by Janet Dexter Storer hangs on the wall. This was her last painting and one she was working on at the time of her death. I saw this painting and immediately knew it was of a high quality, something far beyond the scope of typical folk art where the skyline is below the barn above the lake, or in Maine as it is; the pond. This painting is in the house of Tim Storer, the step-grandson of Janet Dexter Storer.

Maybe in recognition of her aging the tone of this painting is several shades of grays and whites. It is obviously the farmhouse where she and Cola (her third husband) raised their children, but on another level this is a simple composition of geometric shapes. Stripped to its essence this painting is about light, how light reflects off of surfaces (the roof) and how light creates shadows in varied degrees of gray. The detail of the place is not emphasized so much as a way light constructs the composition. The brush strokes are loose and quick, which adds to the spontaneous feel of the work. The salmon colored under painting seeps through the entire background of the work giving it unity, and the salmon colored middle ground leads the viewer's eye into the gray house. The four colors of the painting (blue, green, pink, and gray) portray a sense peace. The painting evokes a still, calm, sunny day where nothing is happening but light and fresh air. The dark rock in the foreground balances the composition with the dark trees on the left and the dark barn on the right.

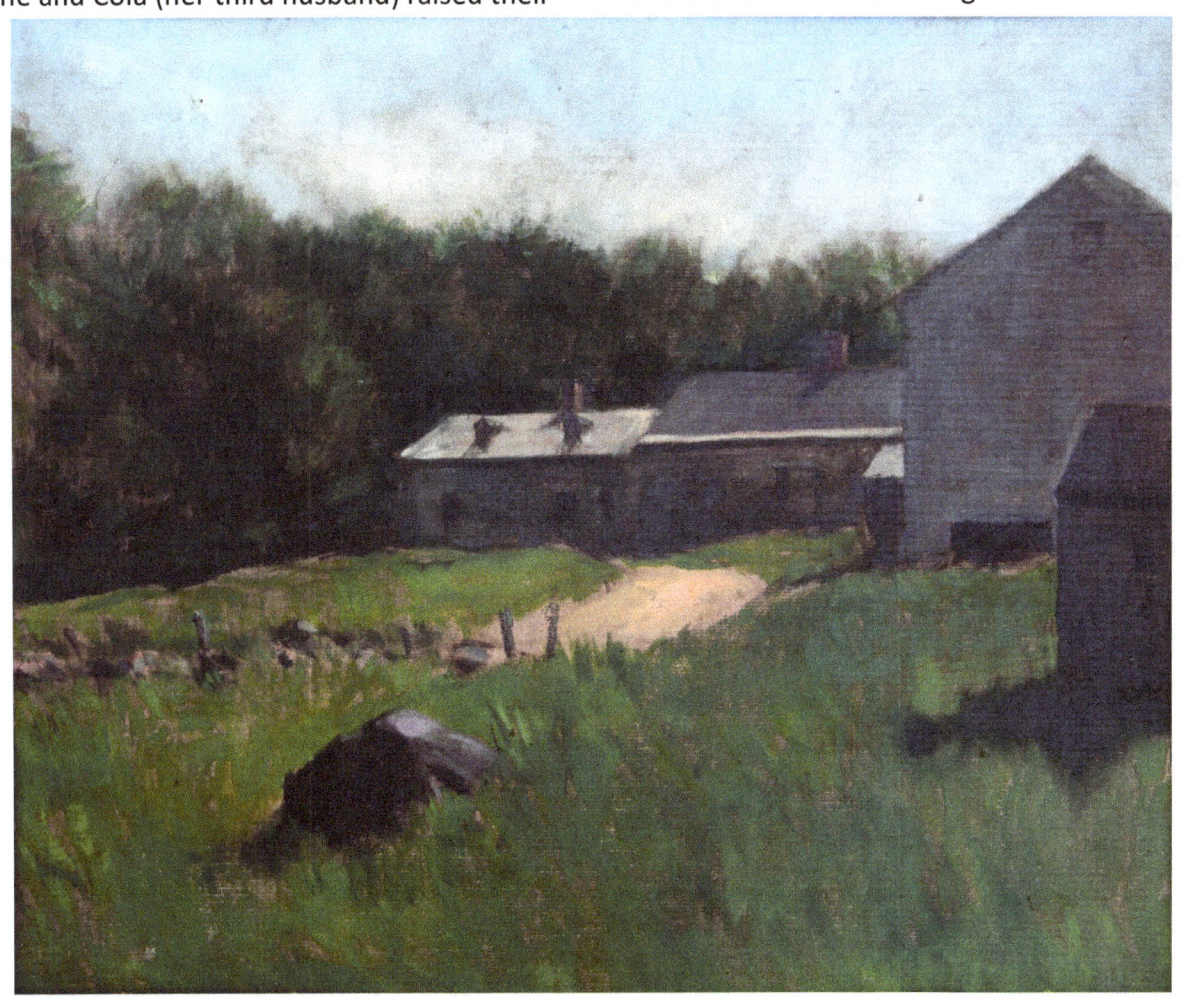

Originally Janet Dexter Storer was not a Maine resident, but a summer vacationer who stayed and took up the local farming culture. As a teenager her family summered in Maine, up from Brookline, Massachusetts. Her father was a well to do businessman that brought up a daughter to mind the profit margin and work hard at whatever she did. The daughter of a wealthy business owner, she studied Fine Art in New York and Paris, yet after moving to Maine permanently, she became the stepmother to fifteen children, and married a hard working farmer named Cola Storer. For what? For love, for love and a revolutionary spirit to get back to the land, back to basics, and back to being a part of a family. When Janet died in 1980 she had fulfilled most of her artistic and physical needs. She saw art as a gift to be shared with others as she raised the children of Cola Storer, but she never stopped creating art and integrated it into her daily life.

How the love story began no one knows for sure. Some say she approached him, other say he approached her. Some family members recall the elders meeting at a dance in town. Some relatives say that Janet first took a liking these outgoing children before she met Cola Storer.

That story goes like this: In Weld, the valley had many poor families around 1940. Janet Dexter was working as a volunteer; she distributed blankets, food, and cloths to the needy. She was of a social class that offered help to the less fortunate. Through the local school Janet was given the names of many families and became acquainted with the community much more than the typical summer vacationer. Her art had given her a quality of life whereby she wanted to return the fruits of her good bounty by helping others. She maintained a studio in Weld

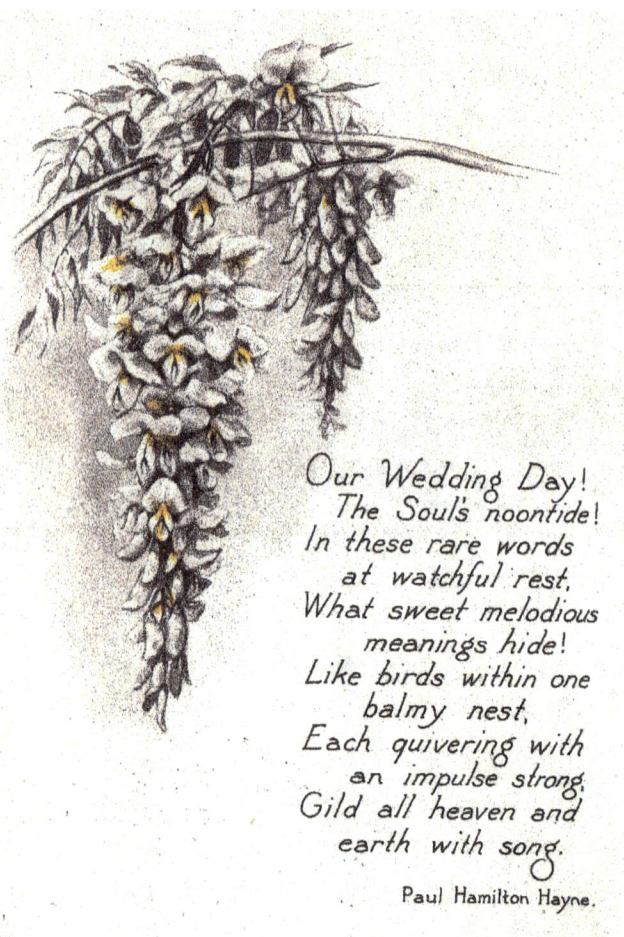

Our Wedding Day!
The Soul's noontide!
In these rare words
at watchful rest,
What sweet melodious
meanings hide!
Like birds within one
balmy nest,
Each quivering with
an impulse strong,
Gild all heaven and
earth with song.

Paul Hamilton Hayne.

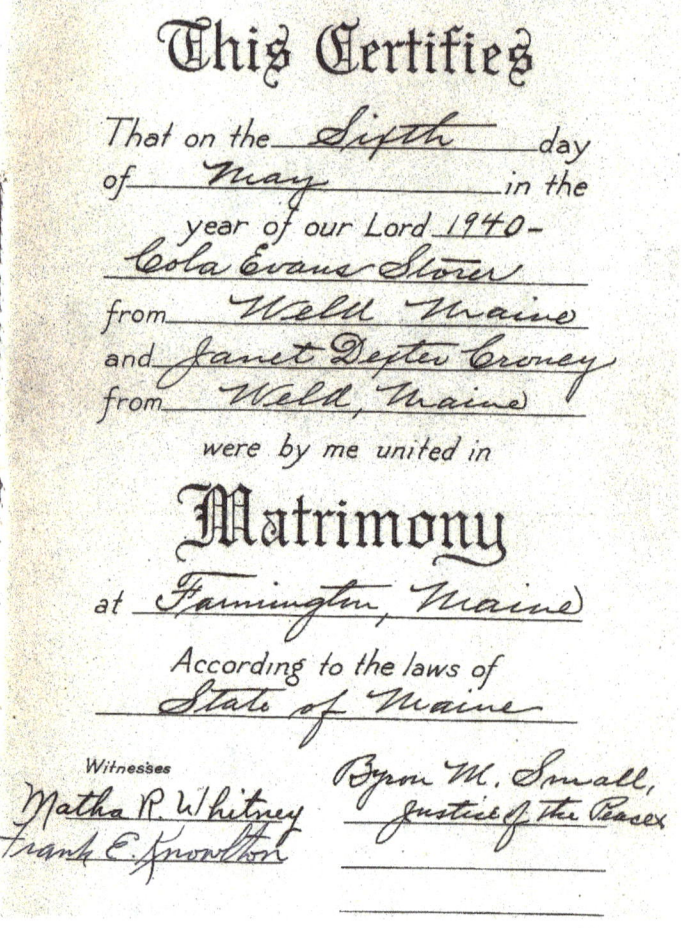

This Certifies

That on the _Sixth_ day of _May_ in the year of our Lord _1940_ _Cola Evans Storer_ from _Weld, Maine_ and _Janet Dexter Croney_ from _Weld, Maine_ were by me united in

Matrimony

at _Farmington, Maine_

According to the laws of _State of Maine_

Witnesses
Matha R. Whitney
Frank E. Knowlton

Byron M. Small,
Justice of the Peace

behind the library. Her mother and she would spend hours at the family lake house, but Janet also preferred her independence and followed her artistic muse.

The exact date Janet and Cola met is not certain, but there are stories of an acquaintance period where Janet sent home baked molasses cookies to a widower with fifteen children. Janet had asked the children what was their fathers favorite baked good, thus the molasses cookies. Some of her famous gingersnap cookies never made it home to Cola; the children had used them as skipping stones on the lakes edge. Yet another version of their meeting was that Janet's brother introduced her to Cola as he worked as a handyman on the Dexter family summer home.

Their courting period was months long. She was smitten by Cola's intellect while another local farmer, and suitor, was posing for a portrait, only to be out-maneuvered by Cola who proposed before the other man's portrait was completed. Janet had asked for complete silence while painting the suitors portrait. She knew she had two men vying for her hand in marriage and chose the least likely, a farmer with fifteen children who lived a few miles from the closest intersection called Weld, Maine.

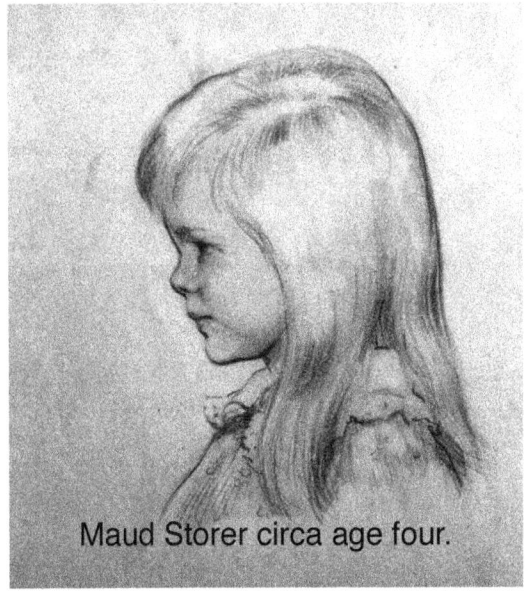

Maud Storer circa age four.

Another story is that Cola rode into town with a team of horses with all the children piled onto the hay wagon. When Janet heard his wife had died due to complications following giving birth to their sixteenth child, she must have been slightly shocked to see such a large motherless family. Yet the story goes that Cola was a handsome man, young looking and full of strength despite his loss of his first wife. Janet had already been married twice. She had been a widow for ten years when she married Cola. Living as a single woman gave her the time to be involved with philanthropic charities. She had already established her independence and full financial stability.

Yet another version is that Janet's cooking was so savory that the word soon spread throughout the neighborhood. In fact people knew Janet for her cooking even though she had once been a star artist among the lights of Broadway. She left the big city to be a farmer's wife in a home that never had electricity or running water. She was keen on investing in the stock market and watching what the most profitable investments returned, she was a worldly woman and a study in contrasts.

During their courtship Janet had a Model A Ford and would meet Cola at the river the runs into Webb Lake. Cola would ride up with his black horse and take Janet onto the horse, across the river and into his domain of farm animals and planted fields. After the marriage she was known to carry water in buckets from the river to the kitchen. She swam in that river; fed her adopted children from crops raised next to the river, where the pigs got the food scraps with love as they were fattened up for slaughter. In 1940 when Janet married Cola she was 40 years old, and she was yet to see her best days.

Prior to her life in Weld and settling down to rural living, Janet Dexter had lived in Paris, New York and Boston. In her twenties she worked in the heart of the Entertainment world doing portraits of celebrities. Before the invention of the printed photograph, newspapers hired artists' illustrators to highlight articles. Janet's job was to frequent back stage dressing rooms just quick enough to get a five minutes sketch of a star. In this fast lane life she executed over 400 published portraits in such notable newspapers as the Boston Globe and New York Times. The body of work left behind is staggering. Her command of the pencil was unique and timeless. Almost sculpting the pencil lines in such articulate swoops, quickly arriving at the essence of her characters, going far beyond the character to a deeply, stunning and realistic portrait. She drew the stars of her day straight from the subjects face, face to face. She captured facial expression in a few, brief turns of the pencil; a squall, a laugh, a sinister look, or an angelic gaze all in a holistic approach to capture reality and the human spirit. Eventually the number of requests for portraits had to be handled through photographic copies, she had skyrocketed to the top of her artistic field by the time she was thirty.

The addition of photography to newspaper publishing put an end to her narrow career path, yet well after her days of illustrating for newspapers she had people paying top dollar for sketched pencil portraits. Life in the big city lights was one thing, but not the solitude one finds in a quiet field in the pastoral summers of Maine. A woman who could have married for money chose love, a woman who had achieved fame in her own career circle found cooking to be as special as painting. A woman who had toured the Continent alone by bicycle, and studied at the prestigious Art Students League came to

settle down in the country, but never give up her lifelong interest in creating superb art. Up until her dying day she was painting and drawing. In the later years she turned more to the difficult task of working in oils and creating larger than life portraits.

While living with Cola and all the children she still maintained a studio where she painted. But at this point in her life she was happy to be cooking for fifteen children and the additional family members; the grandchildren of Cola's Storer. She spent hours entertaining the children and grandchildren and even gave drawing lessons, instructing the children by using a mirror, telling them to look at the object in the mirror, not the actual object.

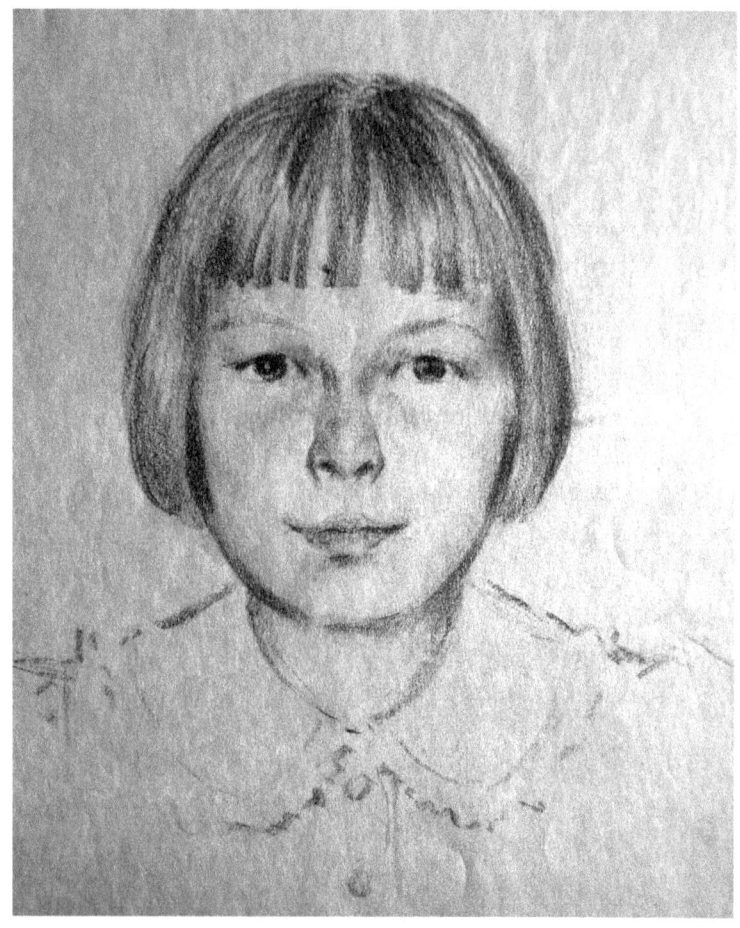

Janice Storer circa age ten.

The house had no electricity, but there was a pipe of fresh water from the creek that ran by the barn where there was a trough for watering the animals. Craps Brook was the name of the creek that fed the family farm. Eventually a continual flow of water from the brook was used to send water to the kitchen where a wood stove had a built-in hot water tank. Bathing was done in a rubber tub with the heated water for bathing. This was the only "modern appliance" this family ever used. At the height of the working season there could have been as many as thirty to forty people to be fed. The plentiful food from the farm satiated many a hungry child and worker during the long hard winters.

Work began each morning long before sunrise at three thirty. The cows had to be milked or they would moo loudly for attention. The chicken and pigs all had to be fed from the scraps of the family meal. After supper there was also more chores, the only day where leisure was permitted was Sunday, but no church on Sunday. The Storer family was not religious, no one was known to professing any specific protestant denomination. Janet Dexter was an atheist who maintained a slightly different spiritual view than her husband Cola. Her independent rebellious streak ran deep. The children had not been raised to go to church on Sundays, but ethics, honesty, and moral character were fostered in the young.

When Janet moved into the house with Cola, she was more proficient at art, piano, violin, and dance than cooking. She learned how to cook for a family of fifteen plus, people each and every day of the week. She surrounded herself with friends who played musical instruments. Janet played the piano and the violin with these local friends. There was enough time to find to play music at birthdays and gatherings. But no matter where the person was working if Janet rang

the dinner bell that meant it was time to stop working and eat supper. Janet made her specialty butter and was known for drawing a cow's head on her handsome handmade packaging. Her sweet butter was popular for local vacationers and year round residents of Maine. She would entertain the groups of grandchildren by giving finger puppet shows to the children. There was always a stash of crayons and coloring books to occupy the grandchildren. A favorite snack she would feed the children was fresh milk in 'Life' cereal. Her homemade donuts were a big hit with the grandchildren. Homemade bread was a common snack, helped with a slather of her sweet butter. The butter churn was a culinary art form for Janet. She knew the correct viscosity of the butter and the proper rhyme to pump the butter in syncopated time.

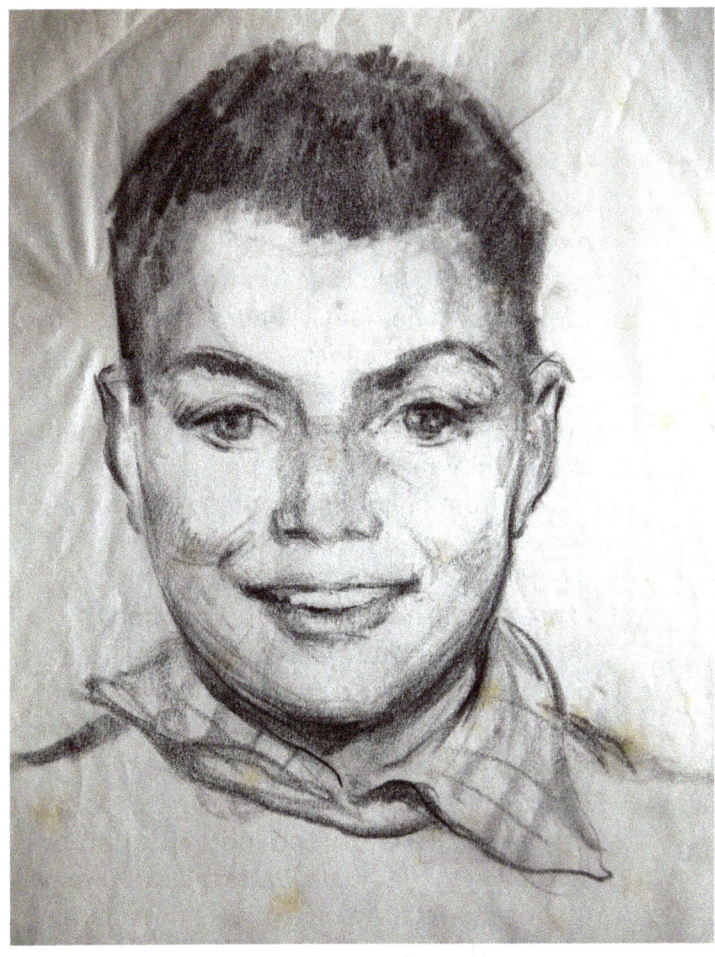

Tim Storer circa age twelve.

Imagine if you will, life on a farm before electricity. Imagine a house full of people, lots of activity, cooking, cleaning, tending to babies and teenagers, and loving every minute of your life. Her fulfillment in life was due to a chance marriage to a widower. She kept many cats and dogs on the farm as beloved pets. She stitched up the worn cloths that became hand-me-downs to the next sized child. The ideal of living close to the land, sharing in the labors of the community, building a life for yourself and your husband was parallel to her political agenda. Her socialistic bent of communal living piqued by her initial interest in the rise of Socialism, was being lived out here by this rurally communal life that her large brood and workers on the farm necessitated. She found bounty and truth in the harvest of the land; she believed she was living a wholly proper and moral life. By entering a romantic land of farmers and laborers, Janet was a part of a community. That community was built on hard labor and a sharing commitment to working the farm for the betterment of the whole family. She was not only a productive member of a community, she was it nexus. We also know that the farm was a losing business and her family inheritance was able to keep the farm afloat.

Being aware of the anti-socialism movement in the United States at the time she chose to retreat from political talk and quietly live her Socialists' dream. Her art was about the dignity of each individual, the truth that is expressed by honoring the human body through using detail and correct form. Her art portrayed the meek, the negro housekeeper, the children, the grandchildren, the musician friends, and even the neighboring game warden in a realistic style. Her subject was people and her preference portraits. Her sensitivity to the human face and capturing emotion gave all her sitters an emotional calm. In that calmness we see strength and resolve. Her subjects are not weak but sensitive self-directed people who know they are individuals living in hard times. Her subjects are not about fashion or style; her subjects are common everyday people who work hard and live in the pioneer spirit. Everyone in town and home called Janet Dexter Storer "Granny", including her portrait

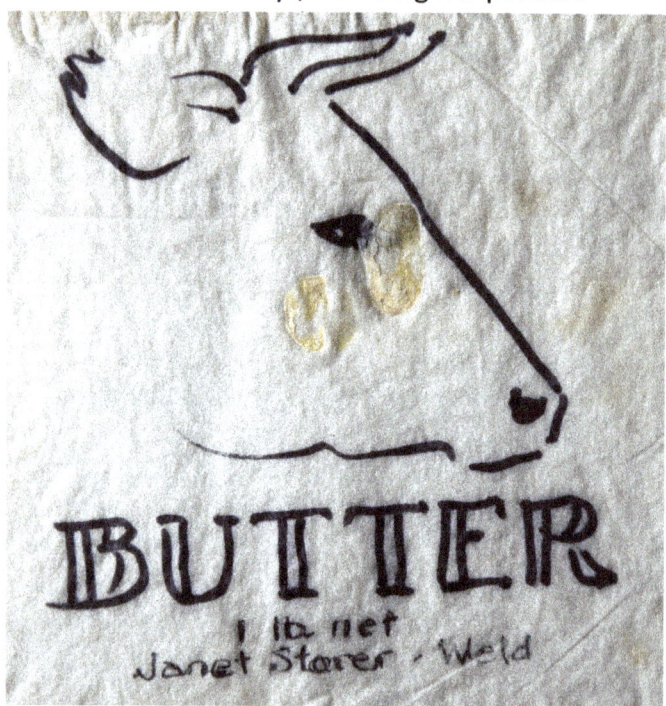

A wrapper from Janet's Home made butter.

Janet passed at the ripe old age of 86. She had outlived her husband Cola by little over one year. She was buried next to her husband in 1980. They both married at age forty and lived an additional forty plus years together. The family farm was sold when Janet died. Her art was given to interested family members and even became disputed by some, as to who should get what and where the body of her work should be located. The Weld Historic Society has the bulk of her newspaper-day sketches. Her paintings have been sold to the public or distributed to family members. The majority of her paintings from later life were sold to one anonymous individual. The findings are still taking place, or the mention of some friend or relative having a painting she did are still coming in. We are lucky to have art works found while researching this project. The exact amount out in the far reaches of Maine and other States is unknown.

Her talent led her to be self-reliant and that reliance became a useful tool to running a farm. She never regretted time not spent painting, not sitting at her easel. Her creativity continued into her sphere of domestic life, the importance of conquering

the art world at an early age was not something she needed to repeat to find happiness. Her early experiences led to new experiences with many more people and a life of loving hard work. She worked hard and had a stern personality with the acting up grandchildren. Both she and Cola had the last word around the farm and no one disputed their authority. Their marriage was that of an equal team effort. Though she died many years ago the memory of her story, talent, and strong character live on long after her passing.

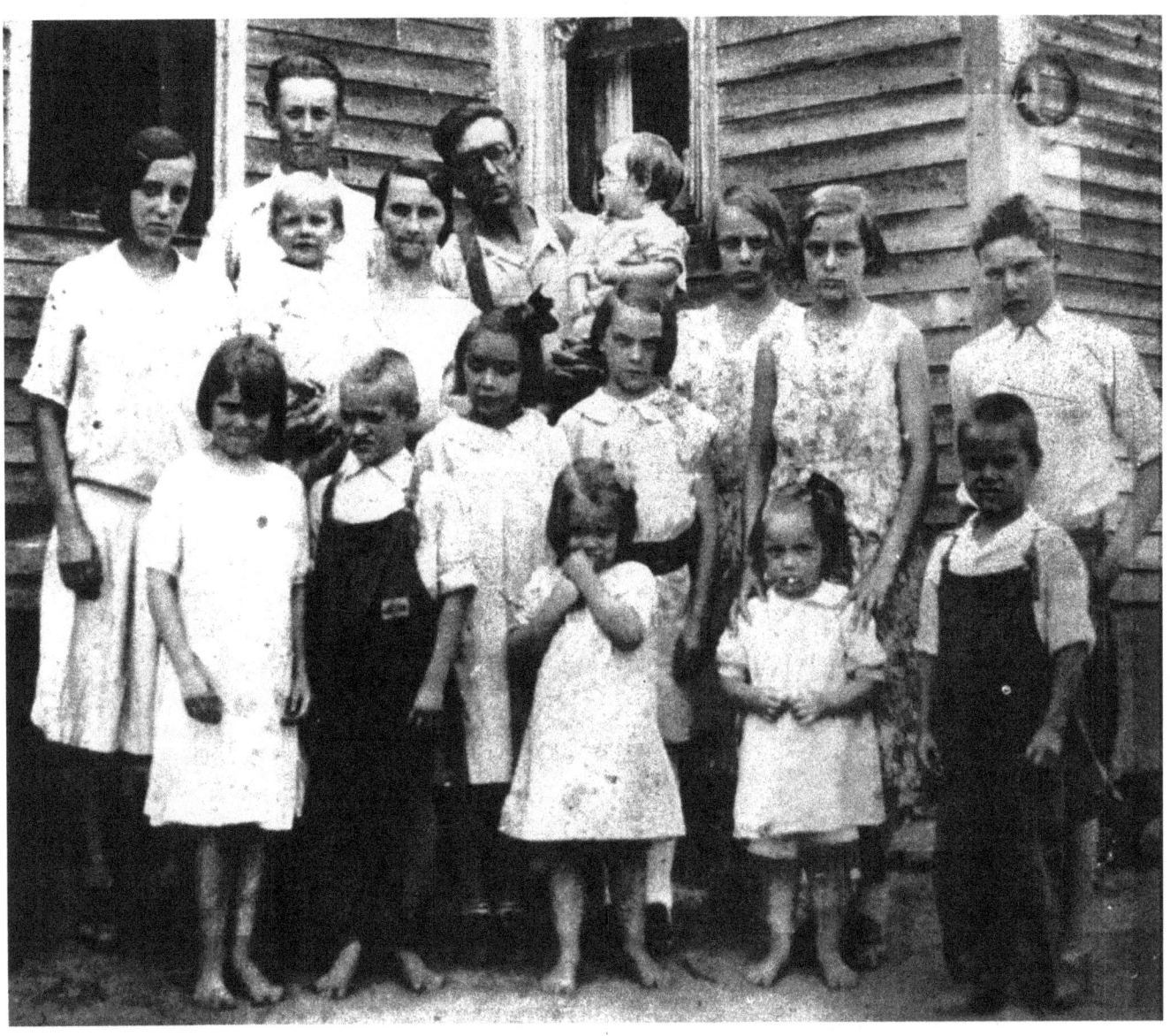

Cola and Esther Conant Storer with their children. Photograph: Weld Historic Society

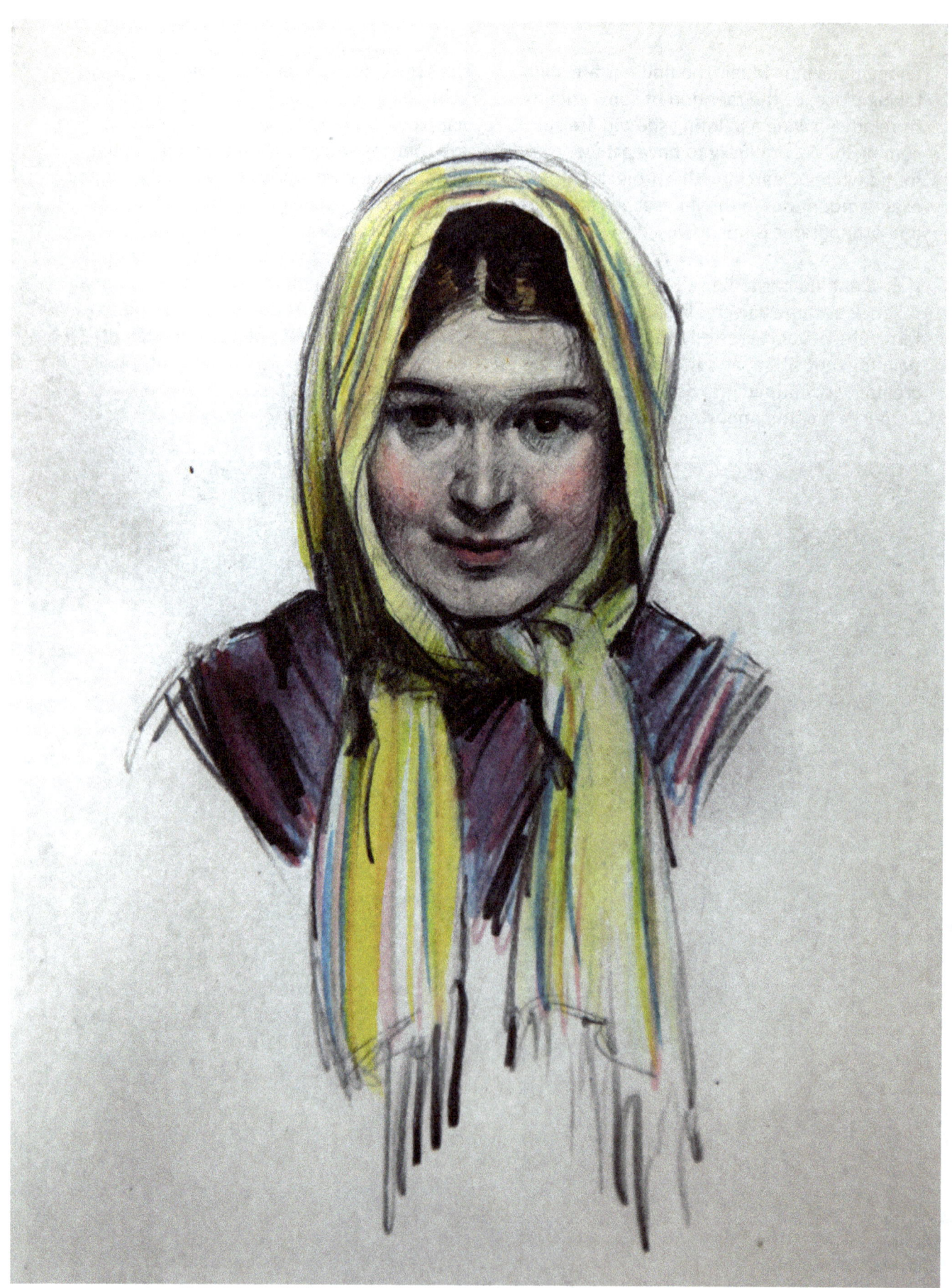

Unknown Model

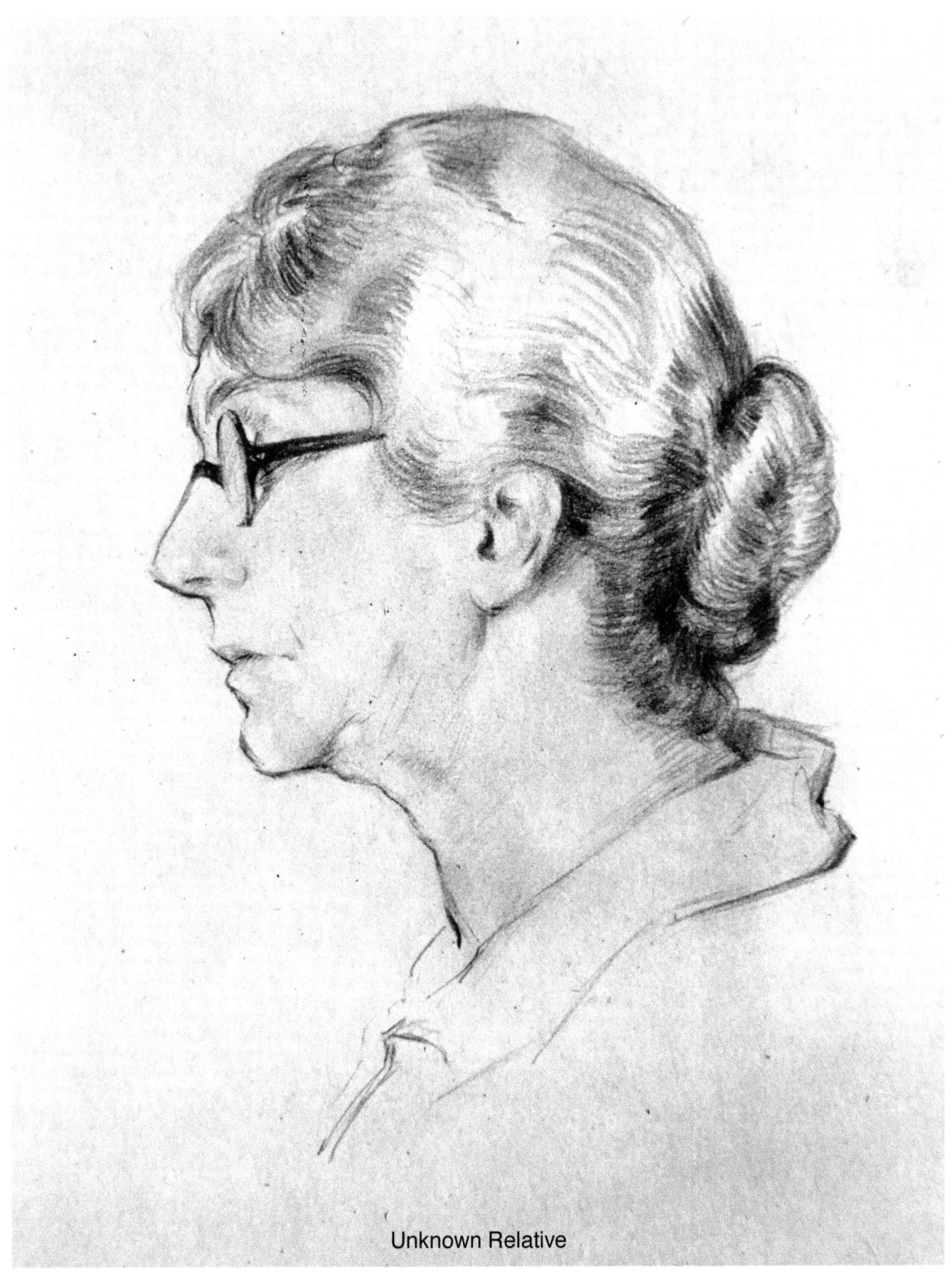

Unknown Relative

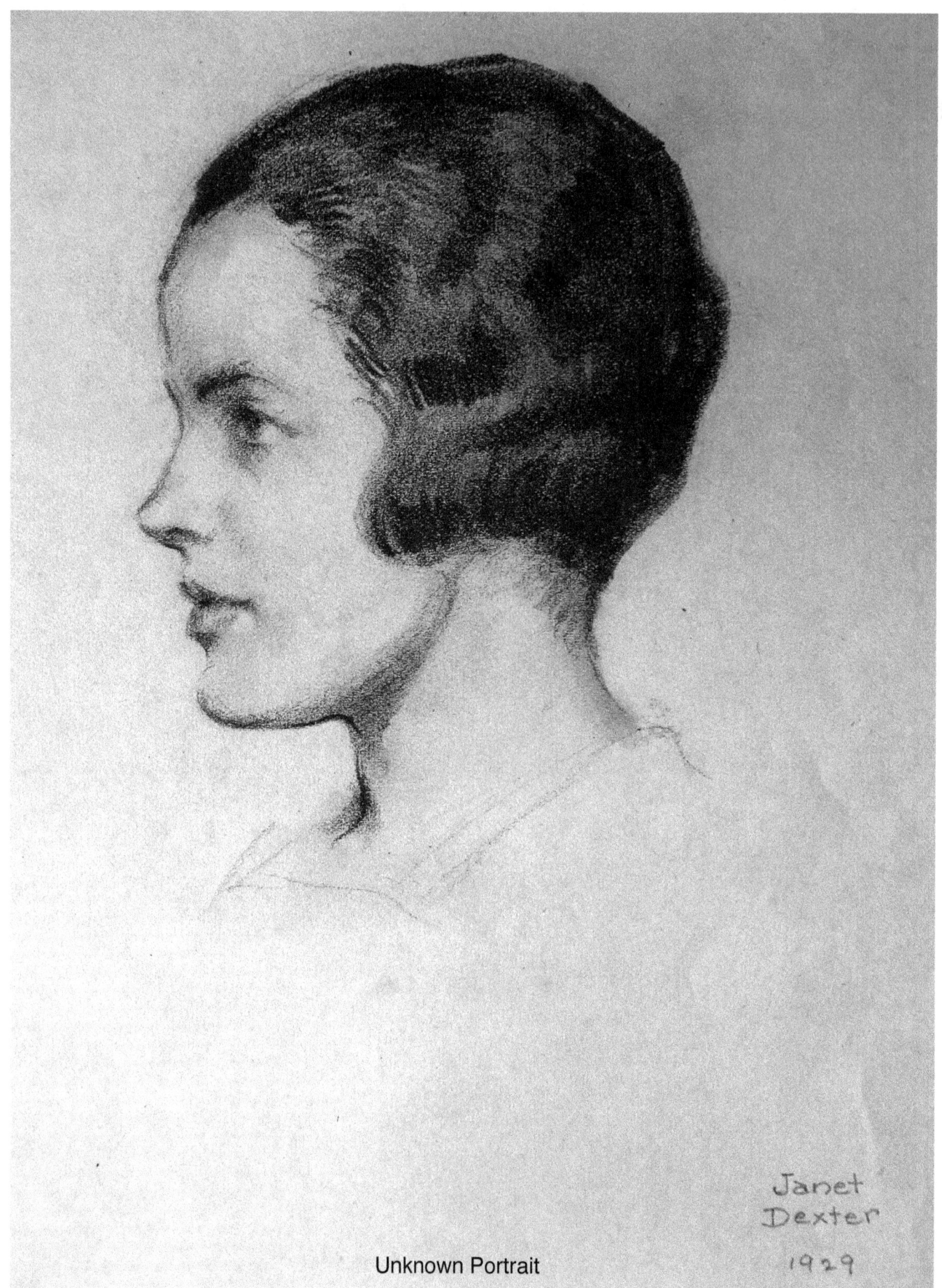

Unknown Portrait

Janet
Dexter
1929

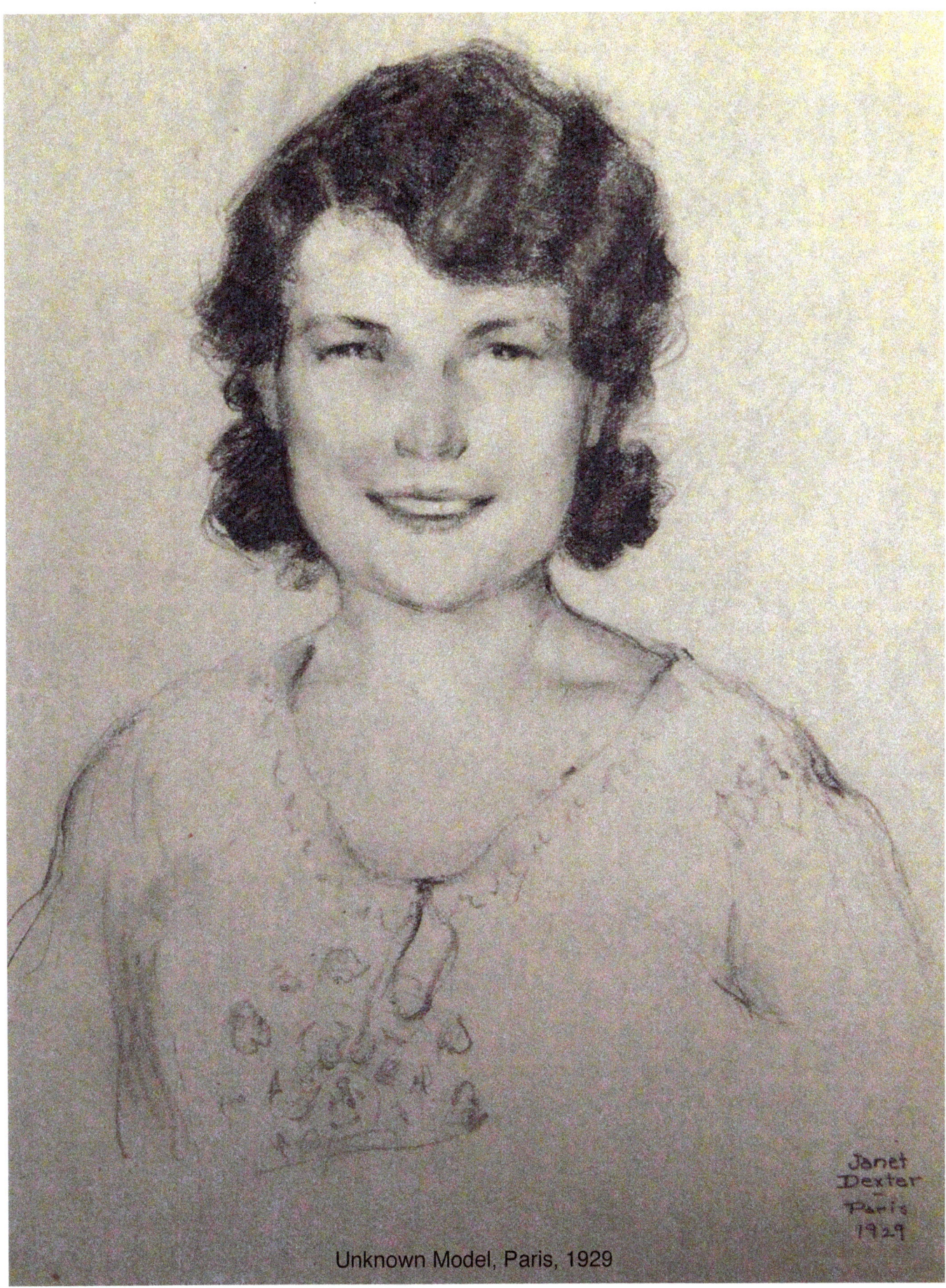

Unknown Model, Paris, 1929

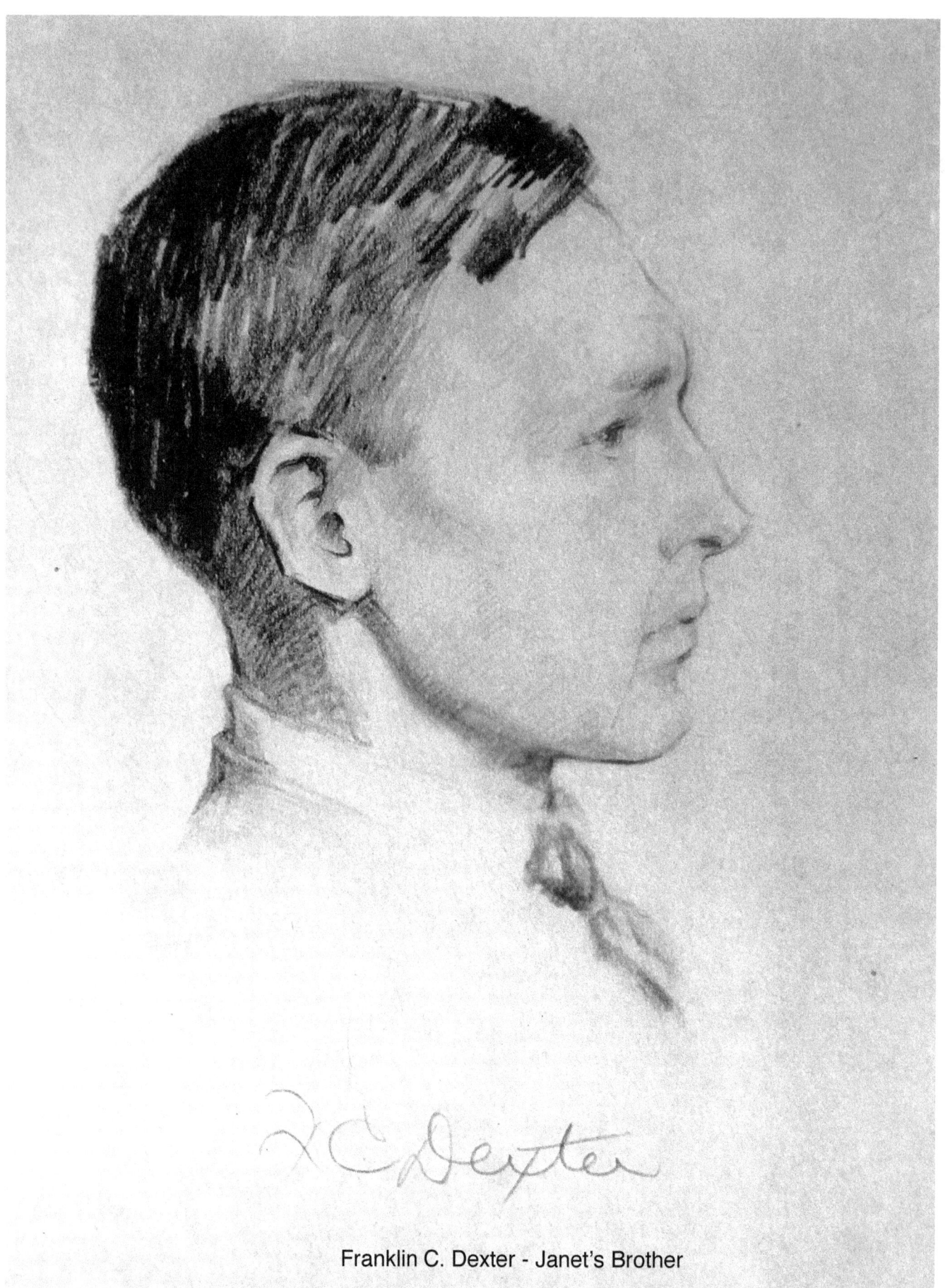

Franklin C. Dexter - Janet's Brother

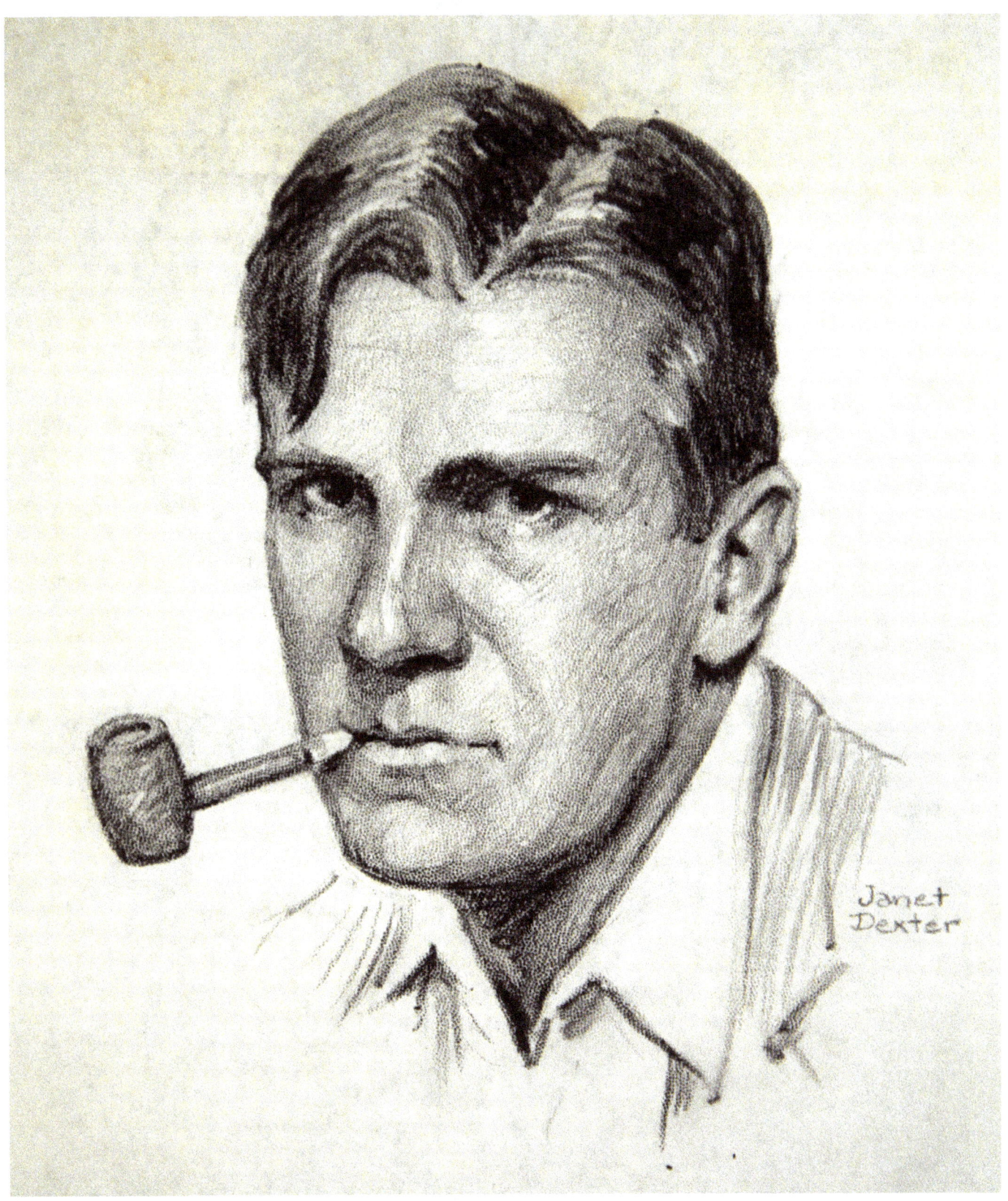

Actor: Glen Anders

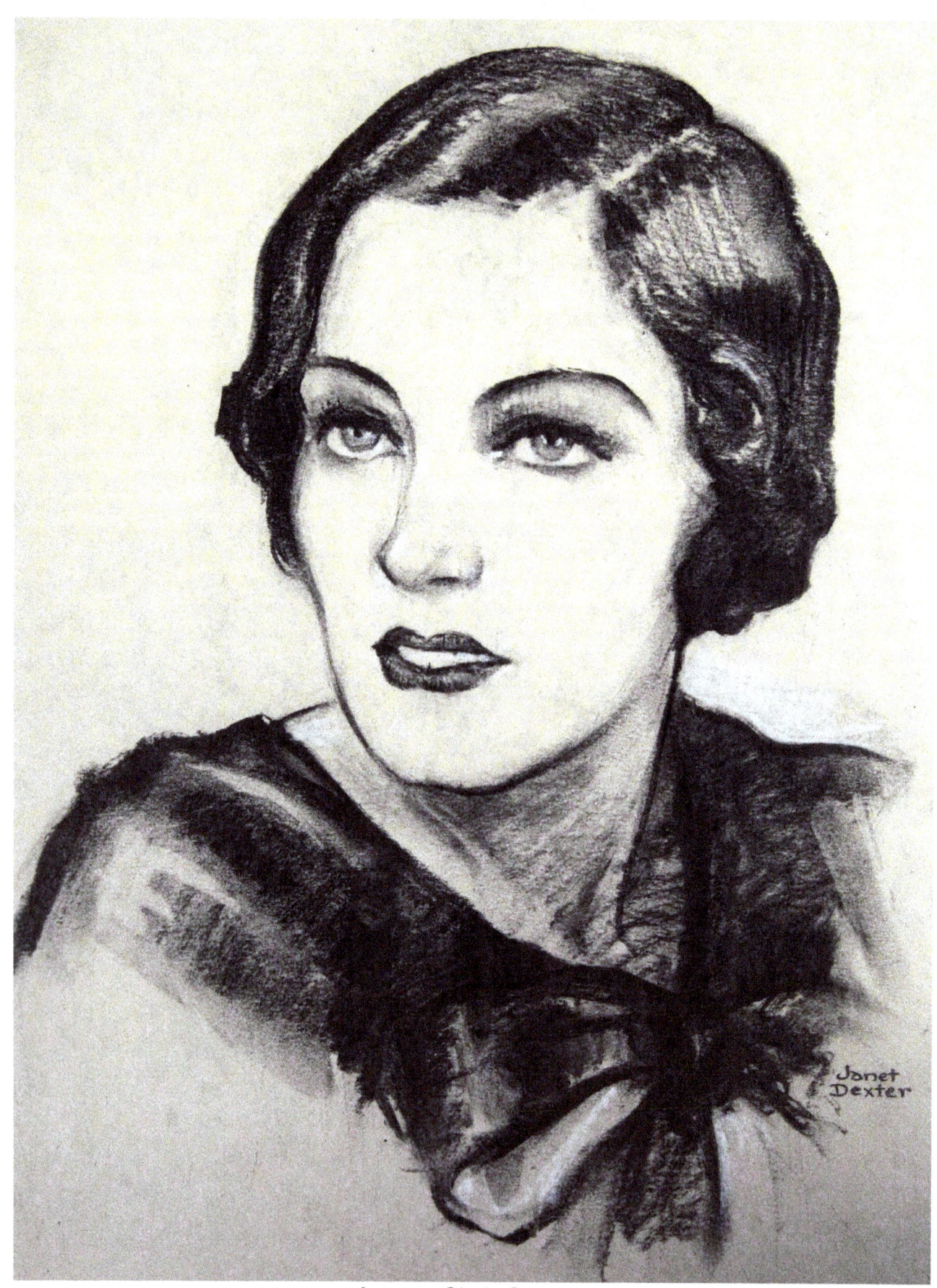

Actress: Gloria Swanson

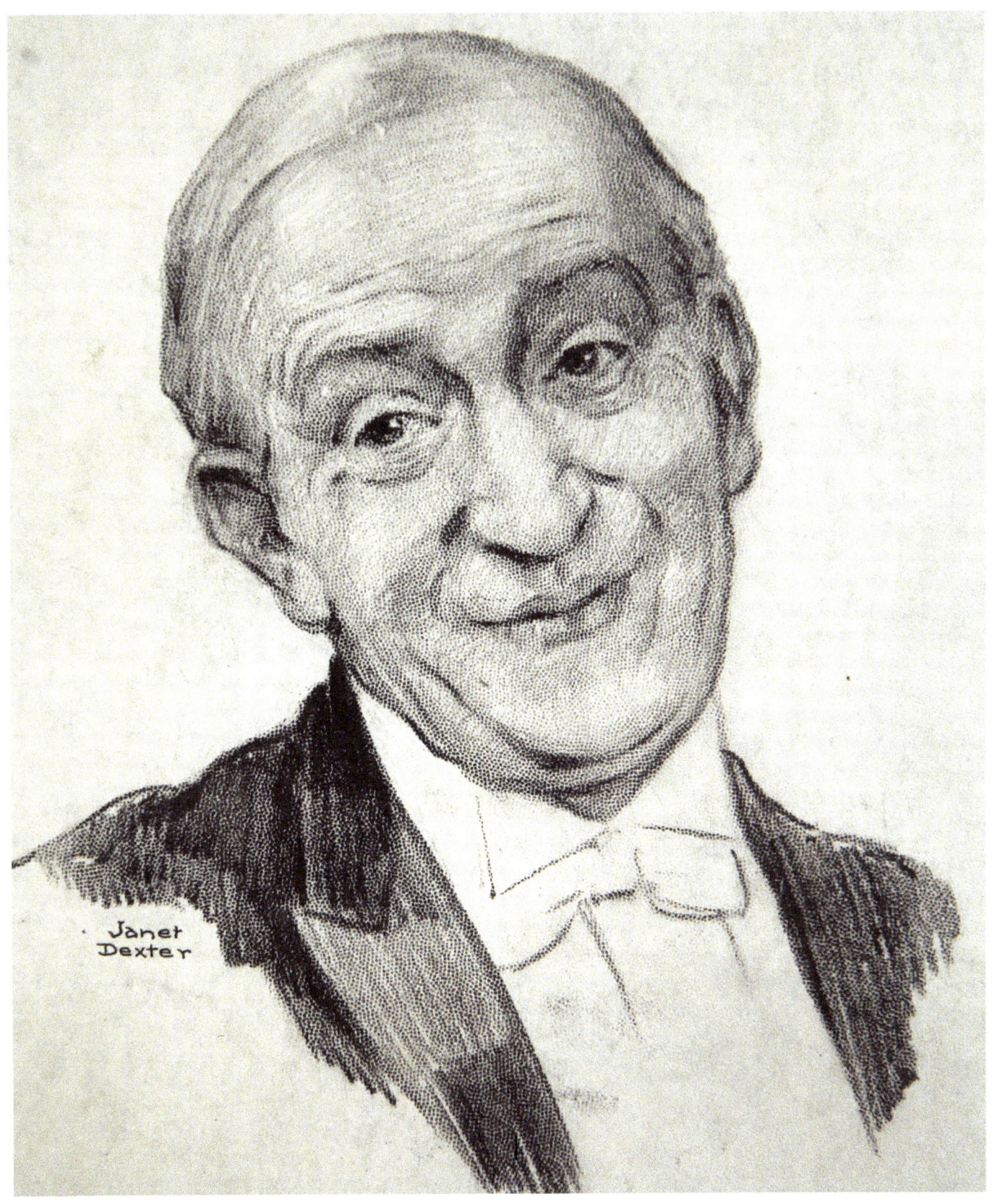

Actor: Lew Fields

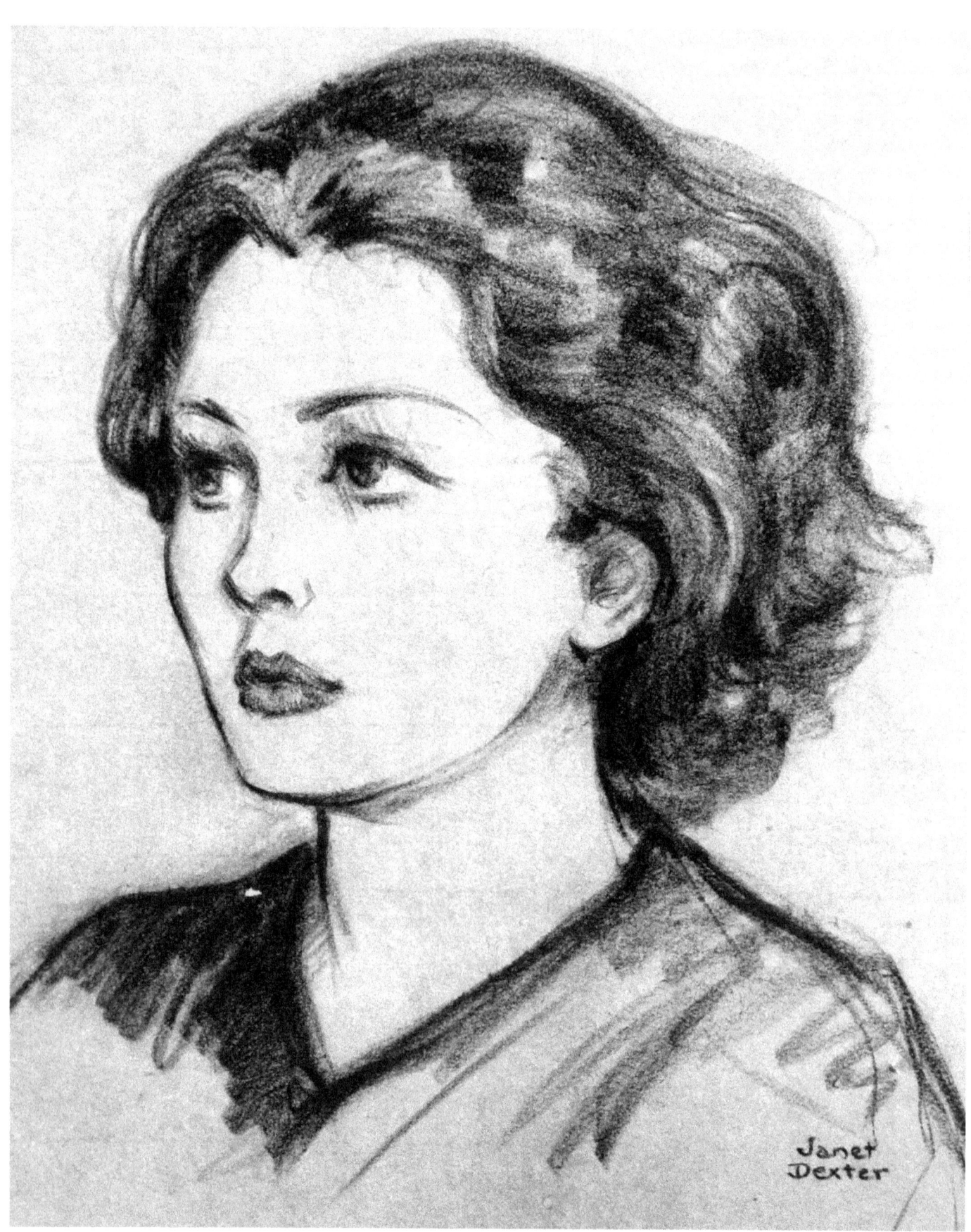

Actress: Alice Reinhart

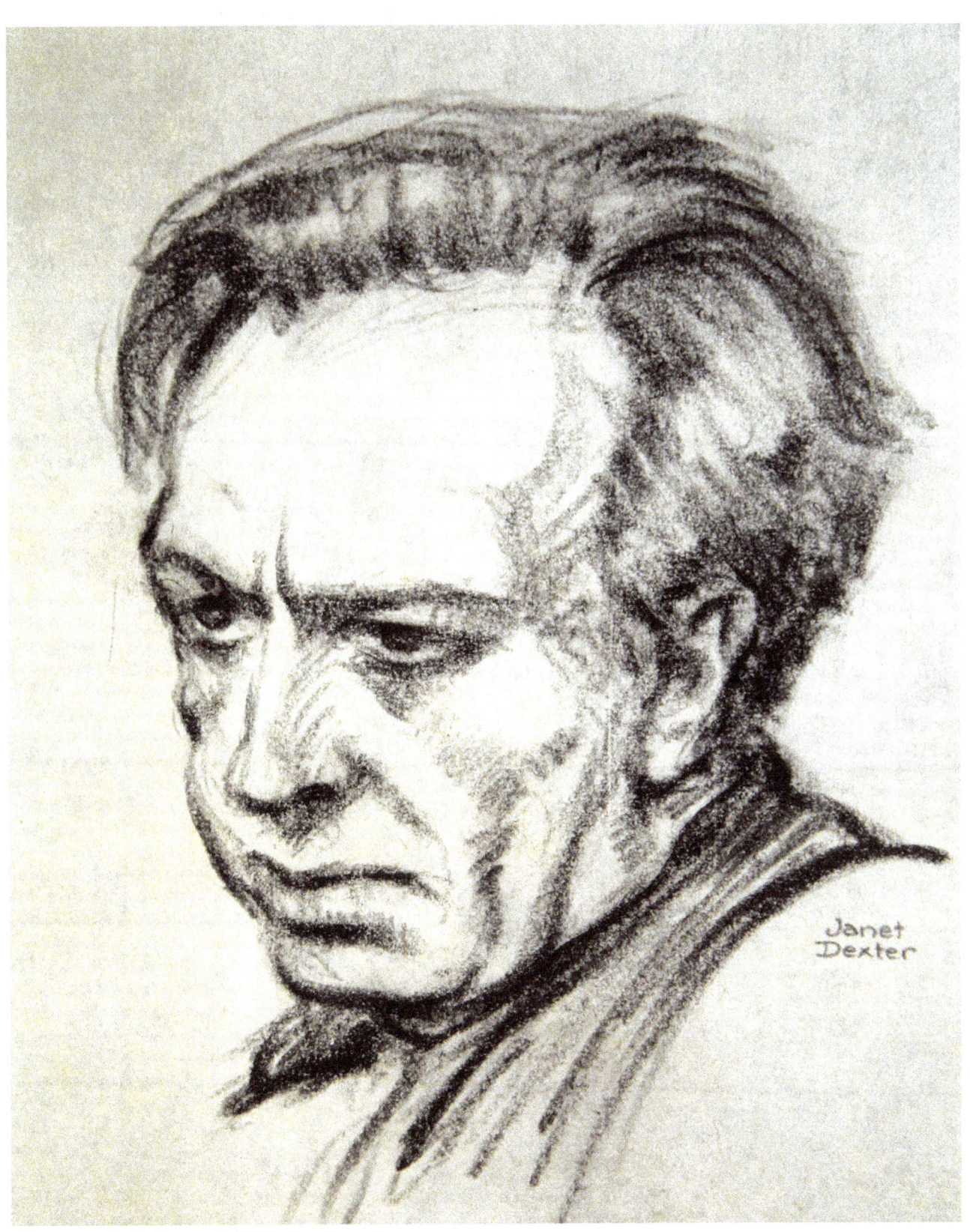

Actor: Bulgakov

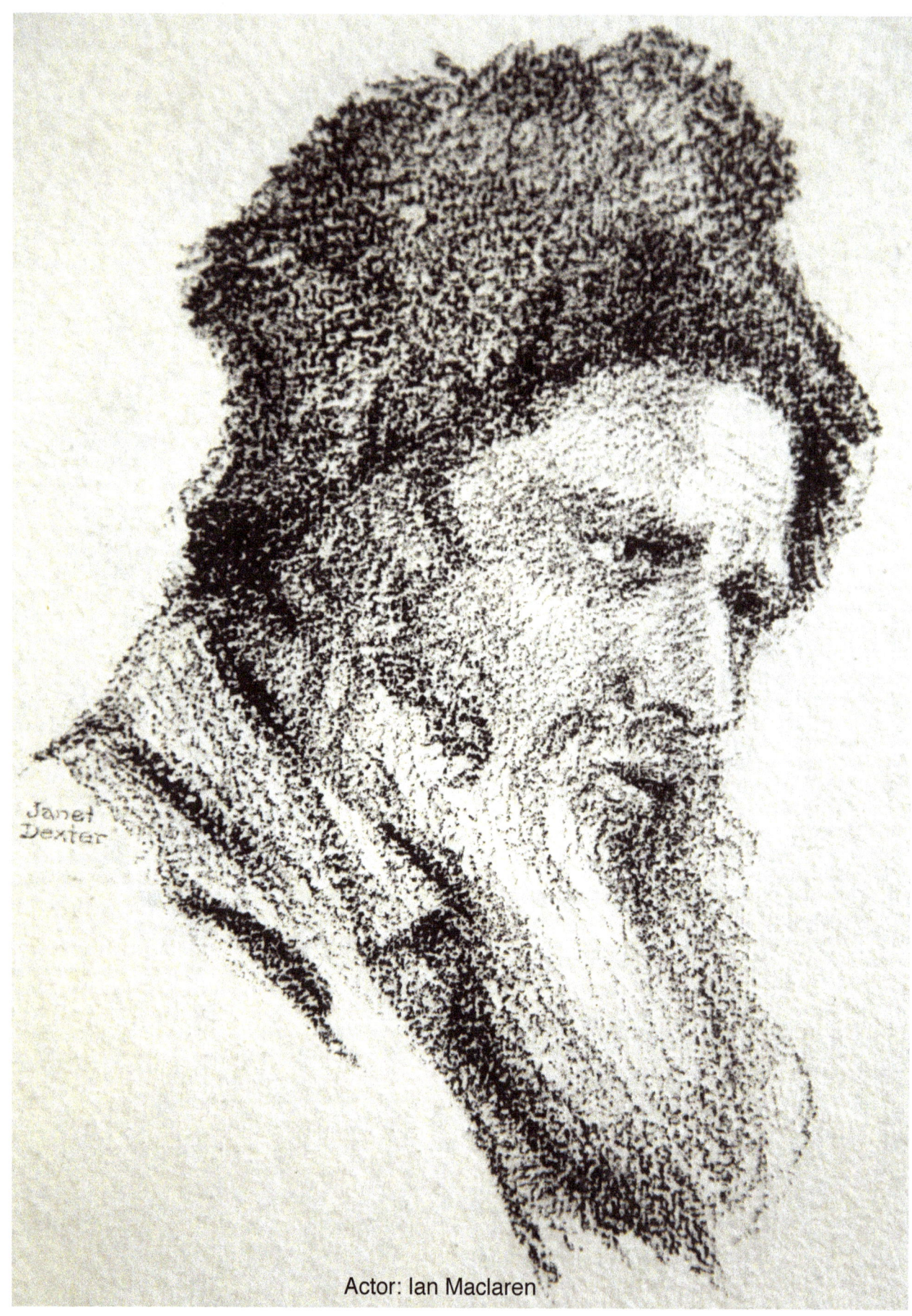

Actor: Ian Maclaren

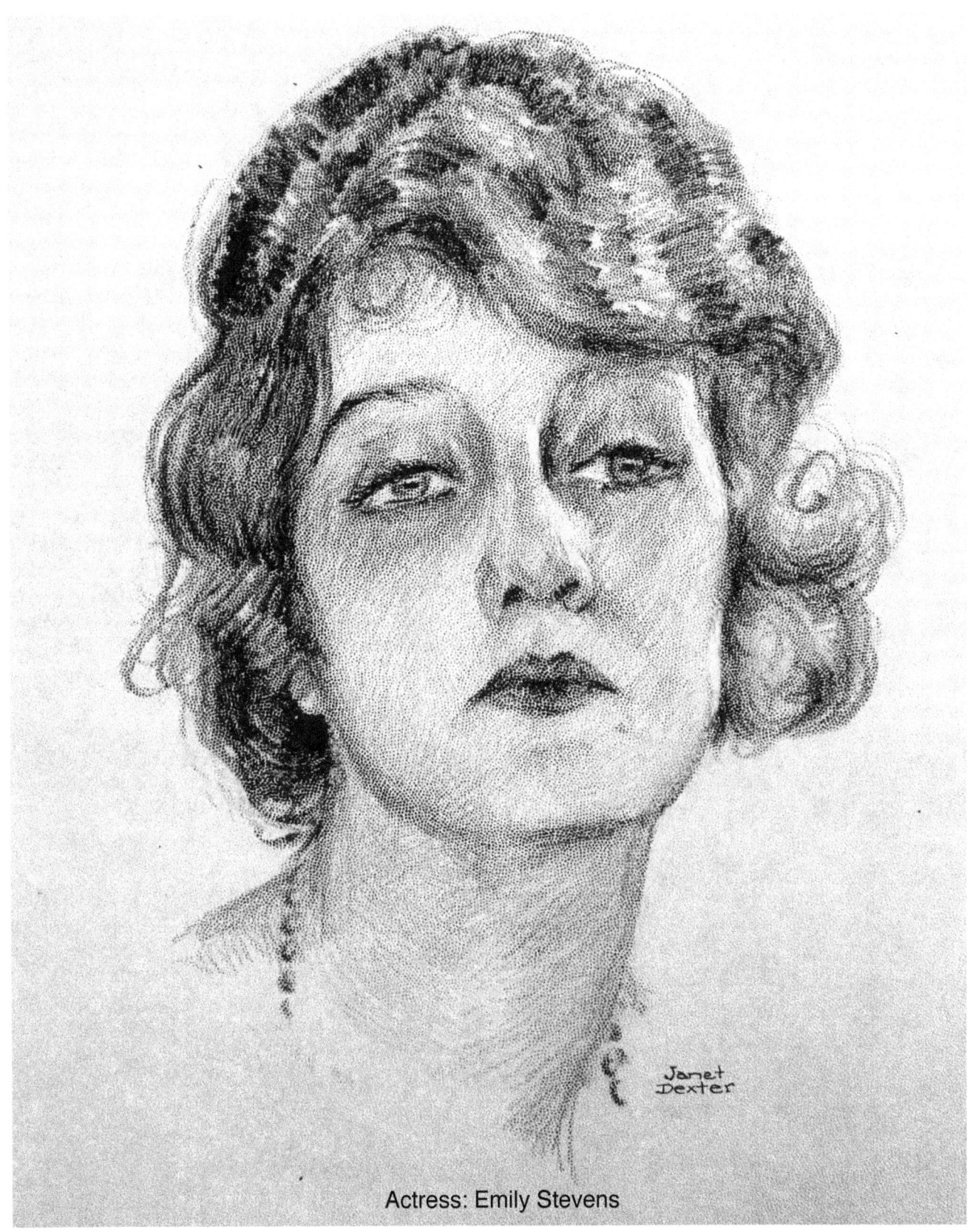

Actress: Emily Stevens

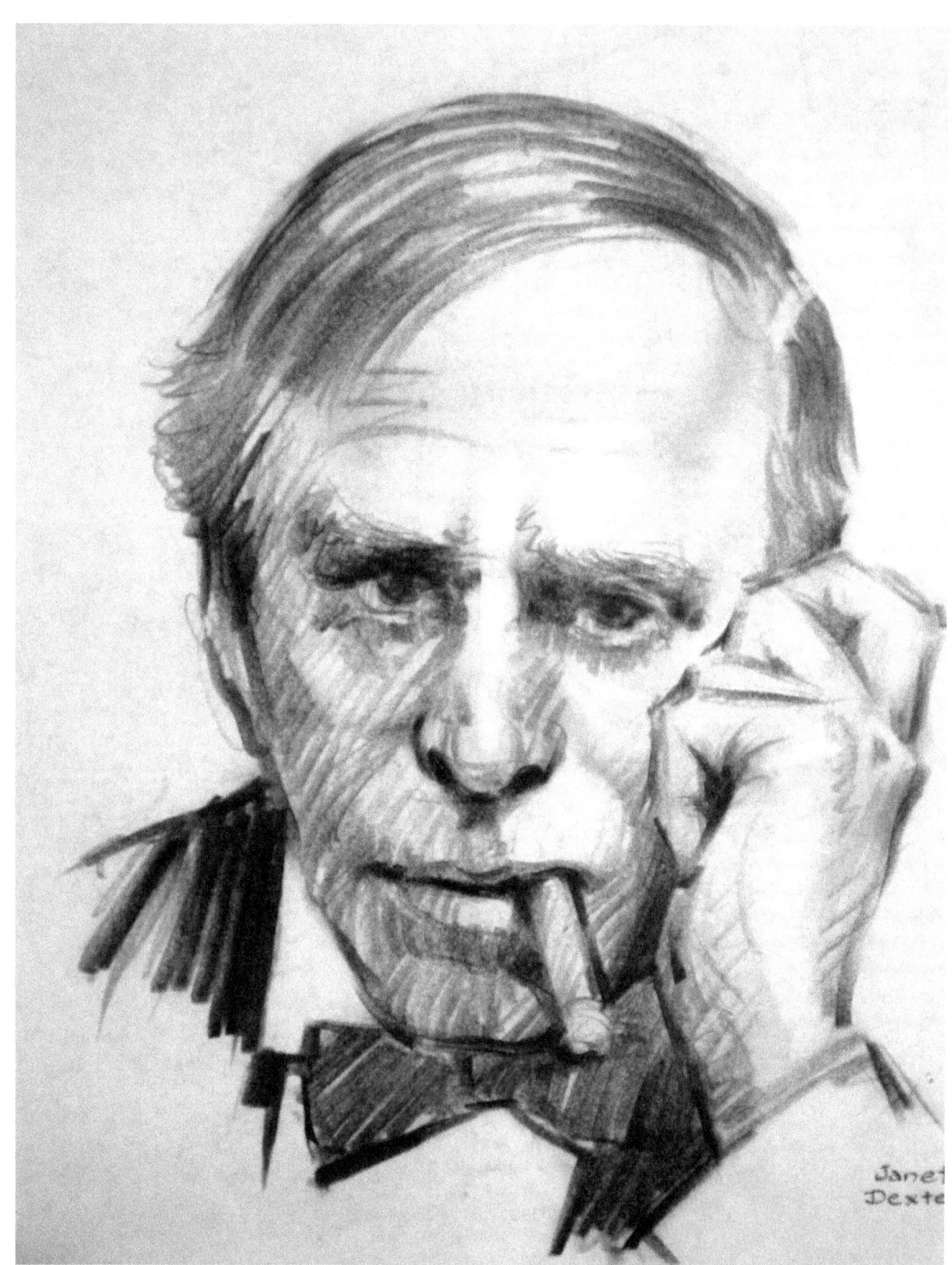

Actor: Louis Mann

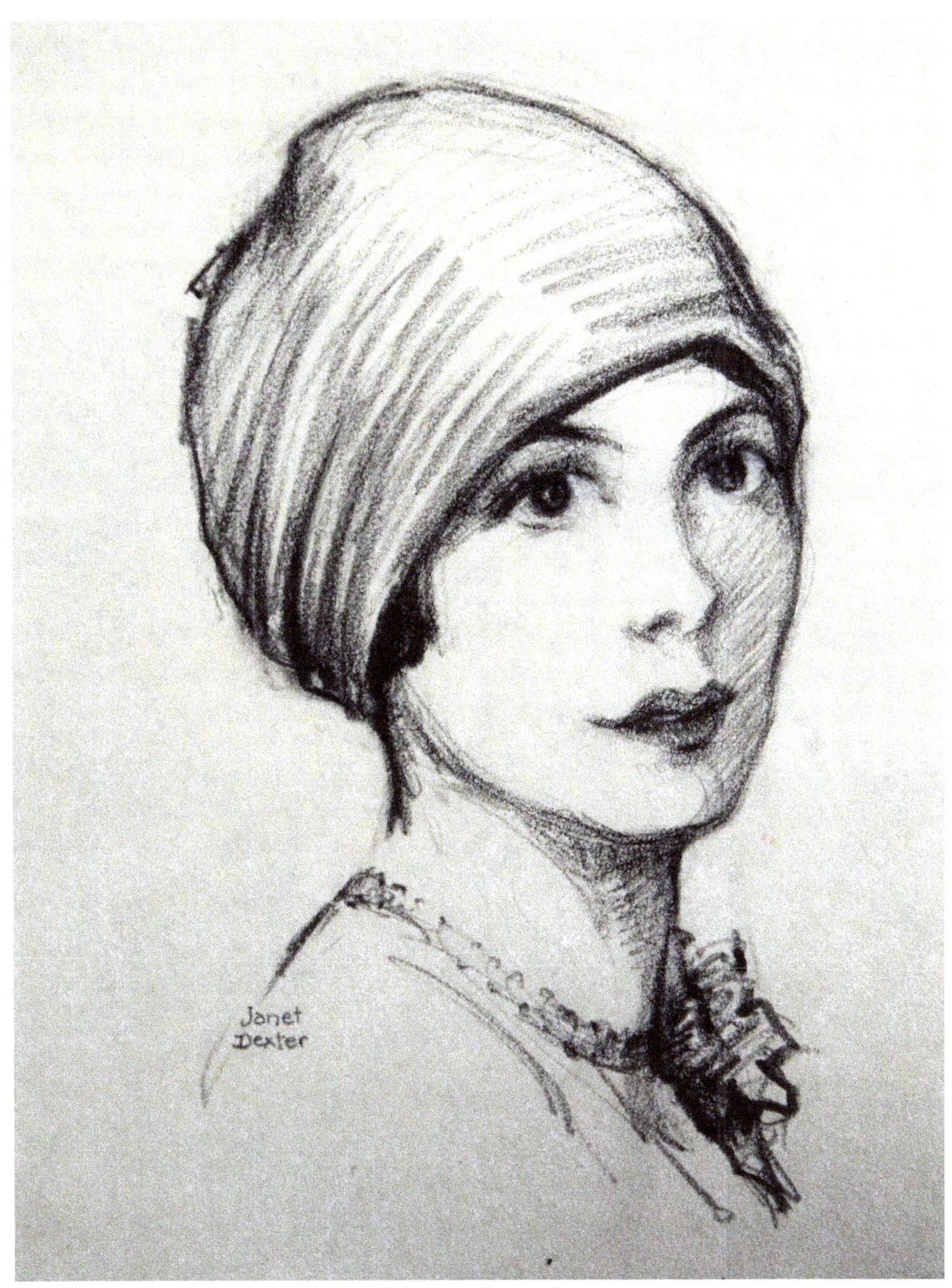

Actress: Sara Haden

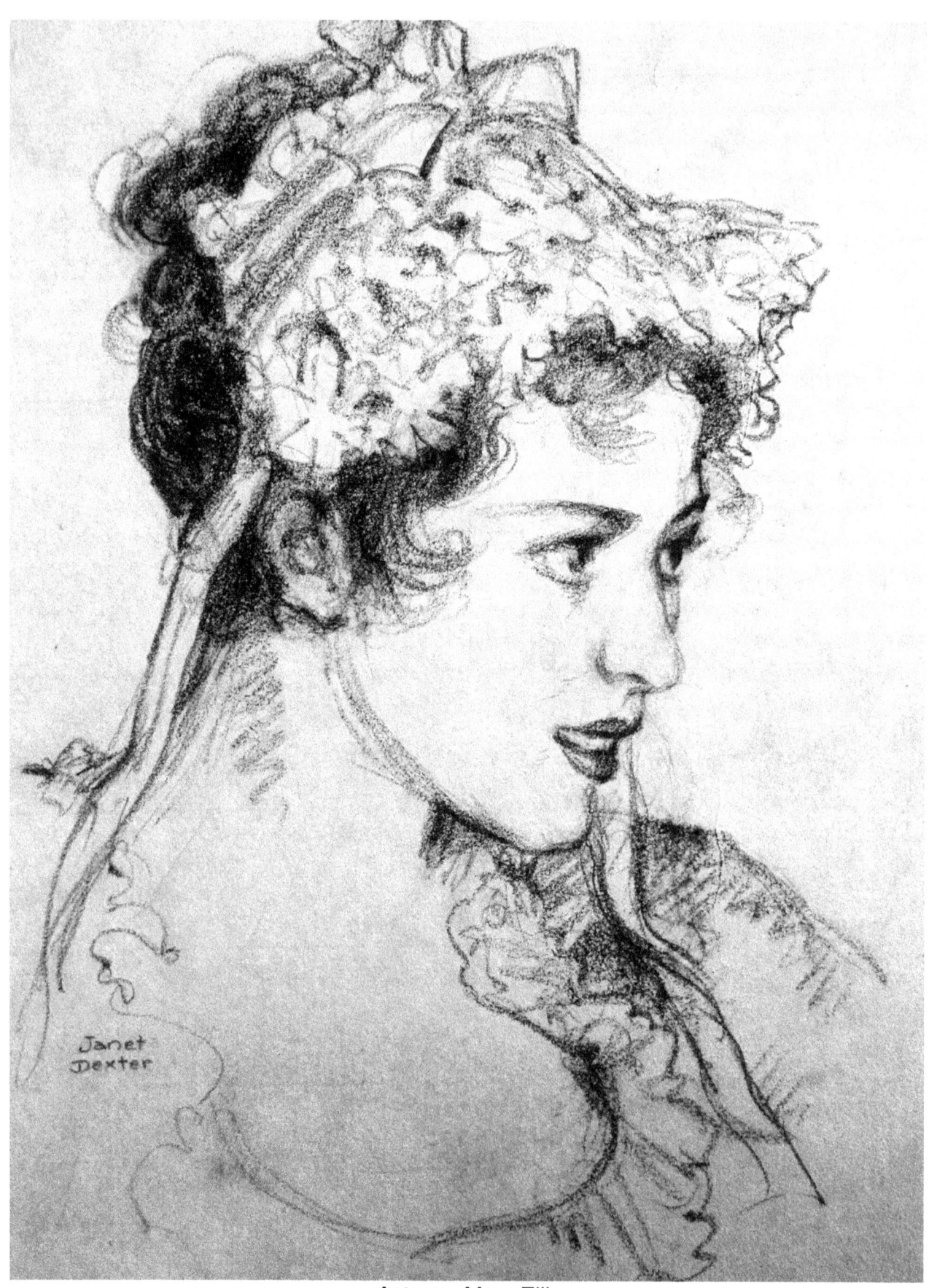

Actress: Mary Ellis

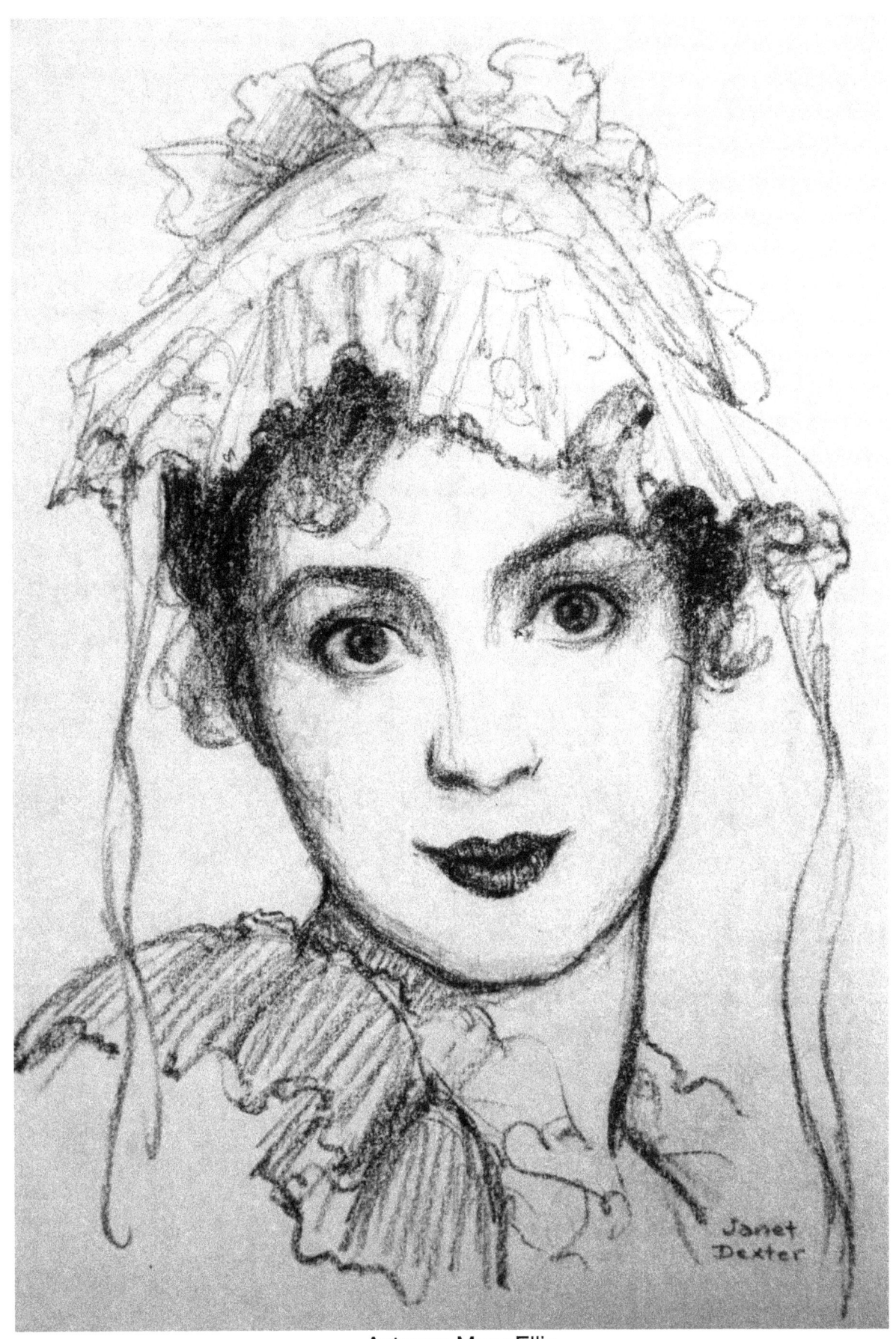

Actress: Mary Ellis

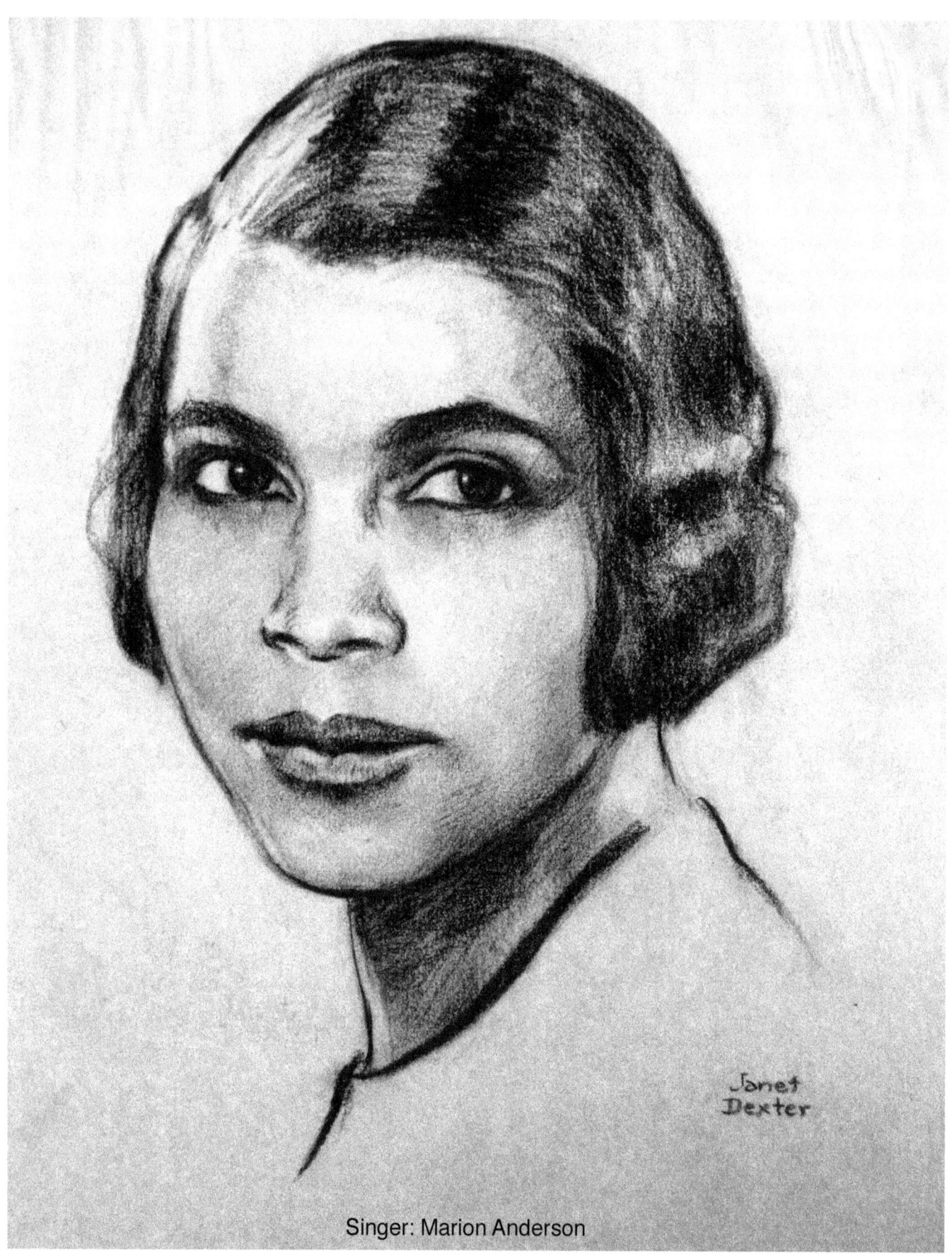

Singer: Marion Anderson

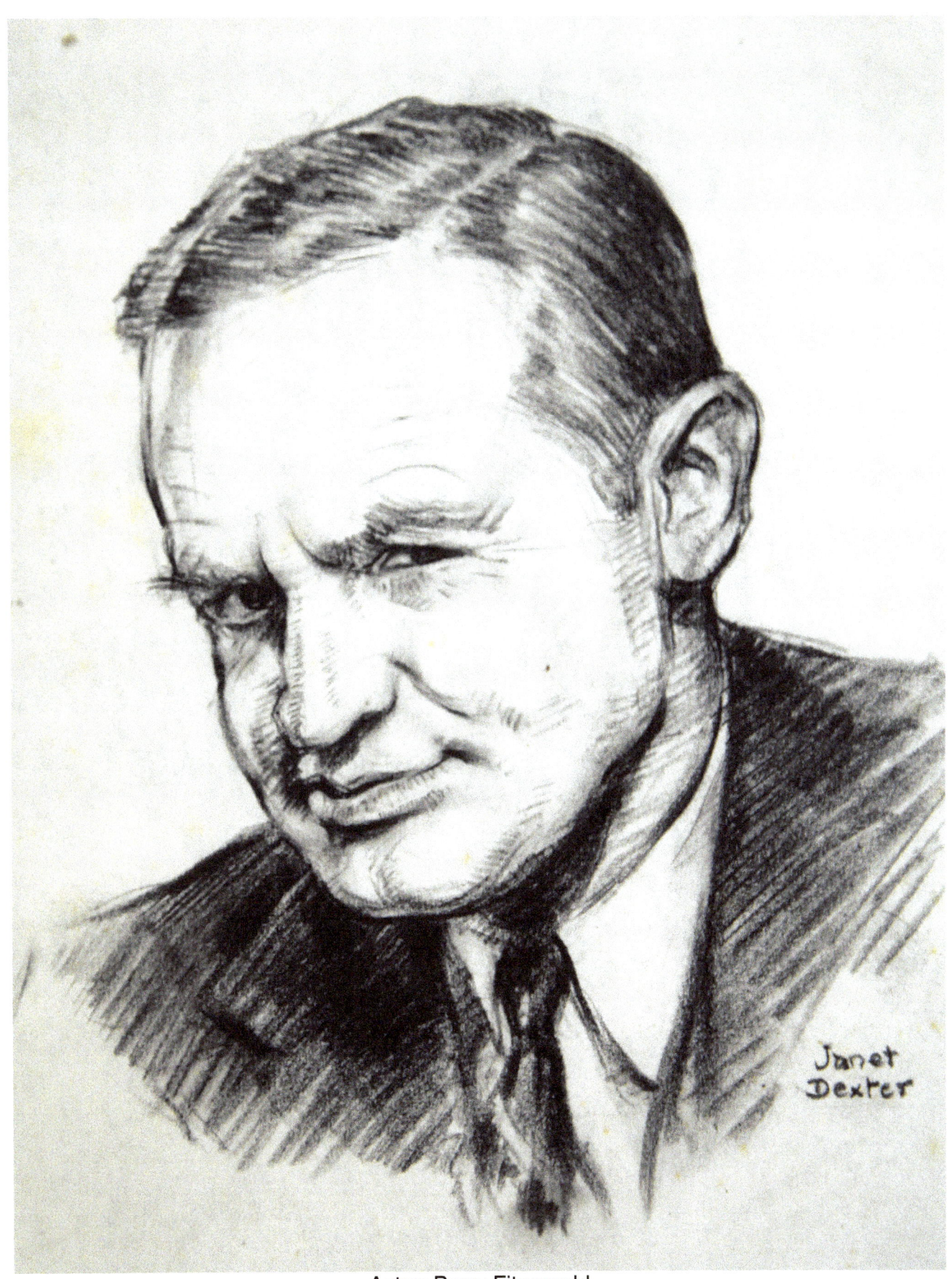

Actor: Barry Fitzgerald

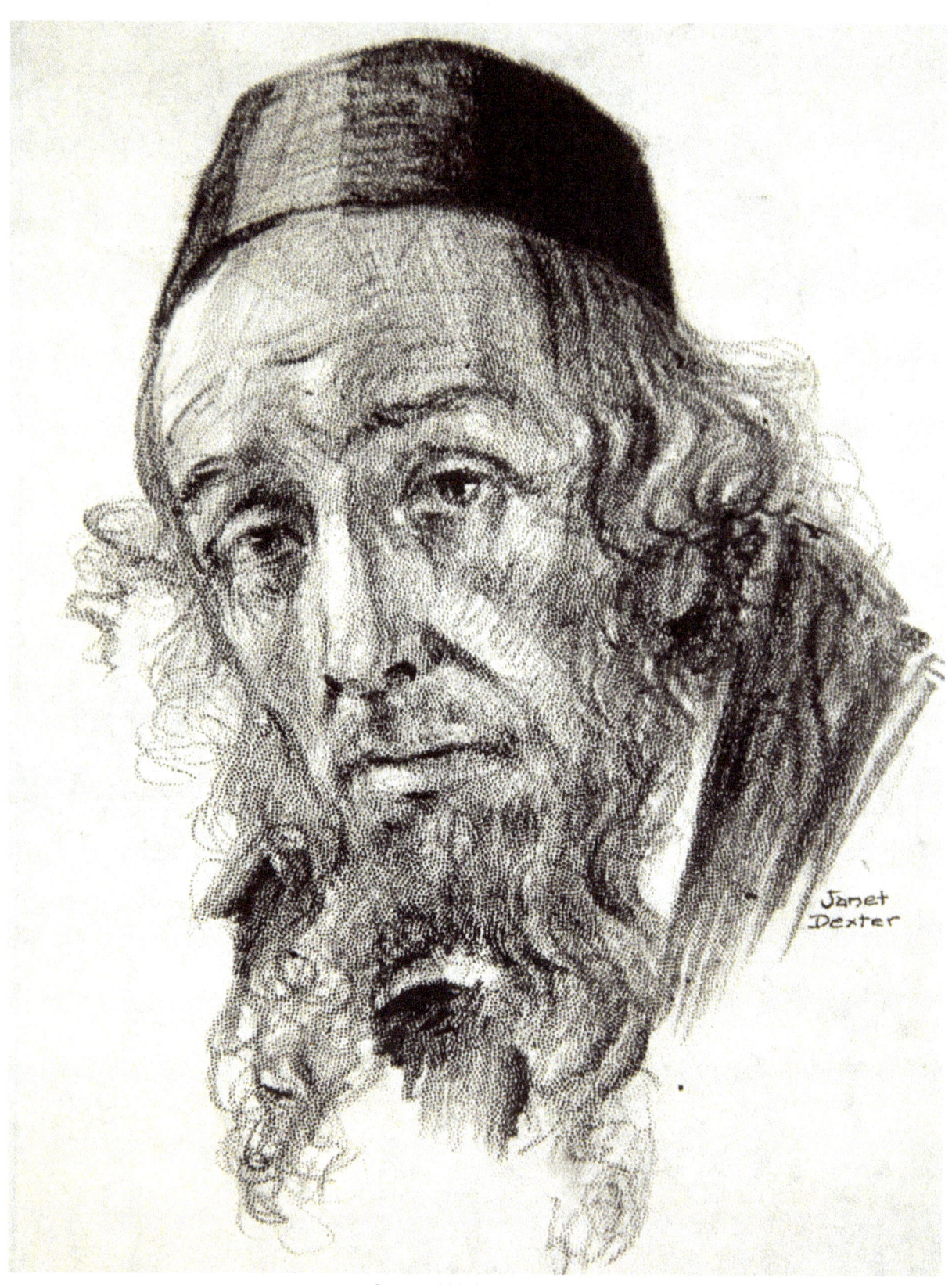

Actor: Walton Har

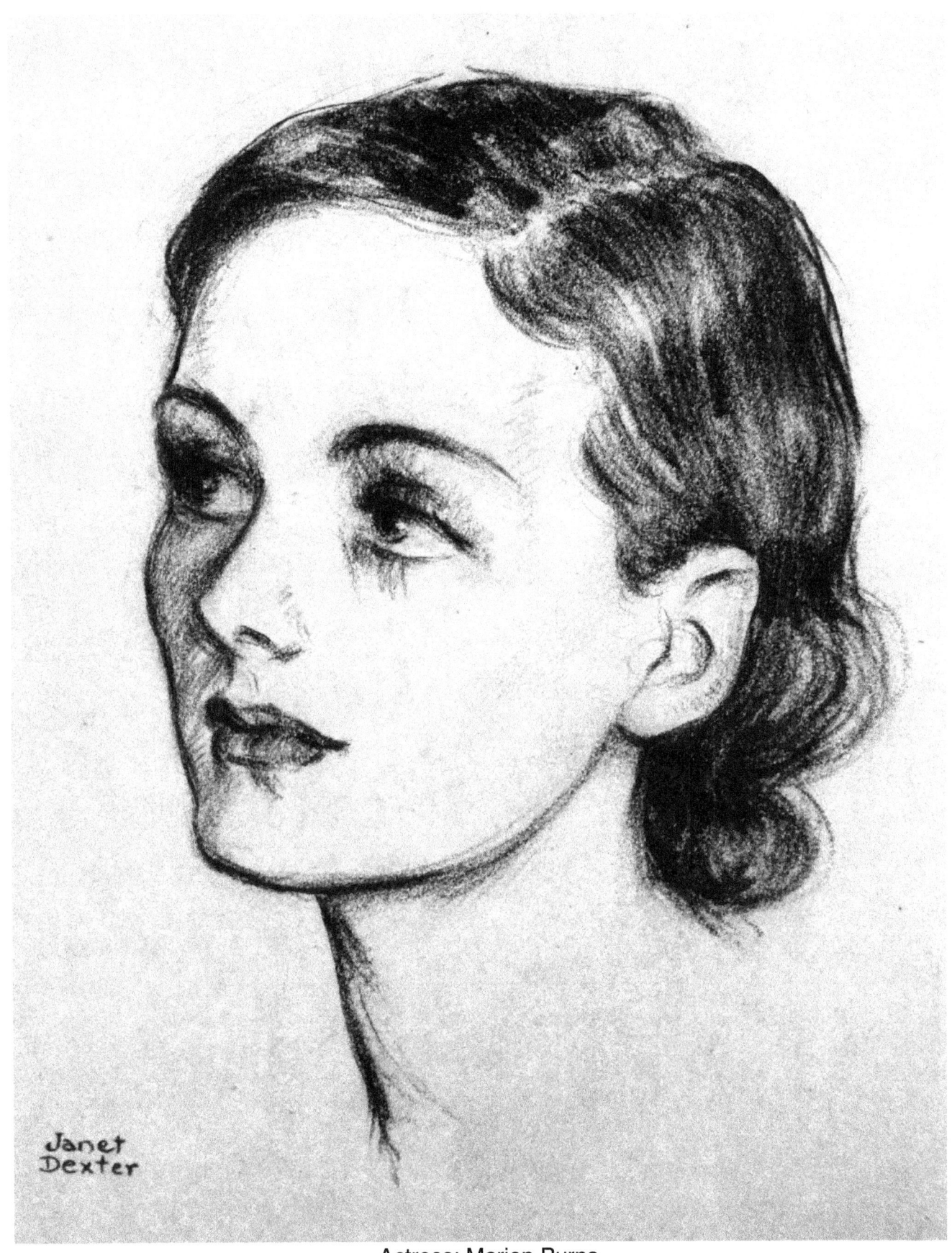

Janet Dexter

Actress: Marion Burns

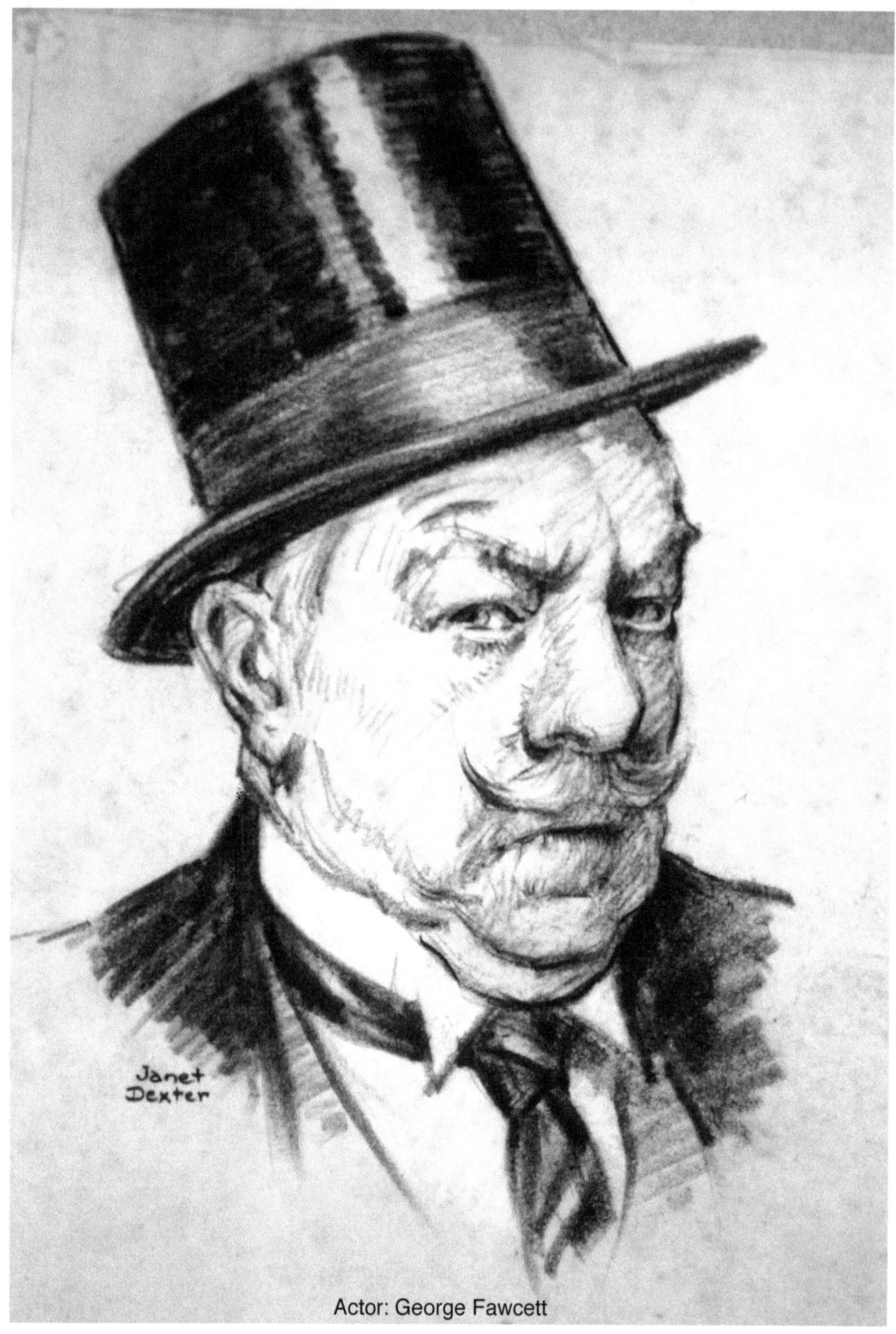

Actor: George Fawcett

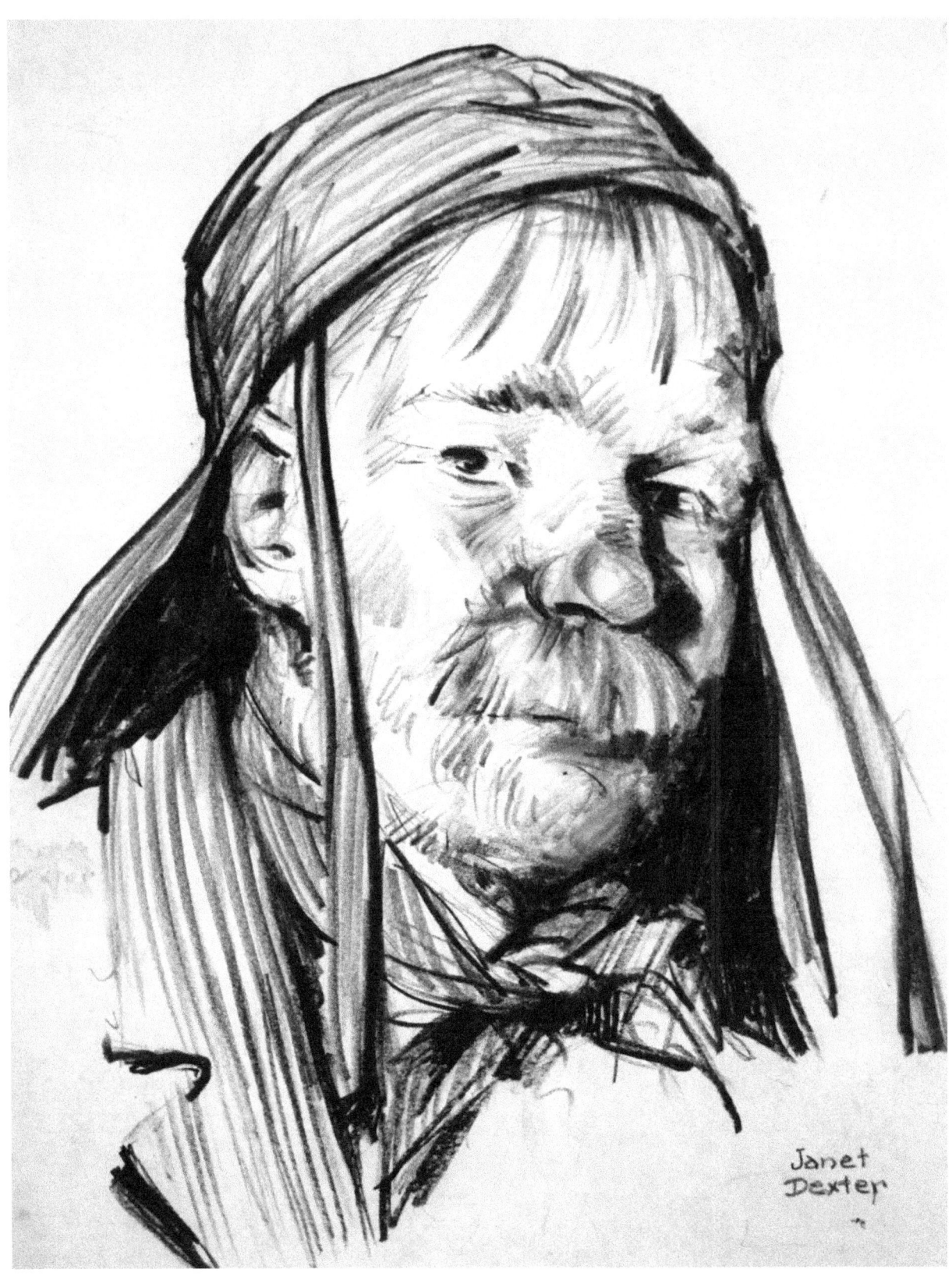

Actor: Henry Travers

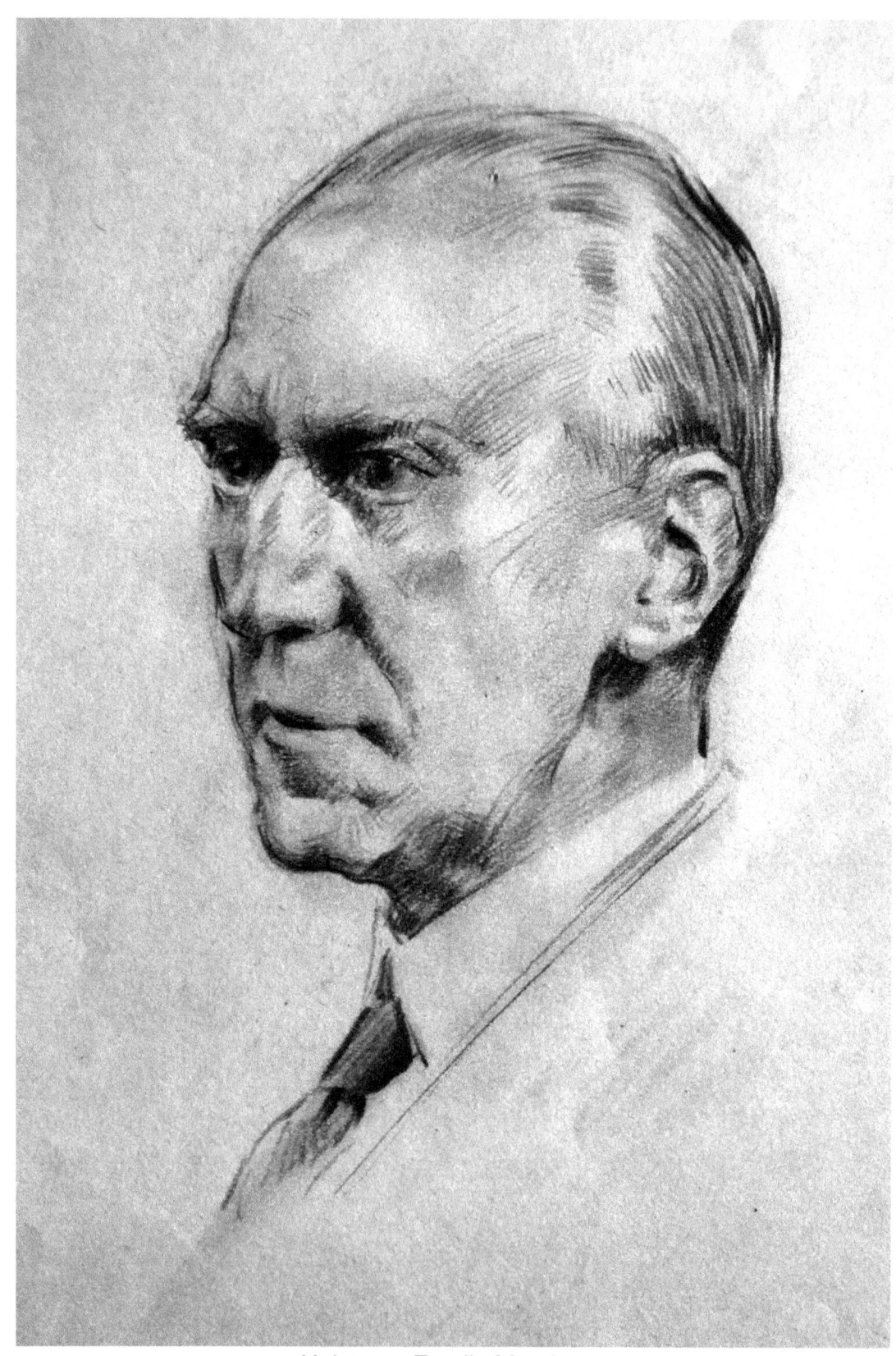

Unknown Family Member

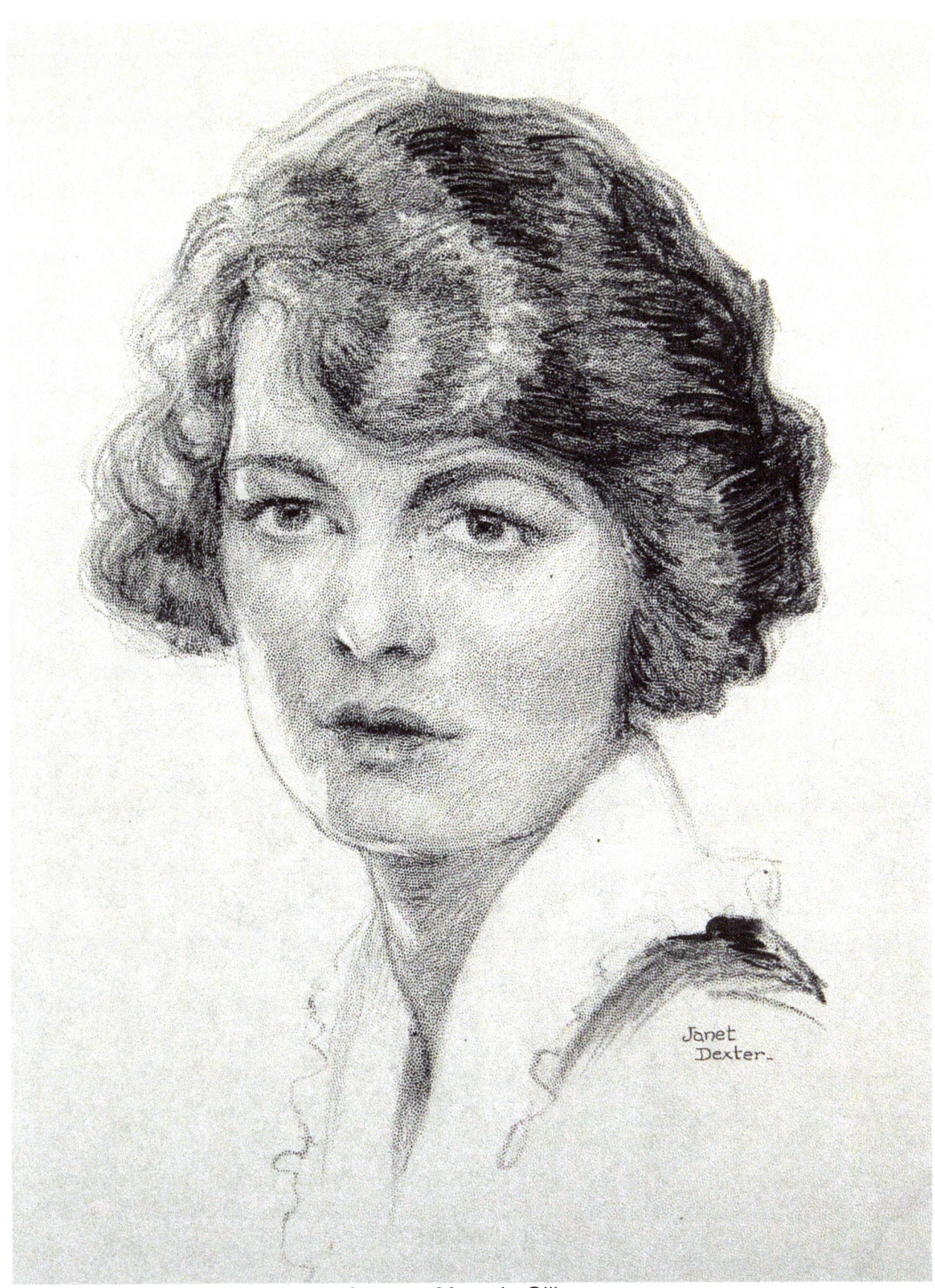

Actress: Margalo Gillmore

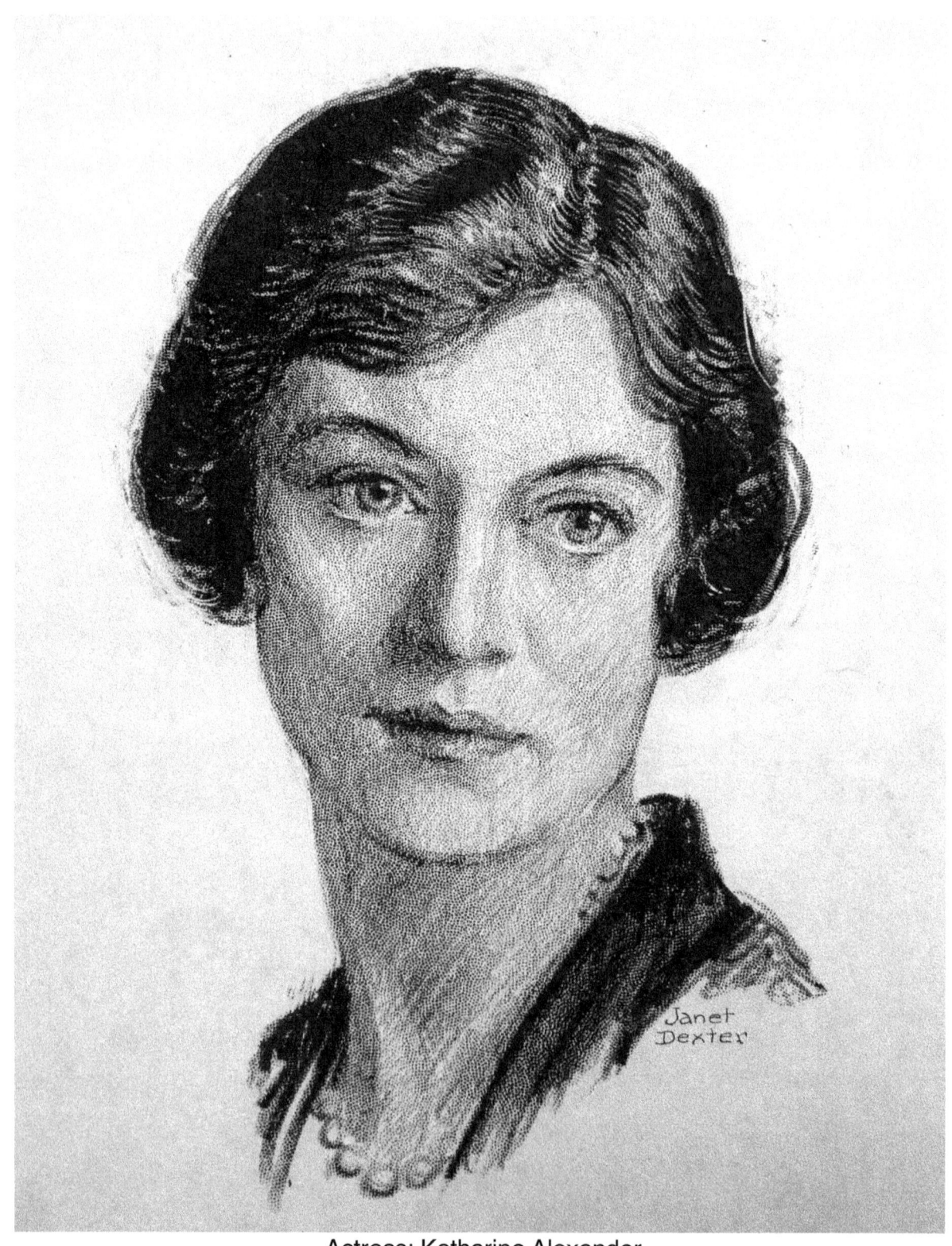

Actress: Katharine Alexander

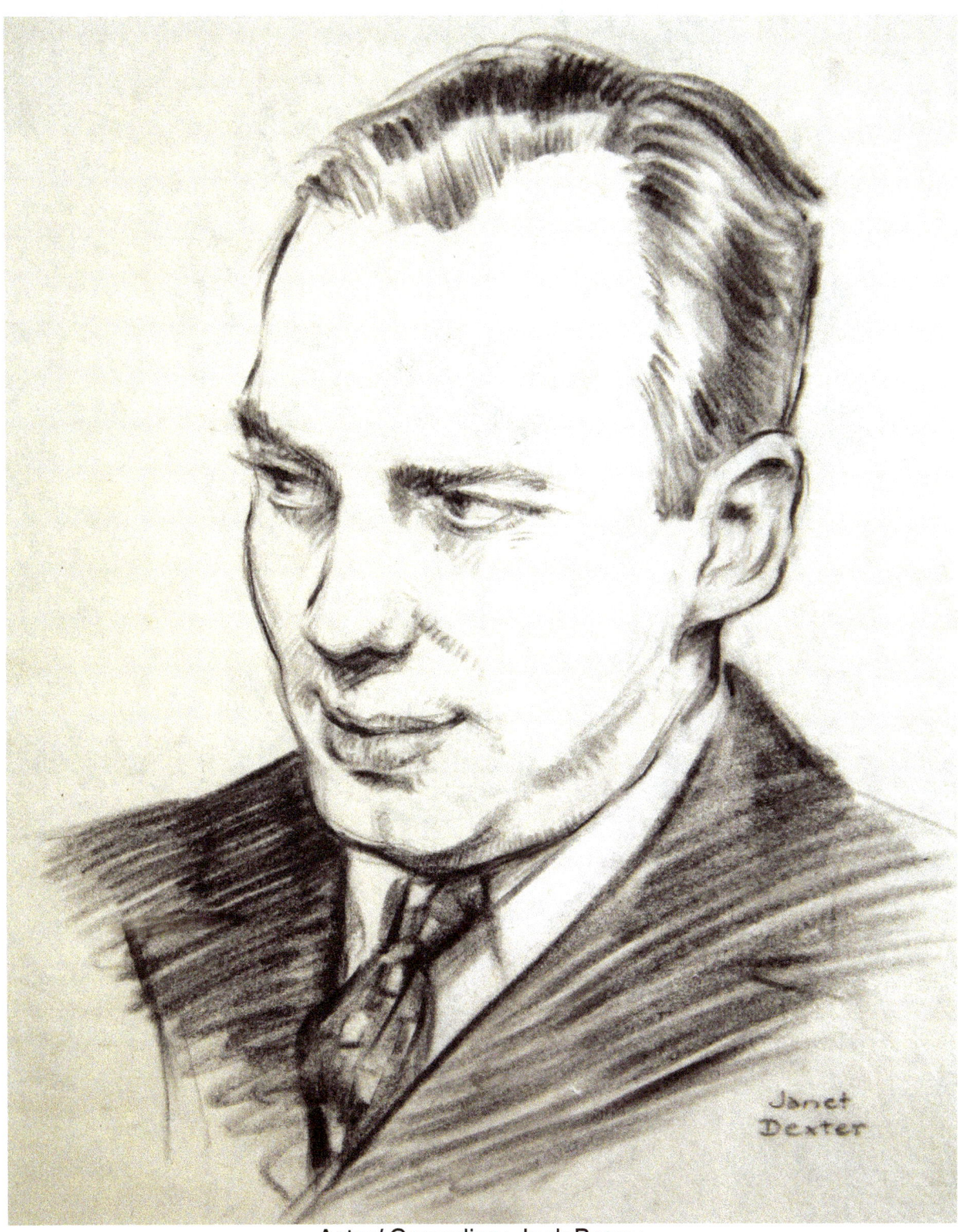

Actor/ Comedian: Jack Benny

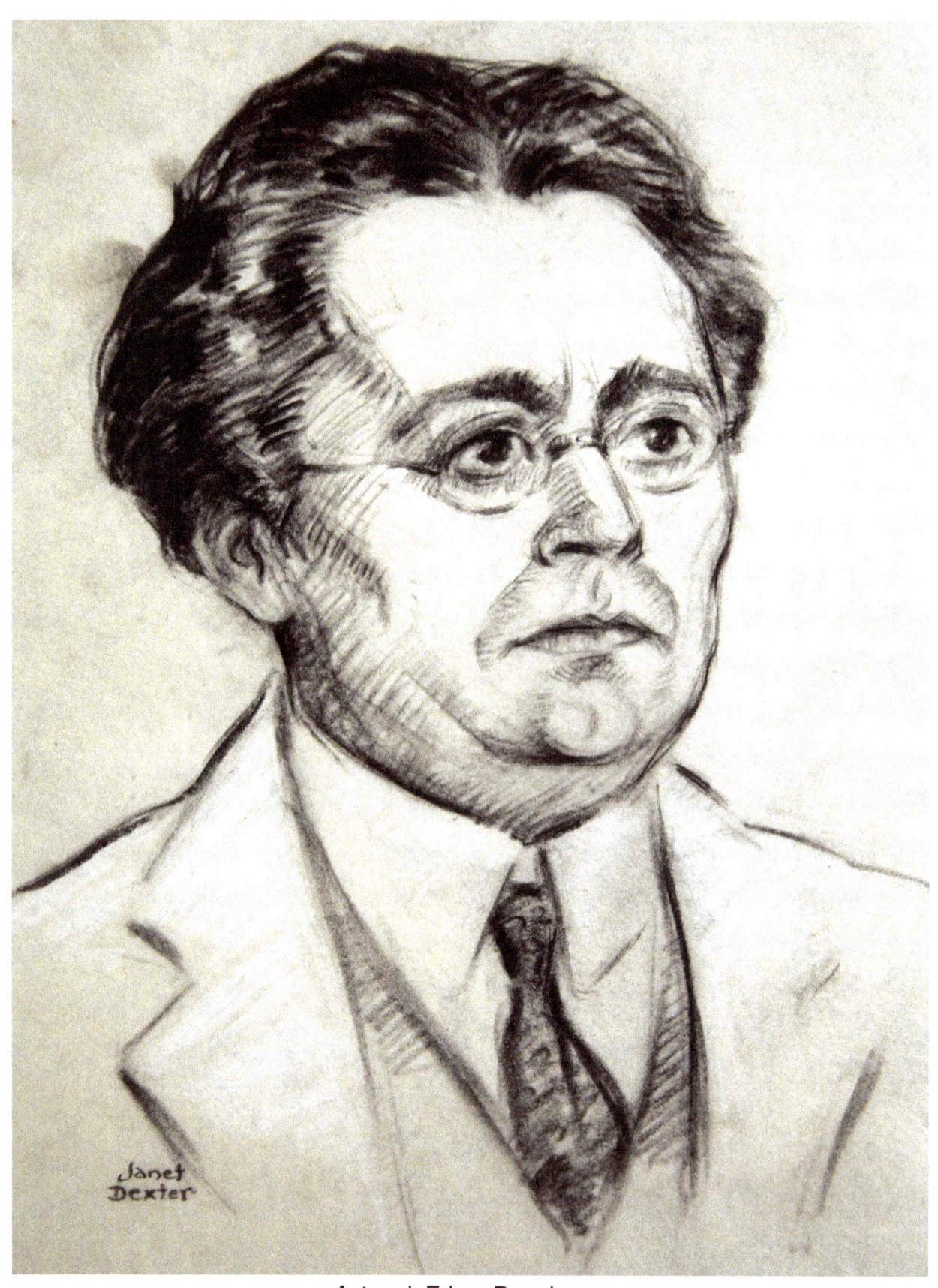

Actor: J. Edgar Bromberg

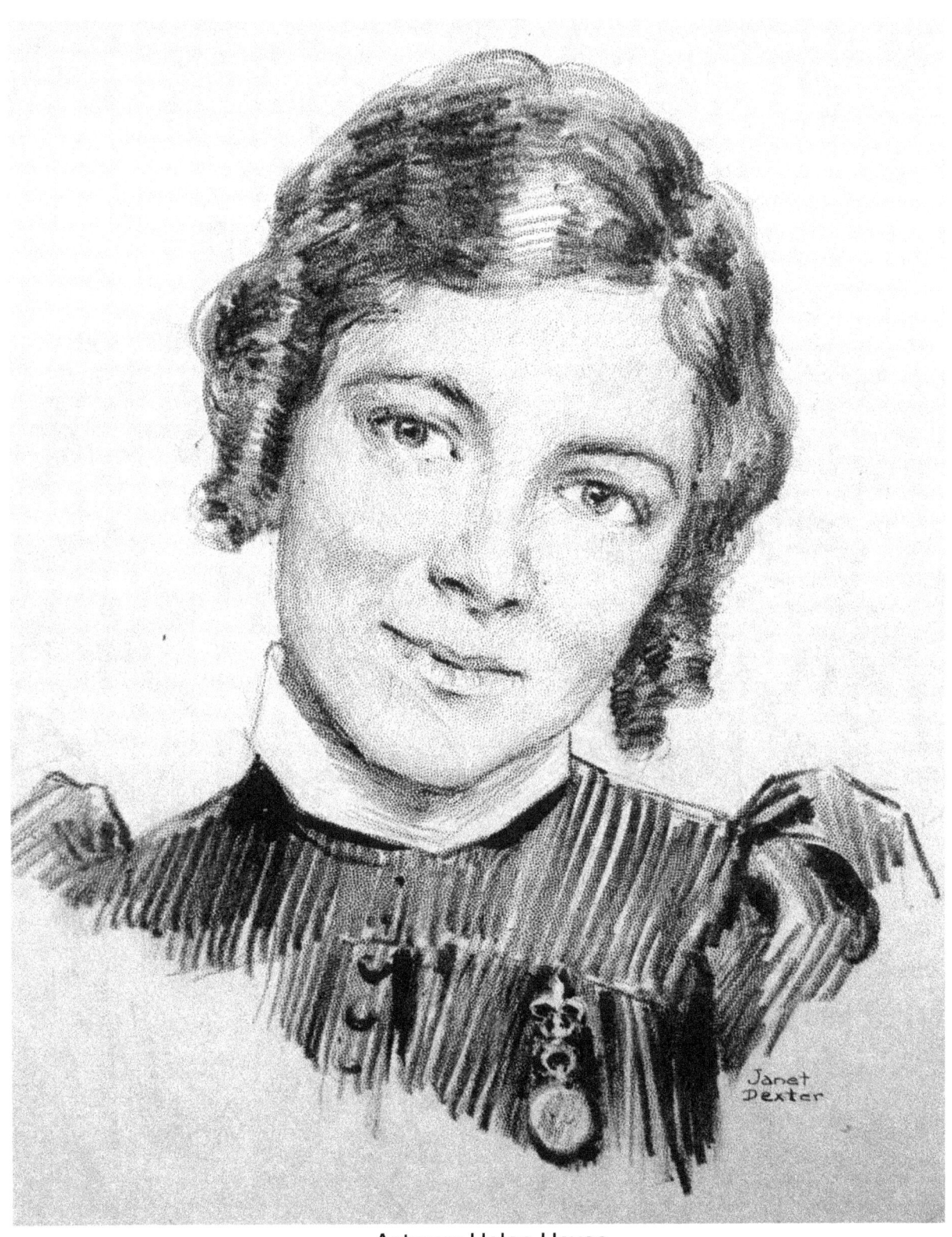

Actress: Helen Hayes

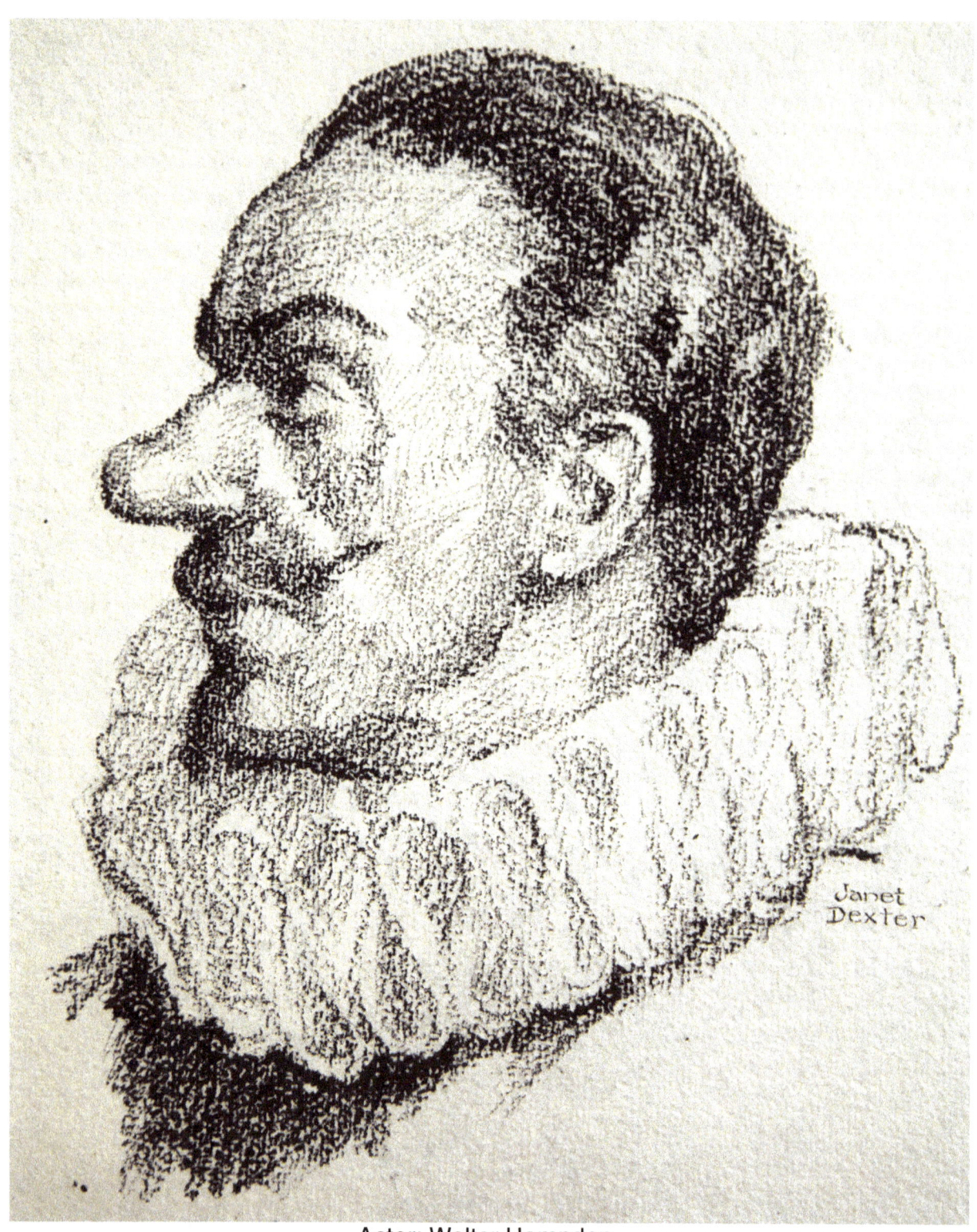

Actor: Walter Hampden

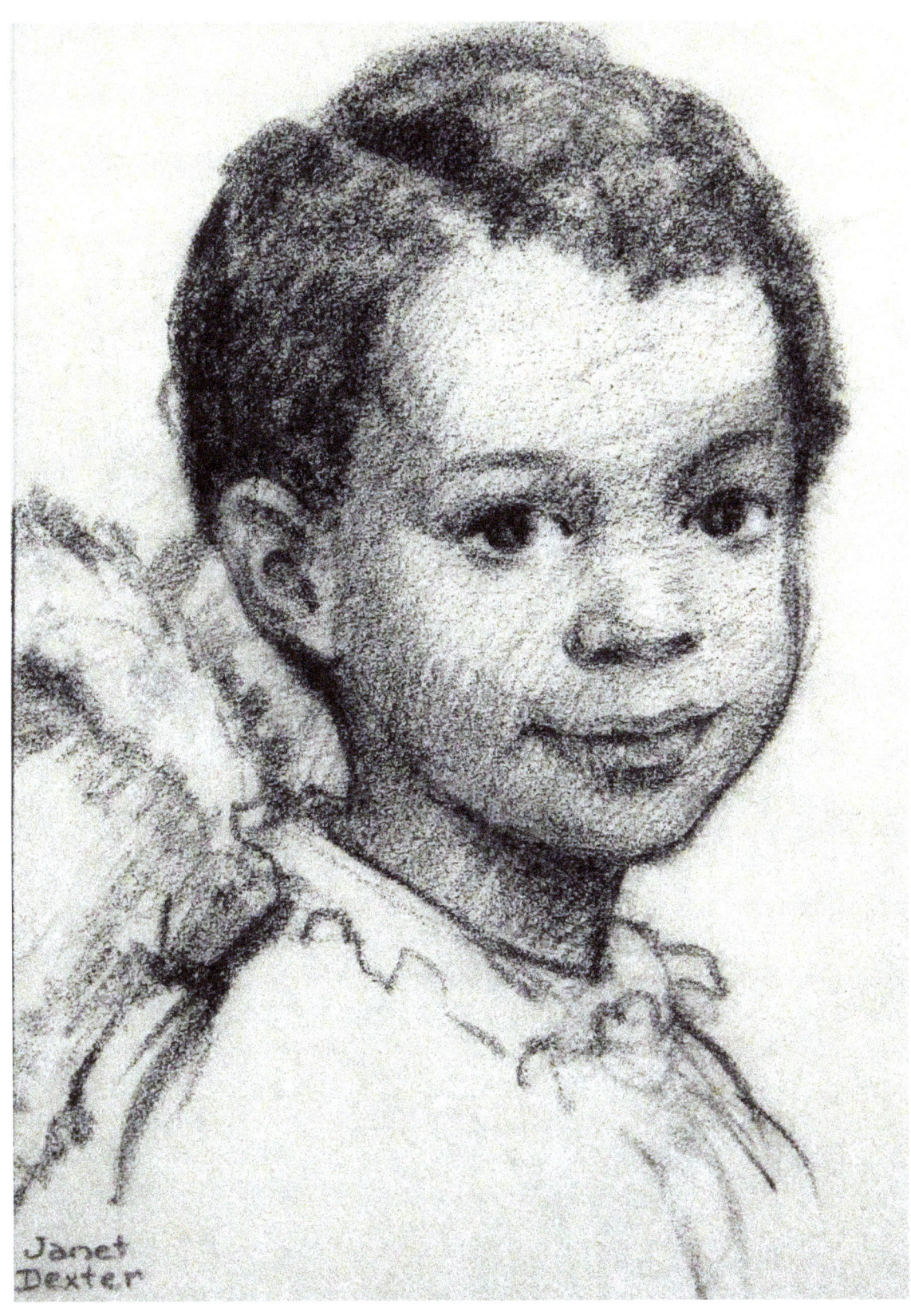

Actress: Gloria Baumgardner

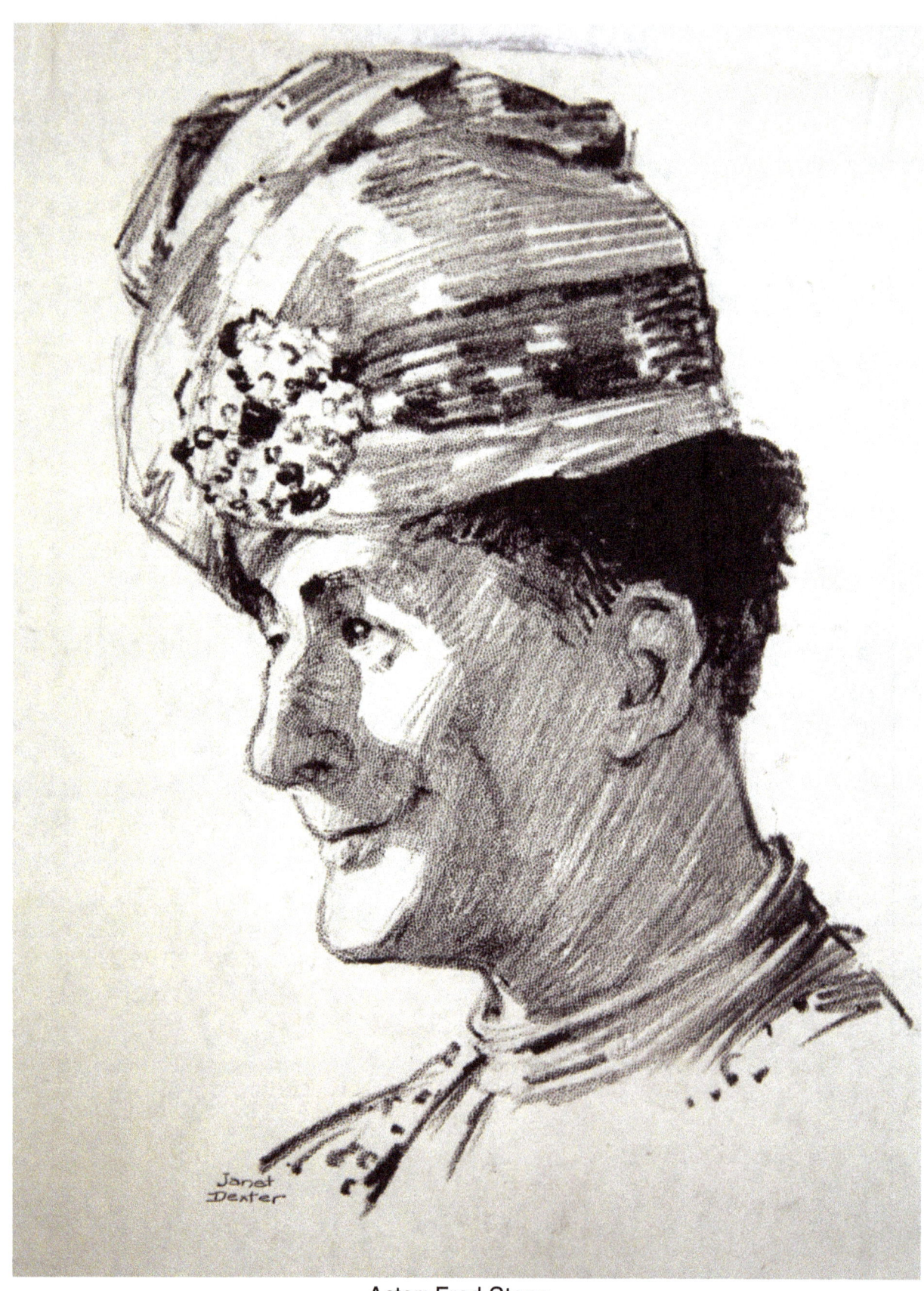

Actor: Fred Stone

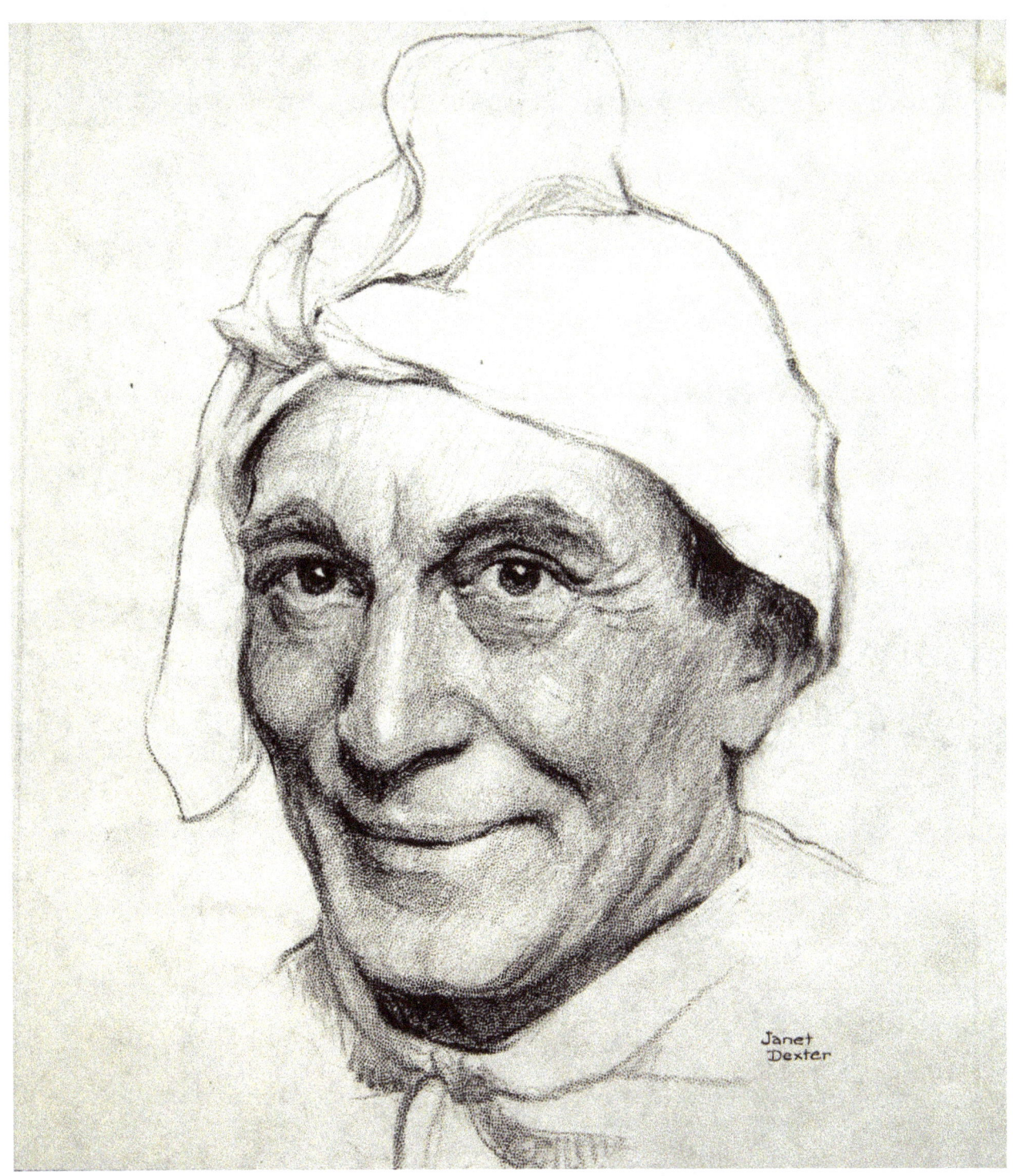

Actor: Firmin Gemier

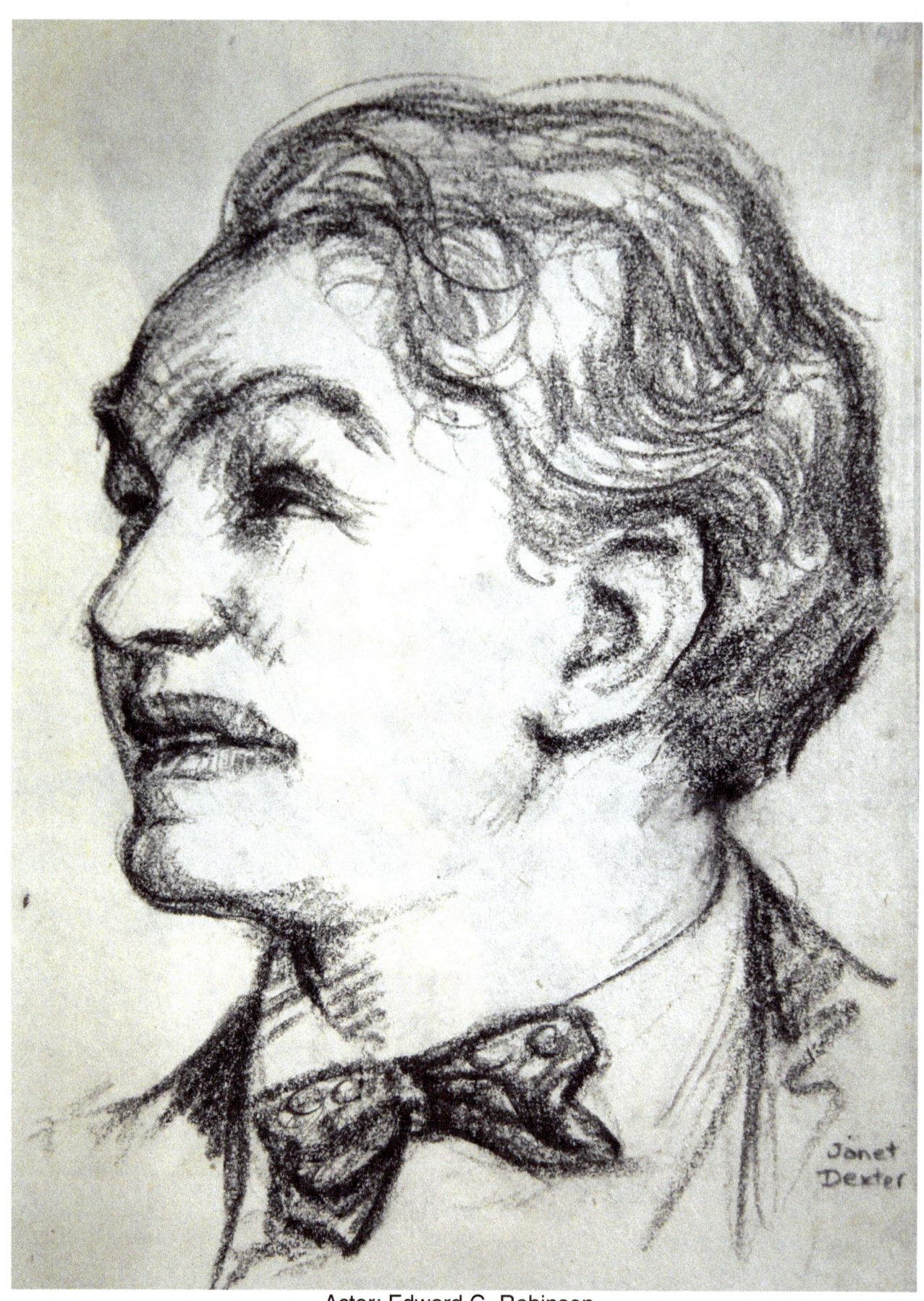

Actor: Edward G. Robinson

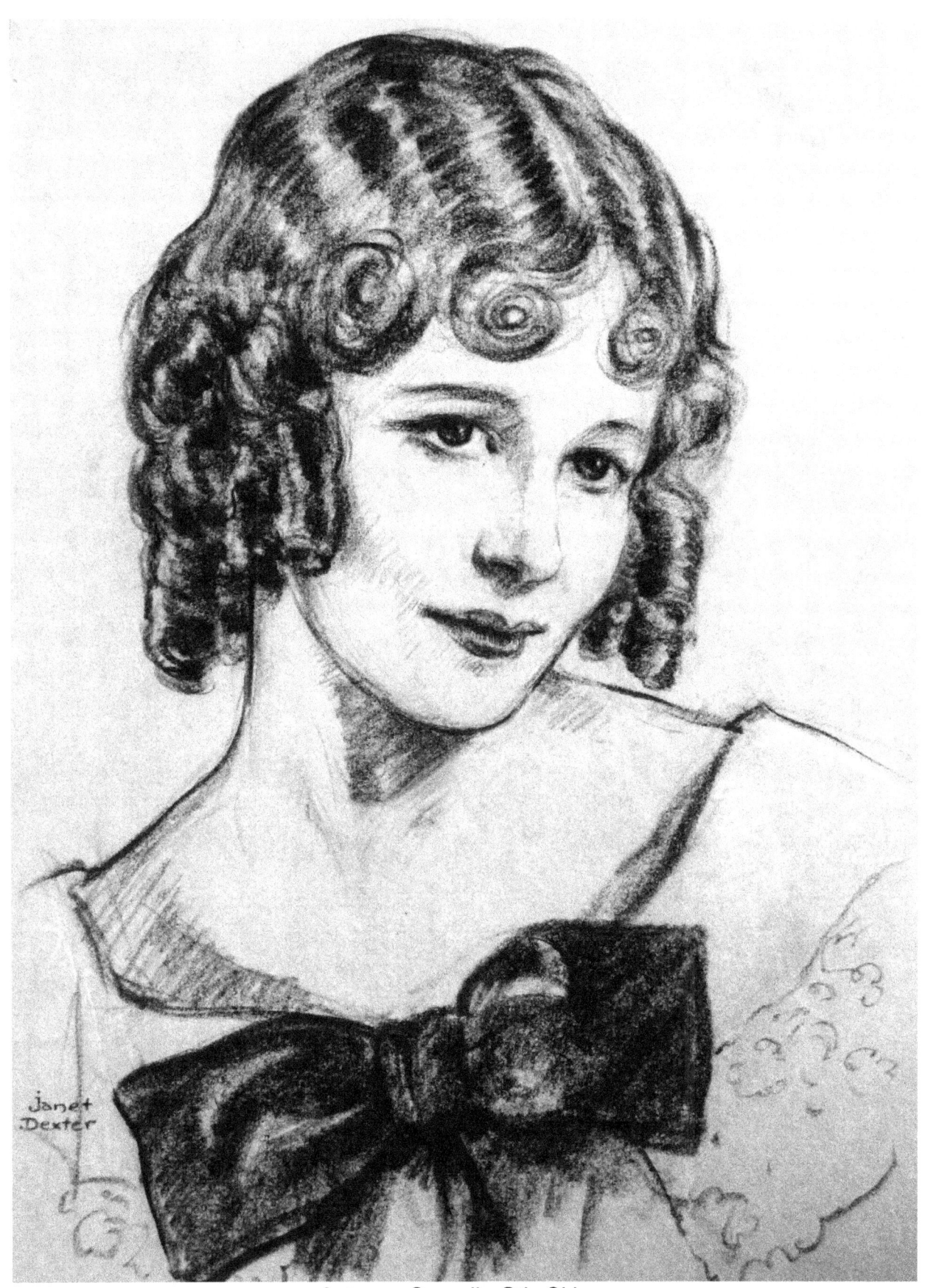

Actress: Cornelia Otis Skinner

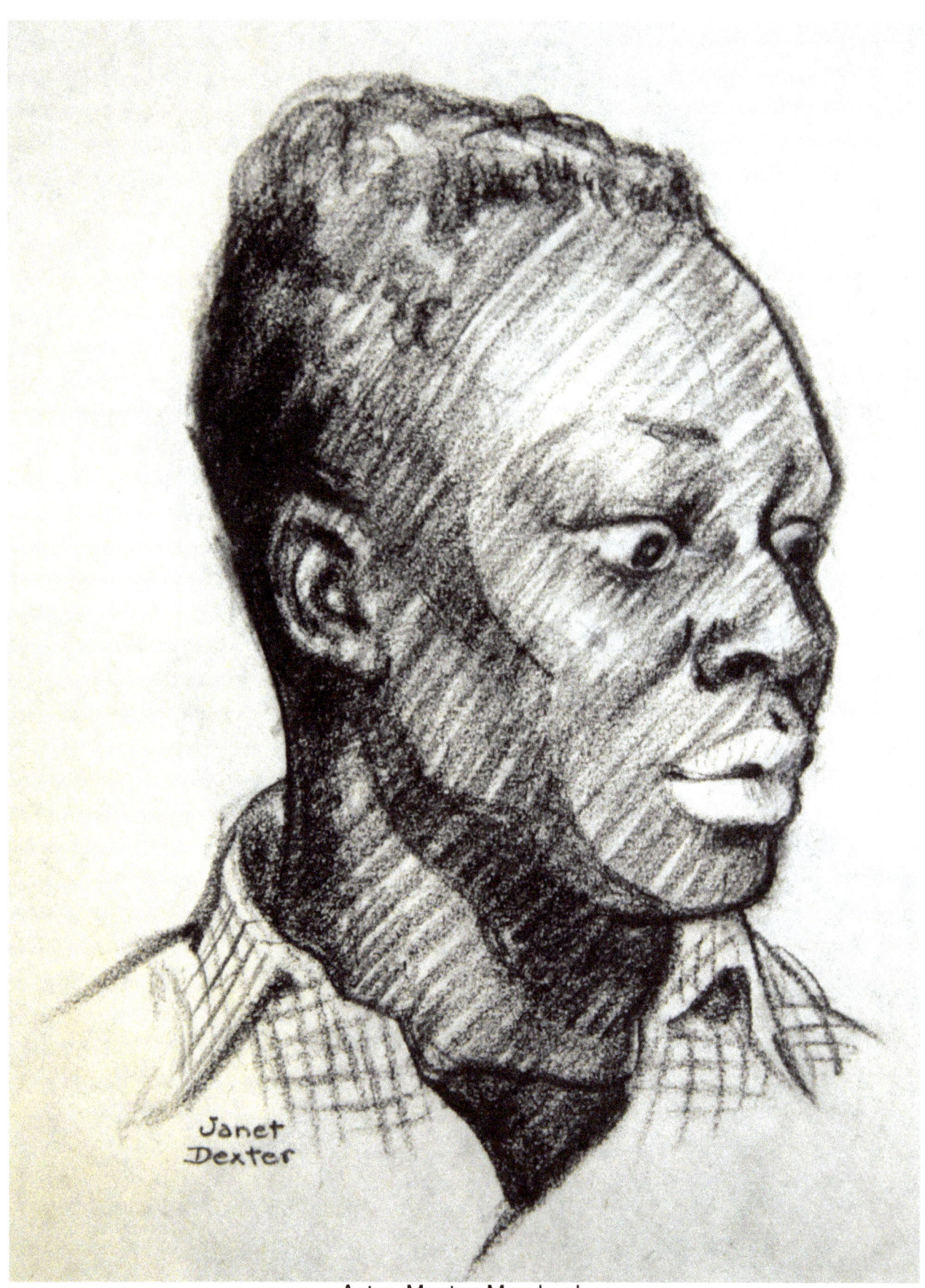

Actor: Manton Moreland

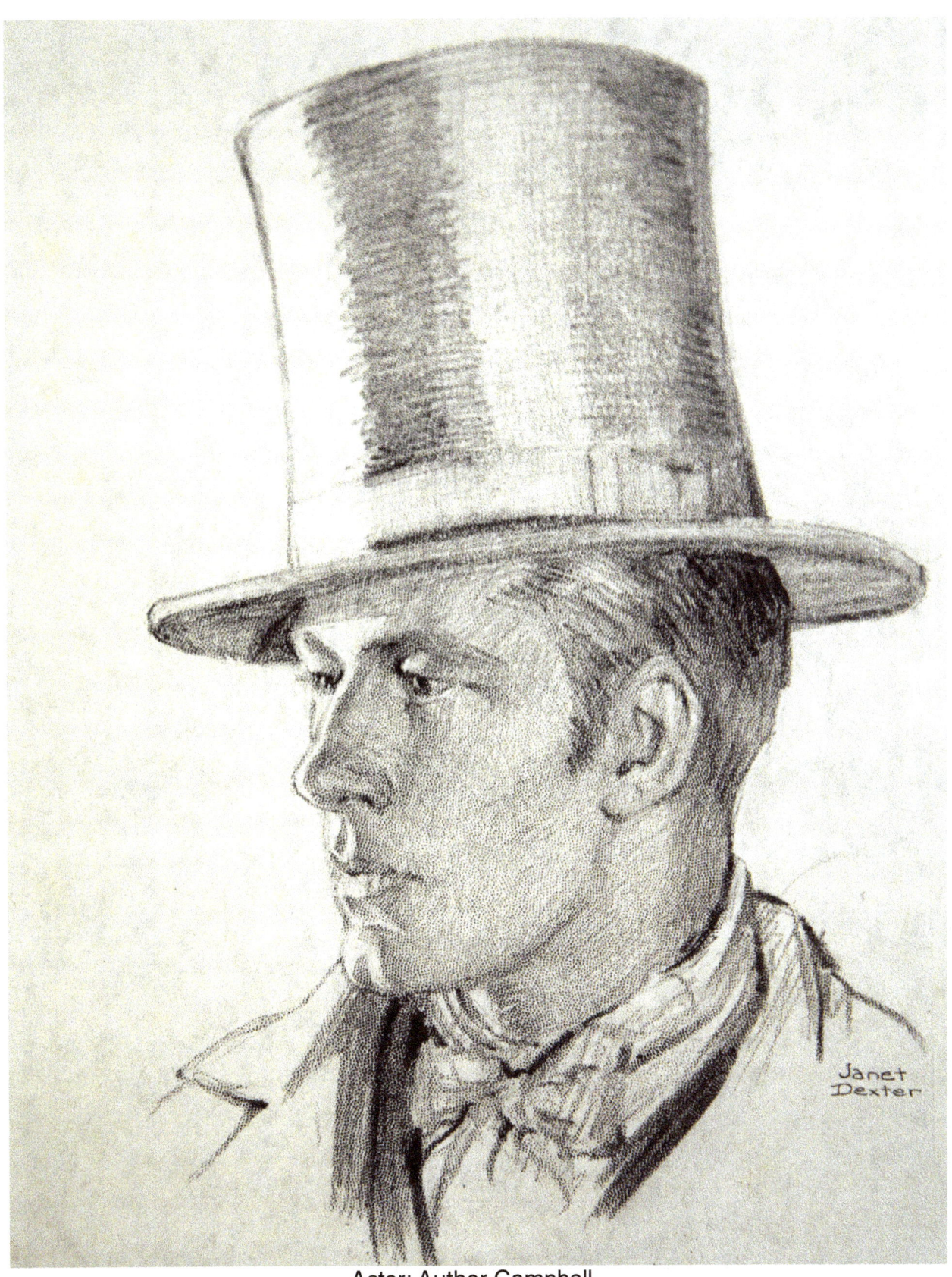

Actor: Author Campbell

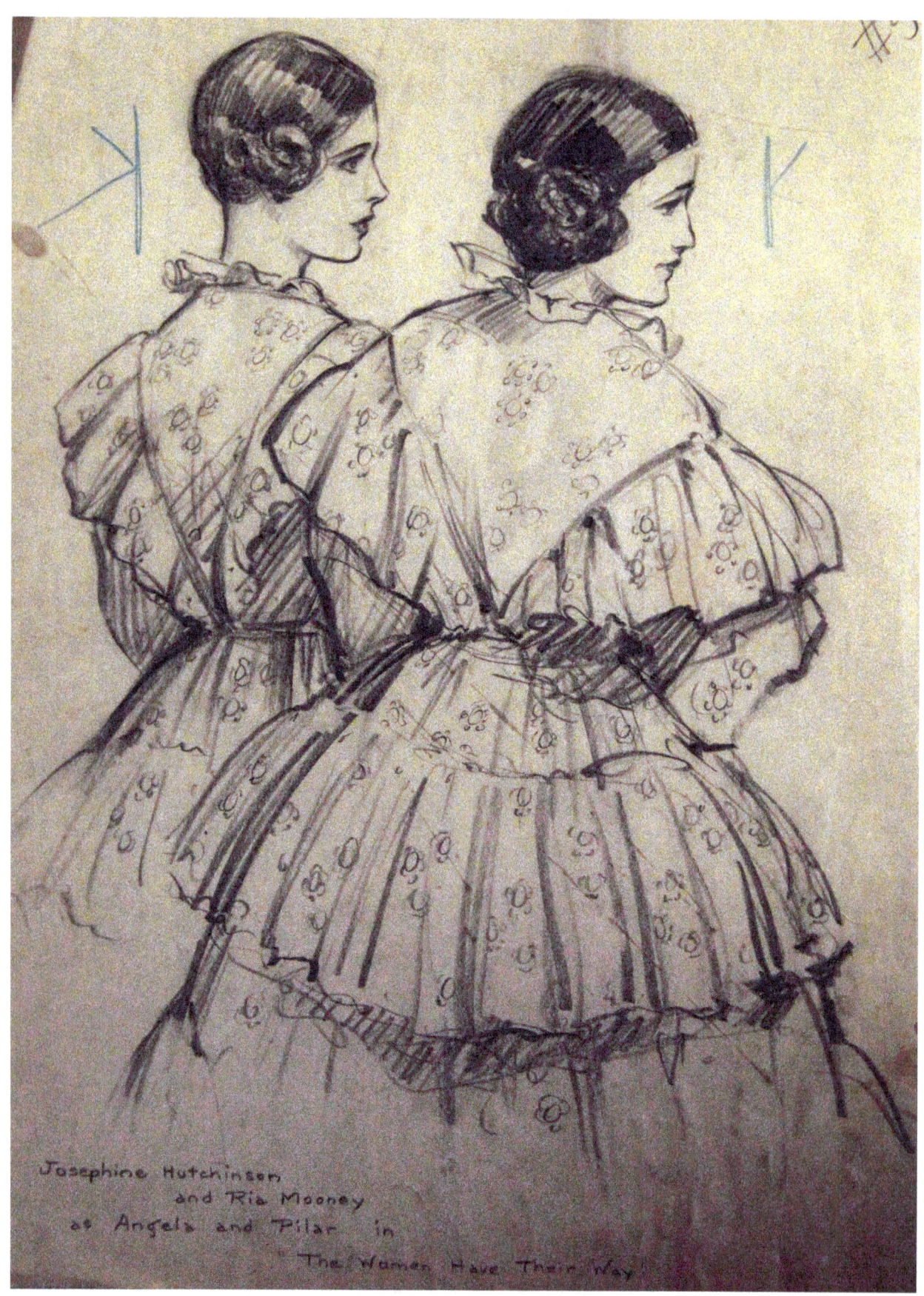

Josephine Hutchinson
and Ria Mooney
as Angela and Pilar in
"The Women Have Their Way"

Actresses: Josephine Hutchinson / Ria Mooney

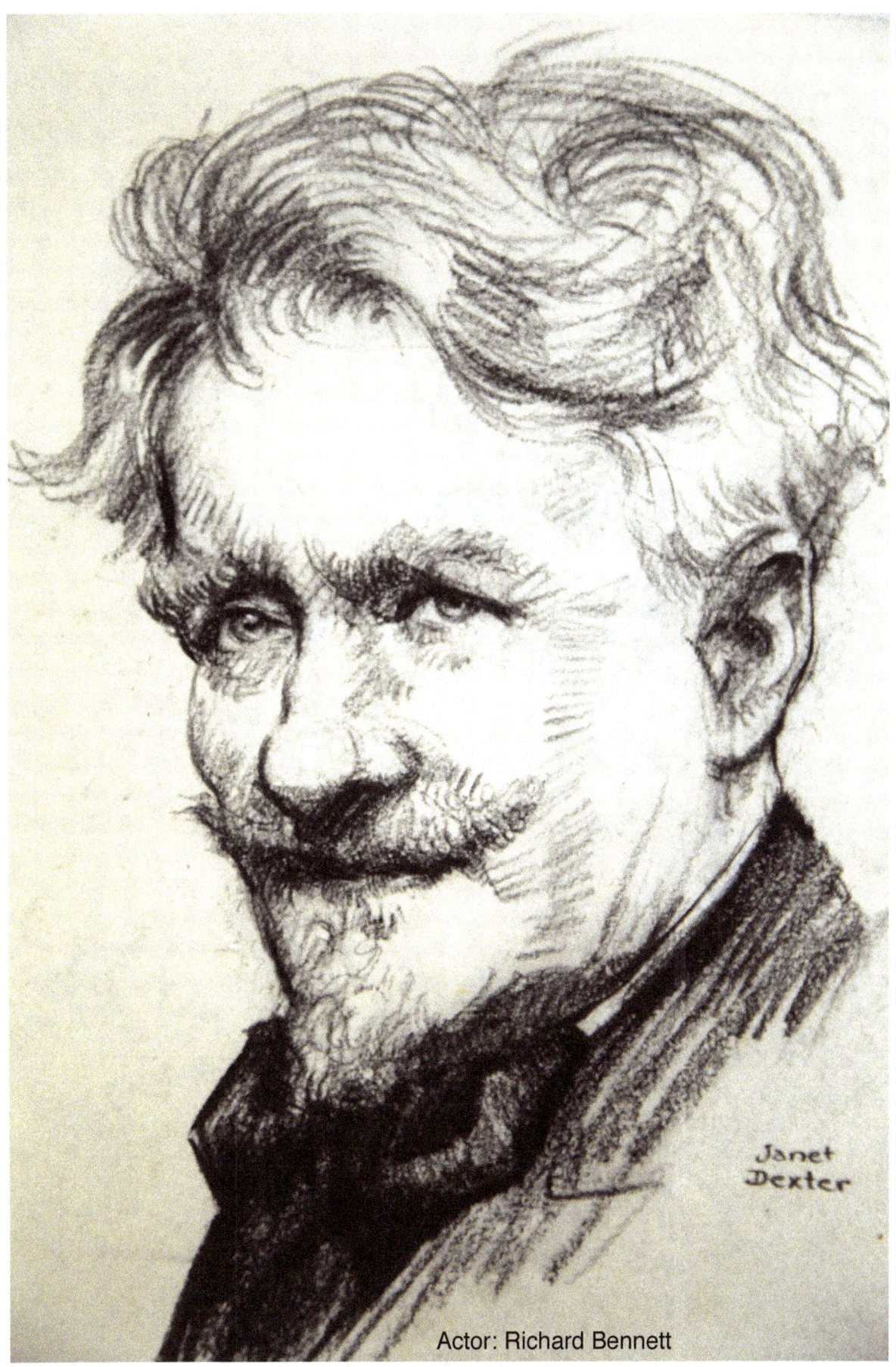

Actor: Richard Bennett

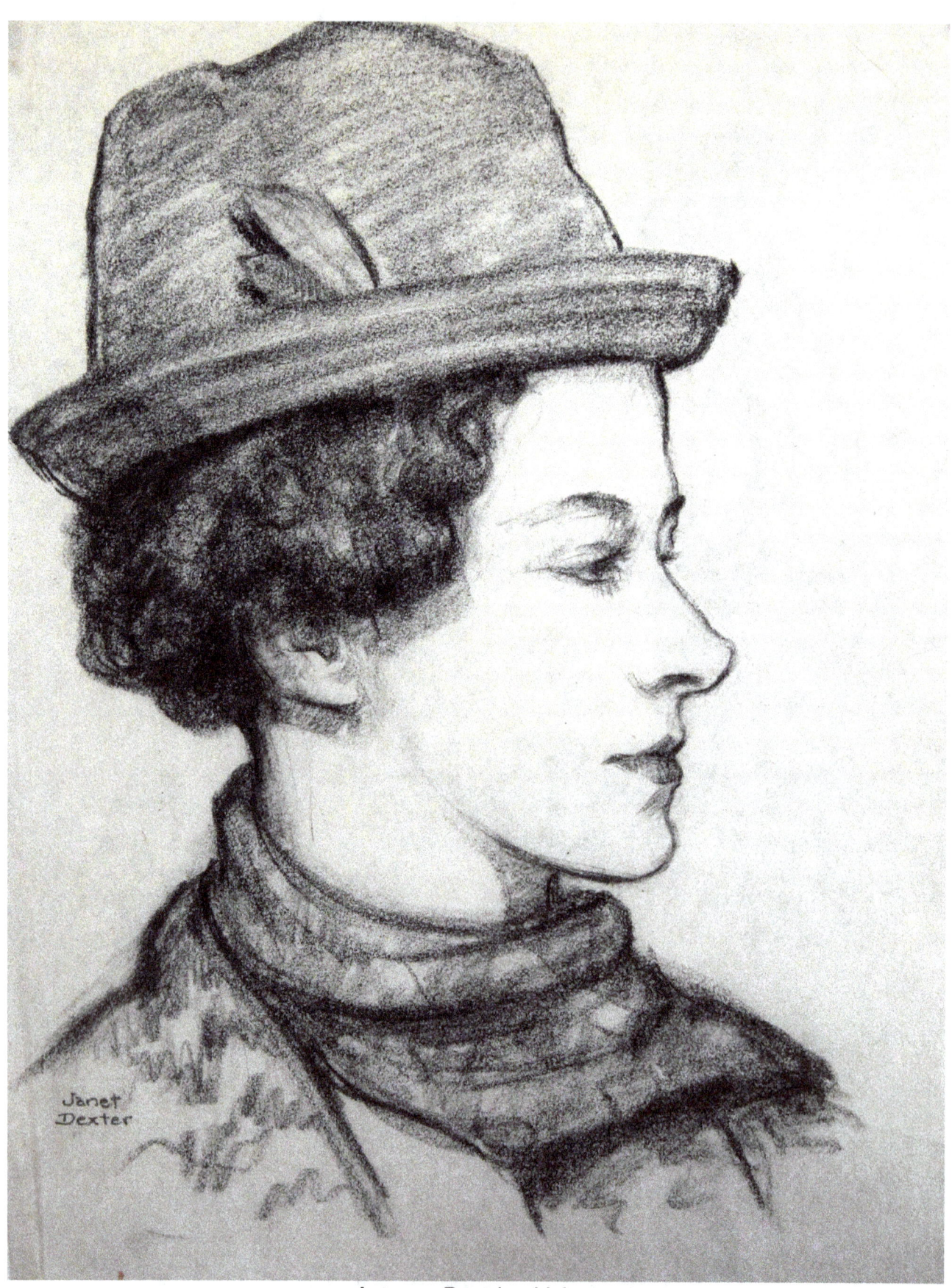

Actress: Beatrice Lisie

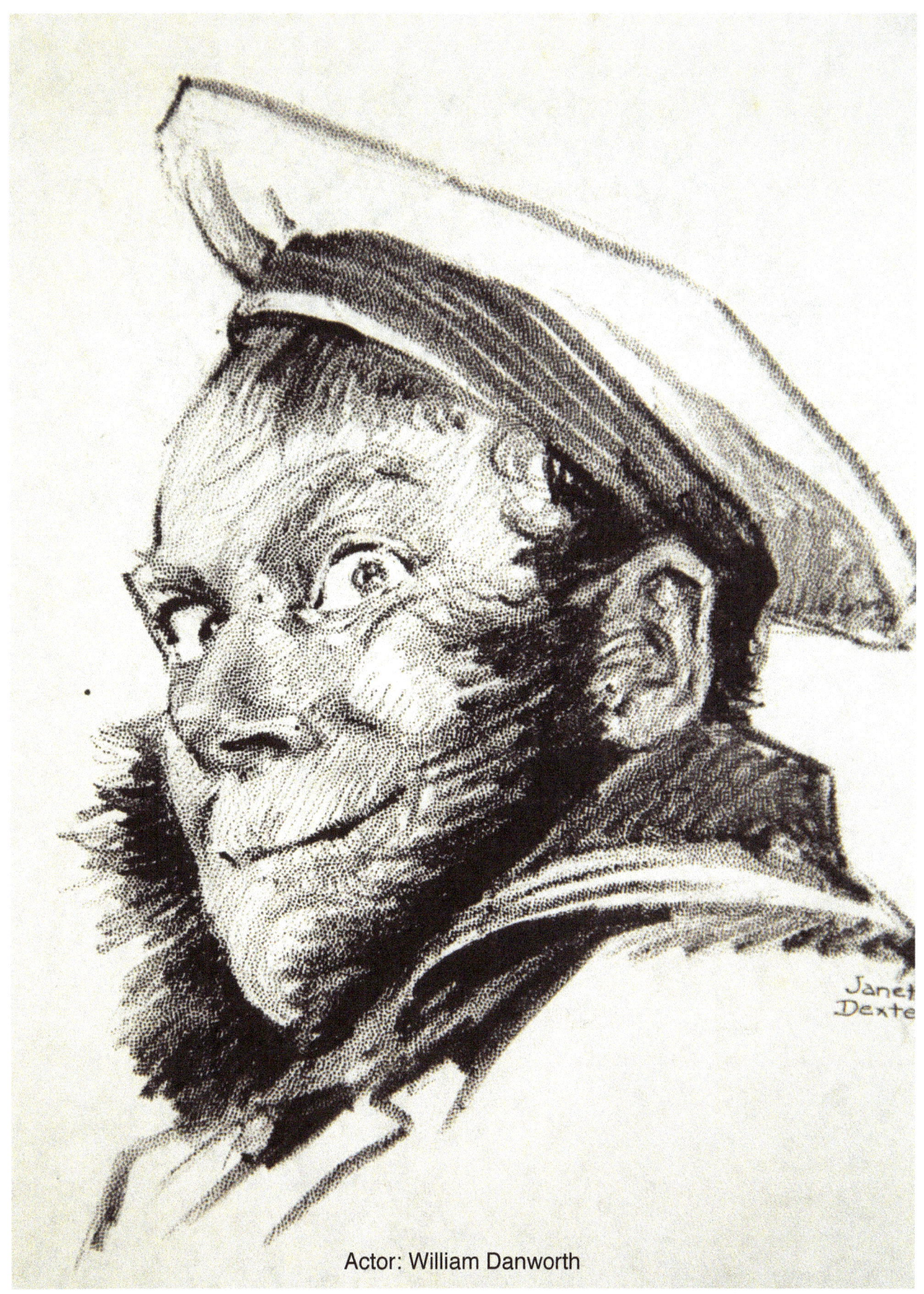

Actor: William Danworth

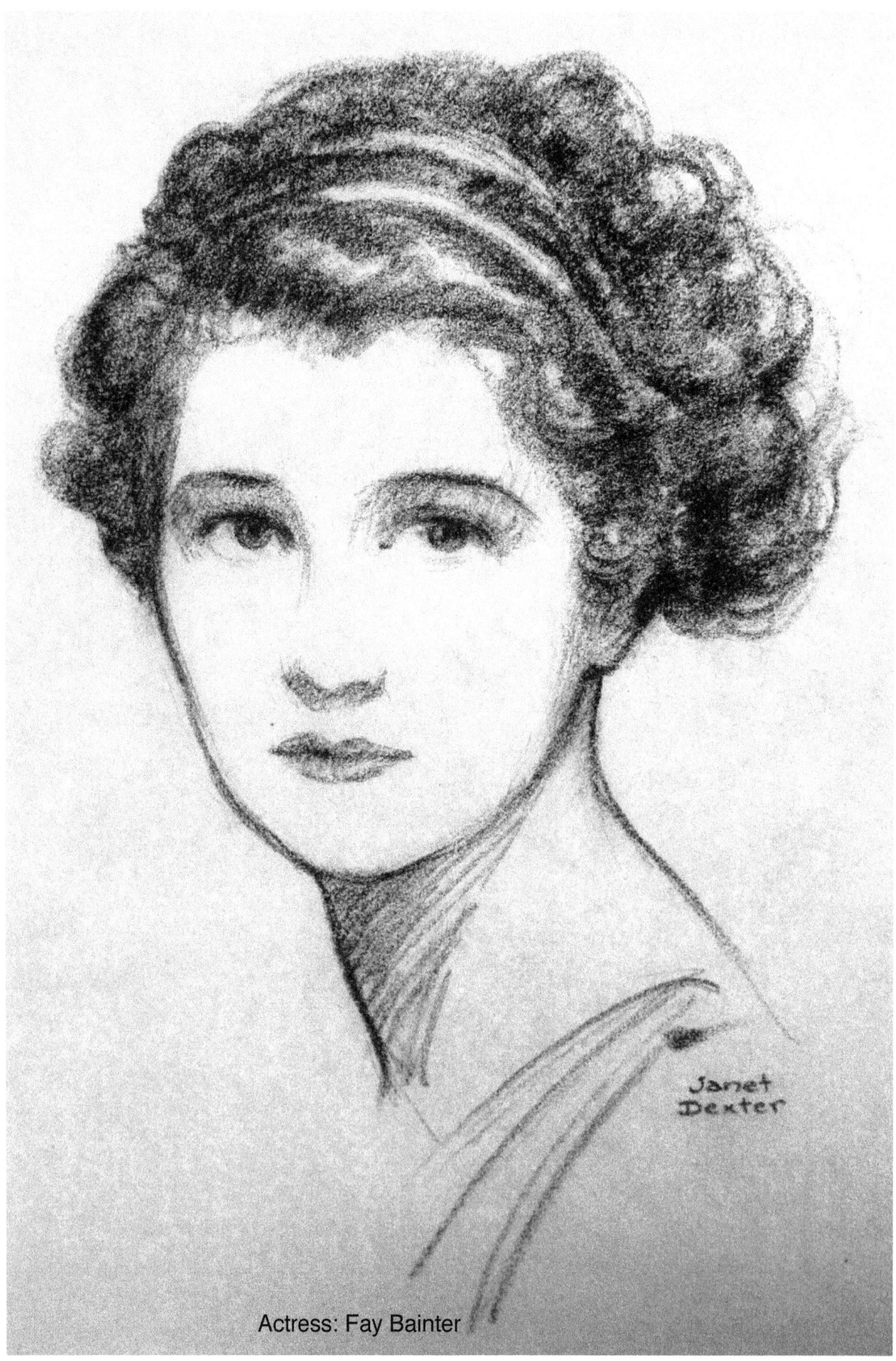

Actress: Fay Bainter

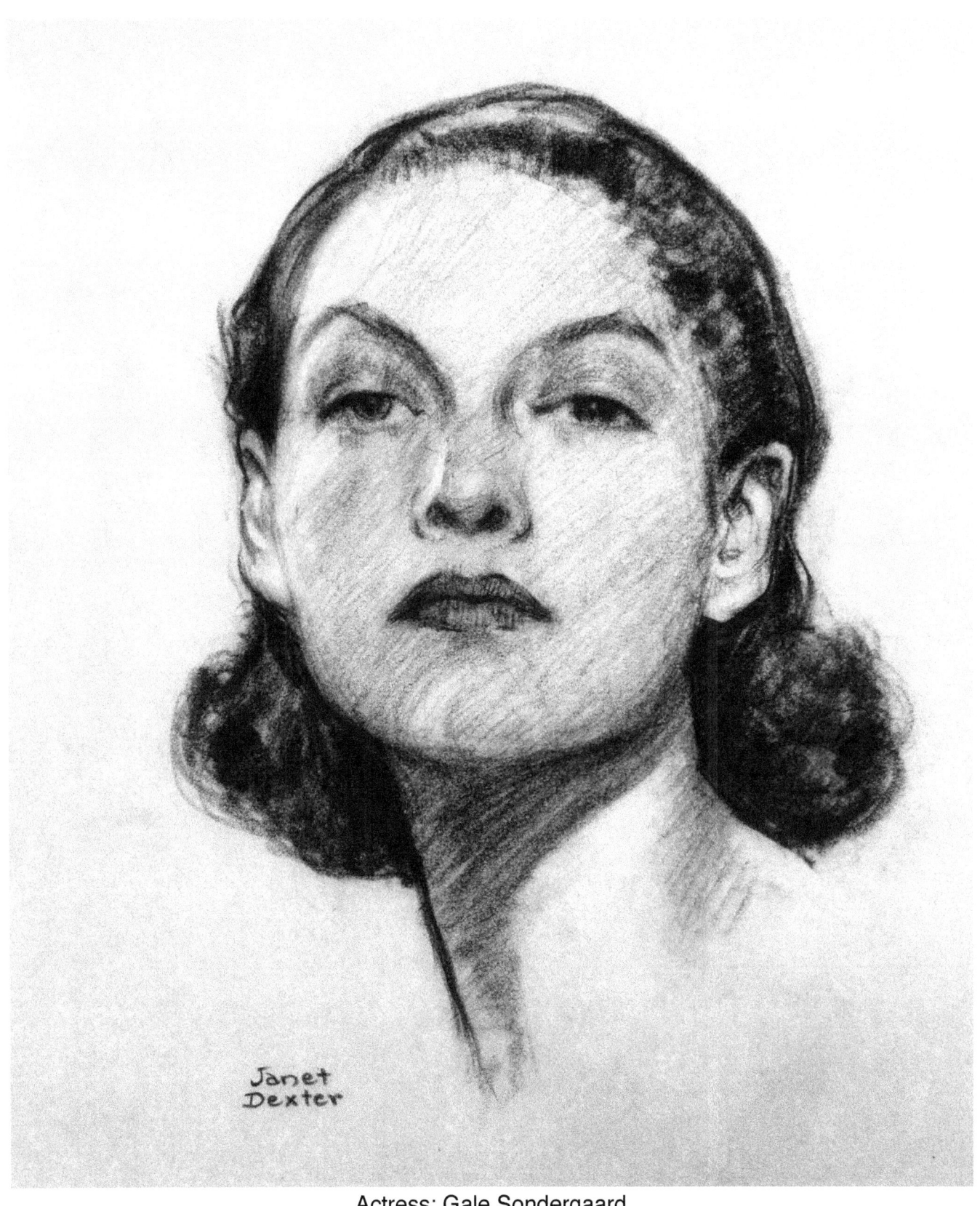

Actress: Gale Sondergaard

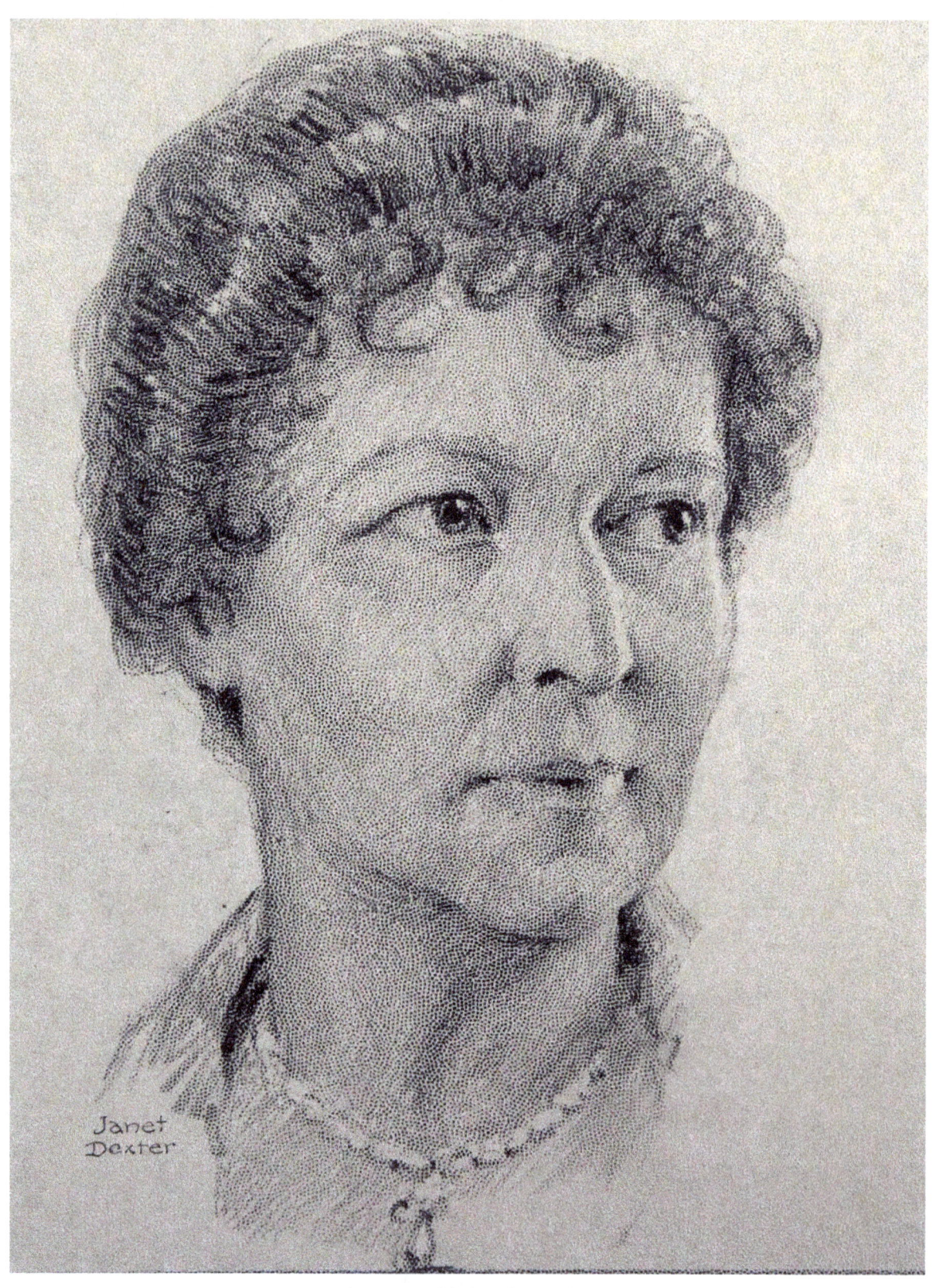

Actress: Helen Lowell

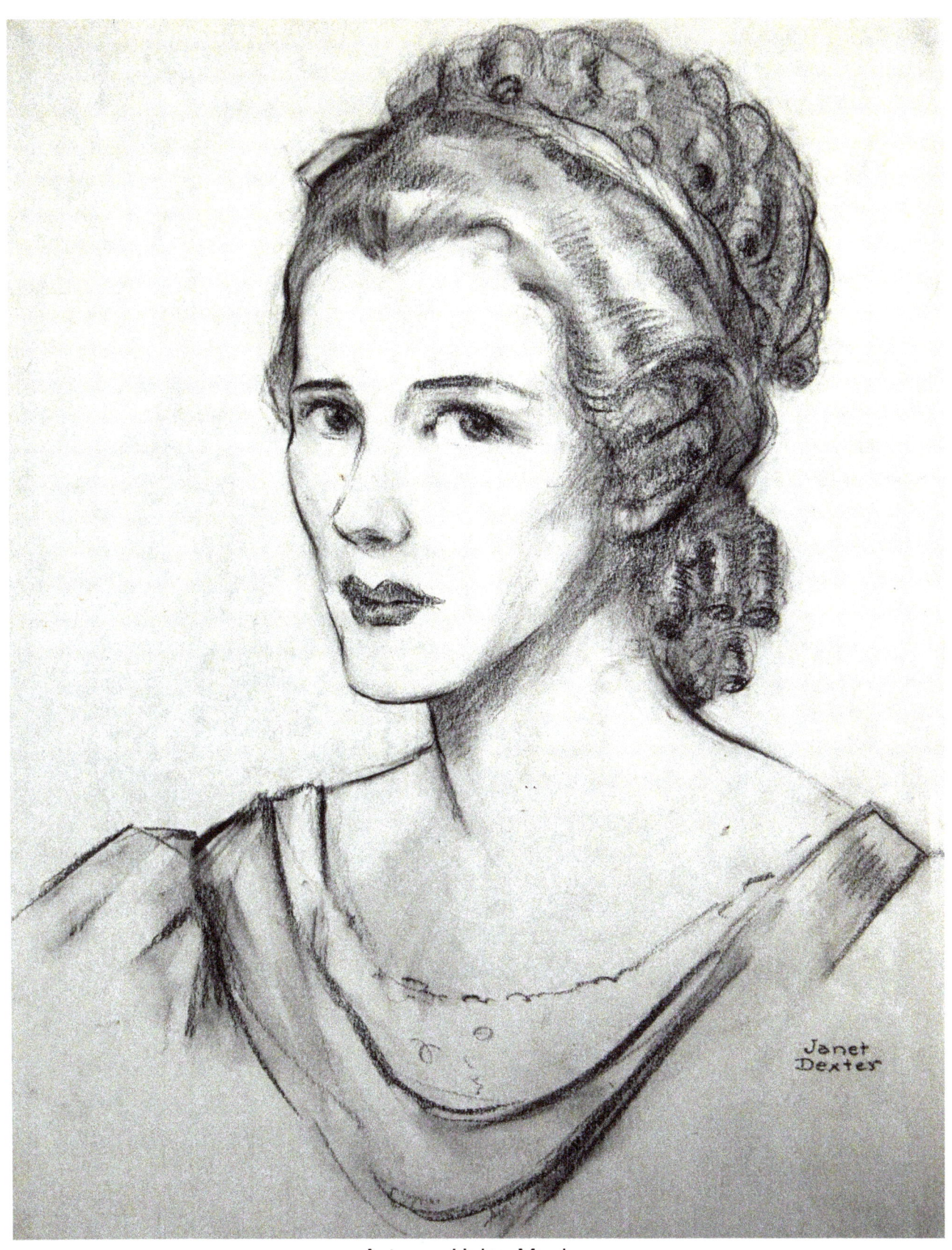

Actress: Helen Menken

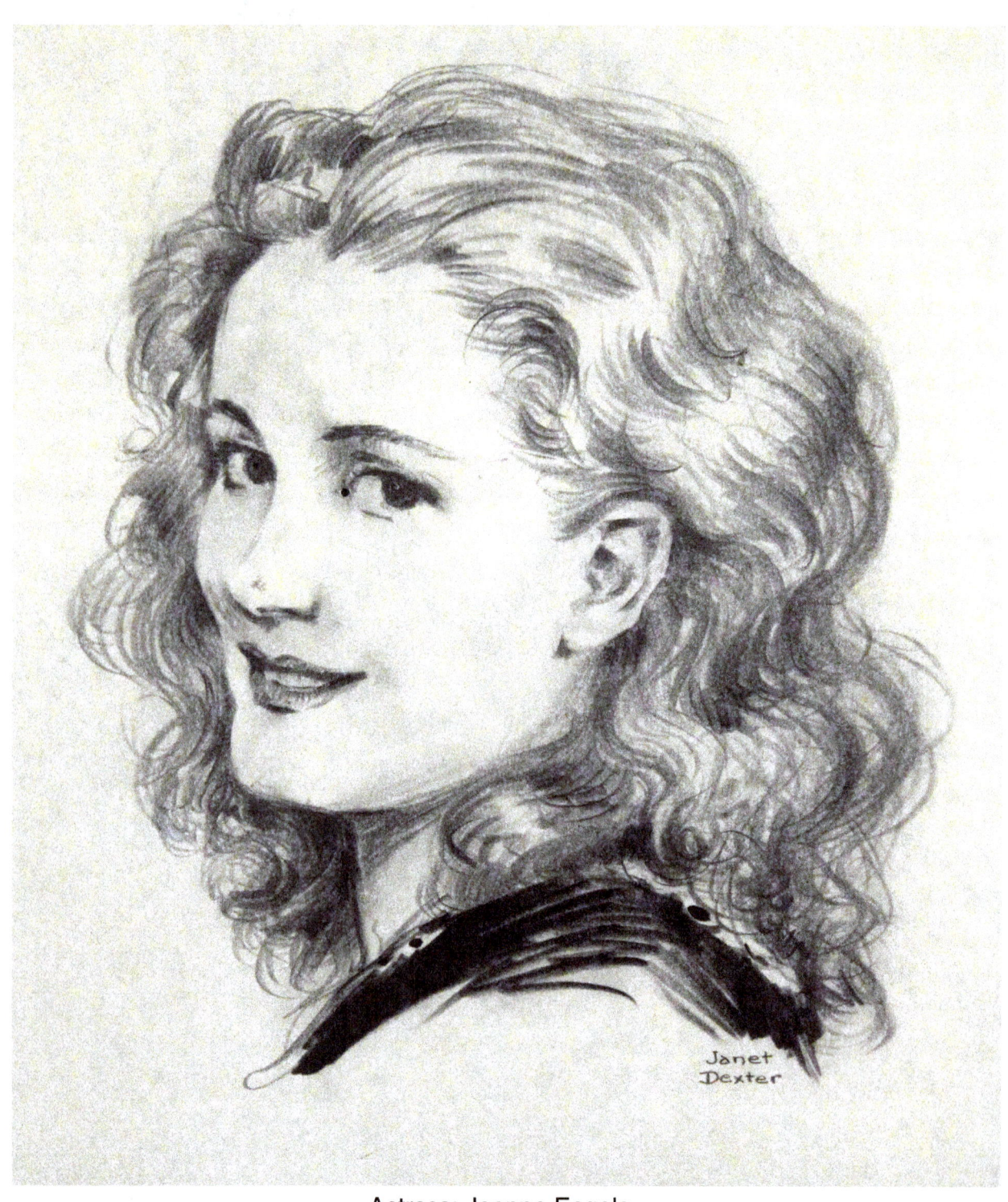

Actress: Jeanne Eagels

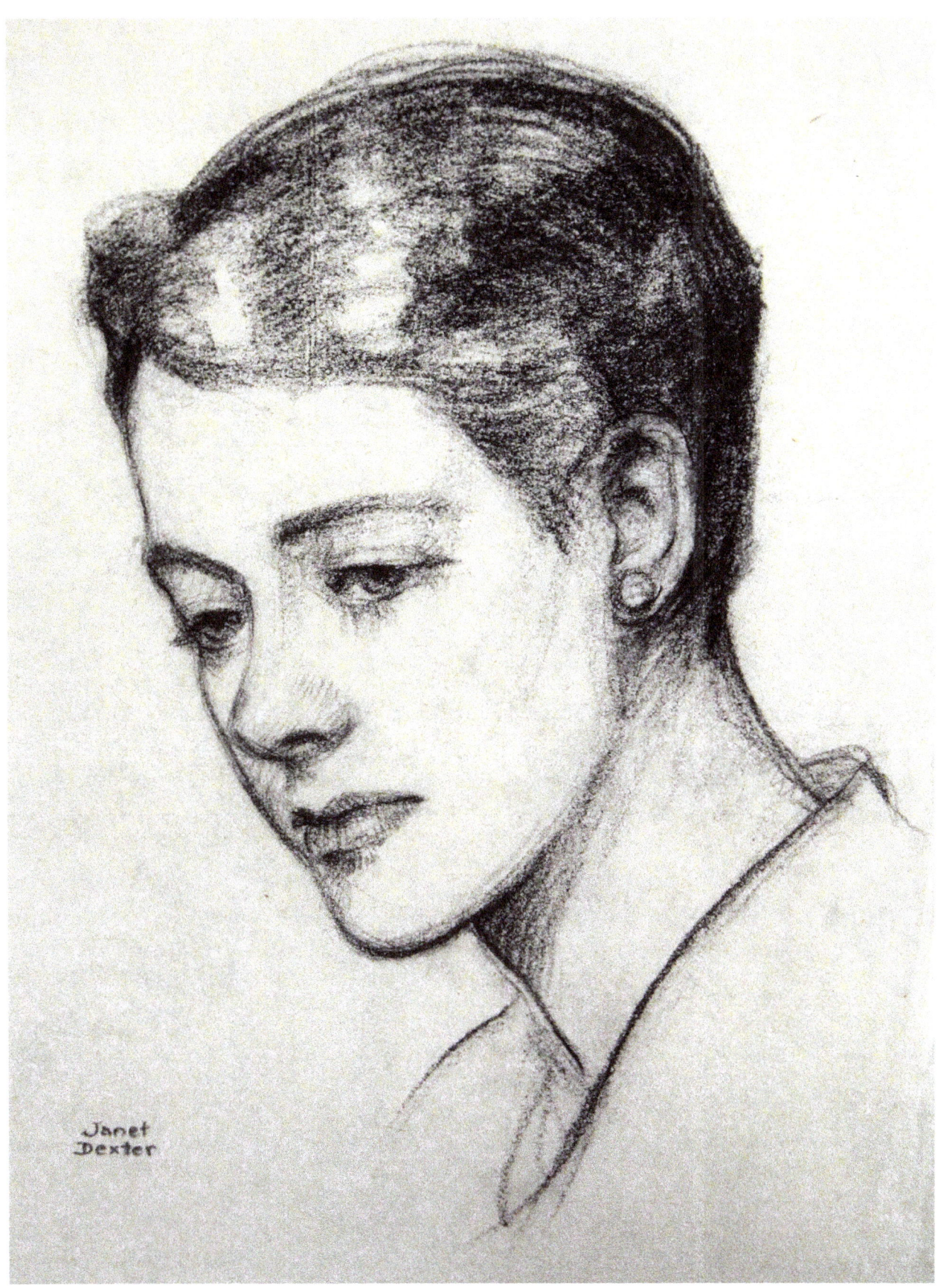

Actress: Hope Williams

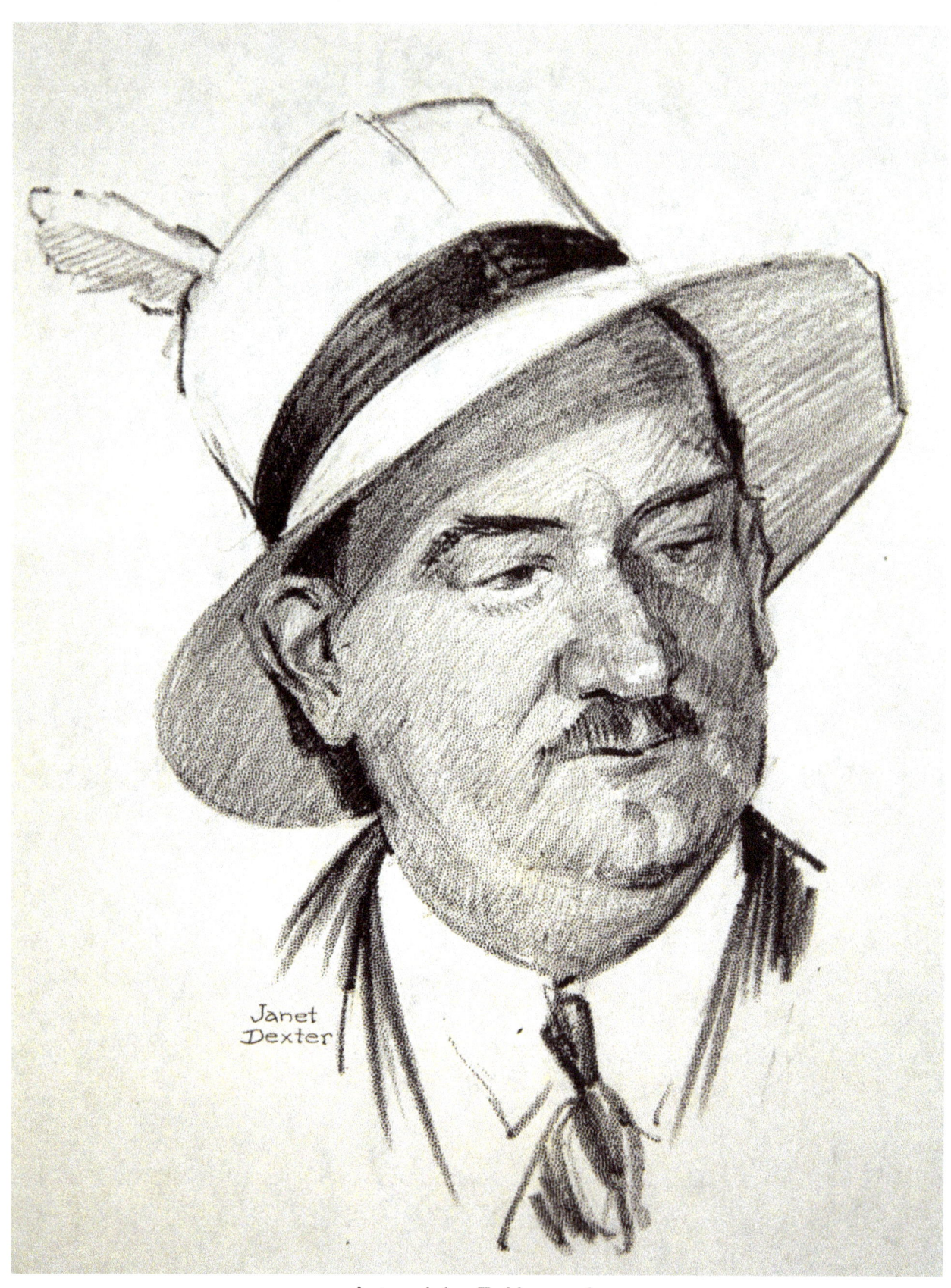

Actor: John E. Hazzard

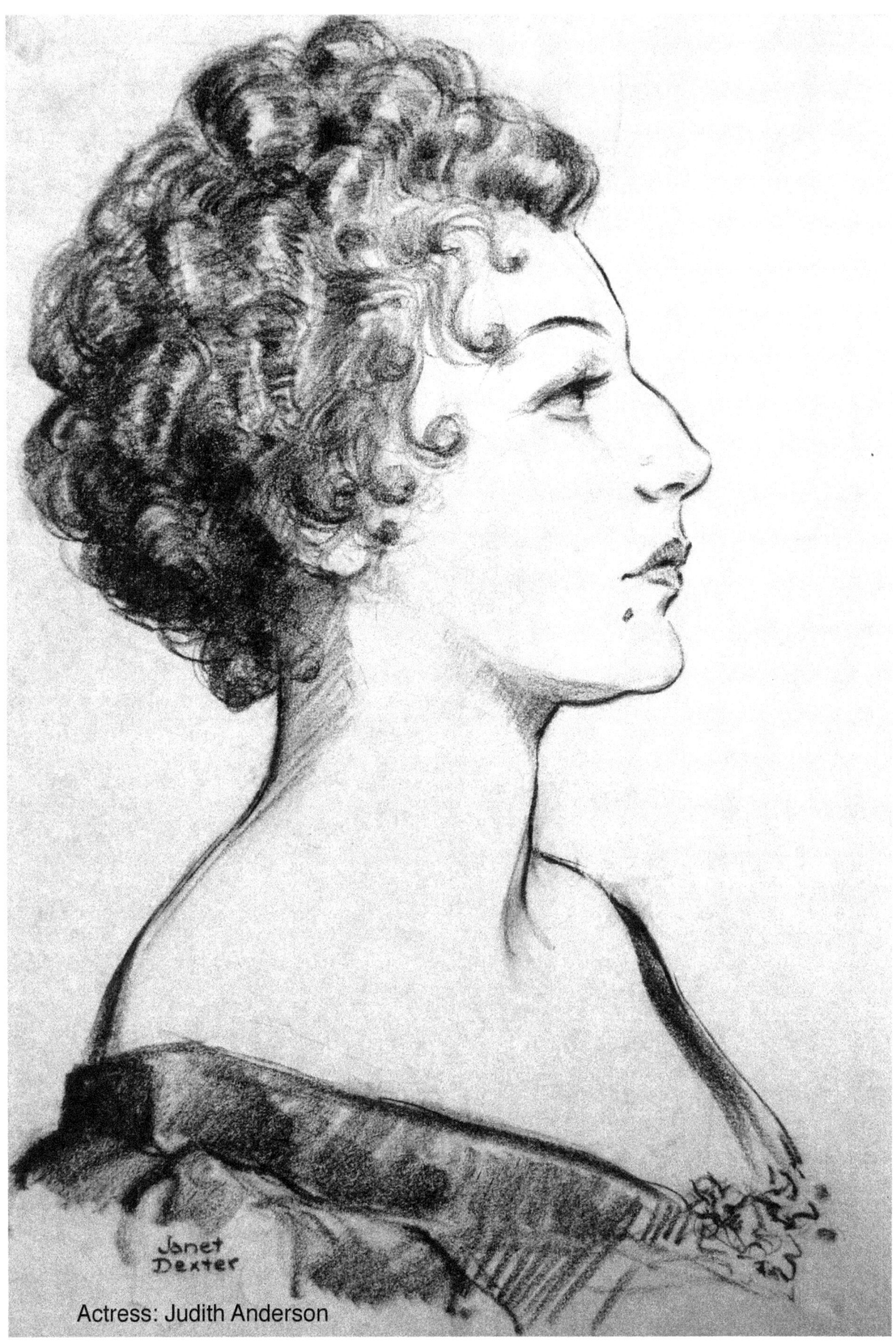

Janet Dexter

Actress: Judith Anderson

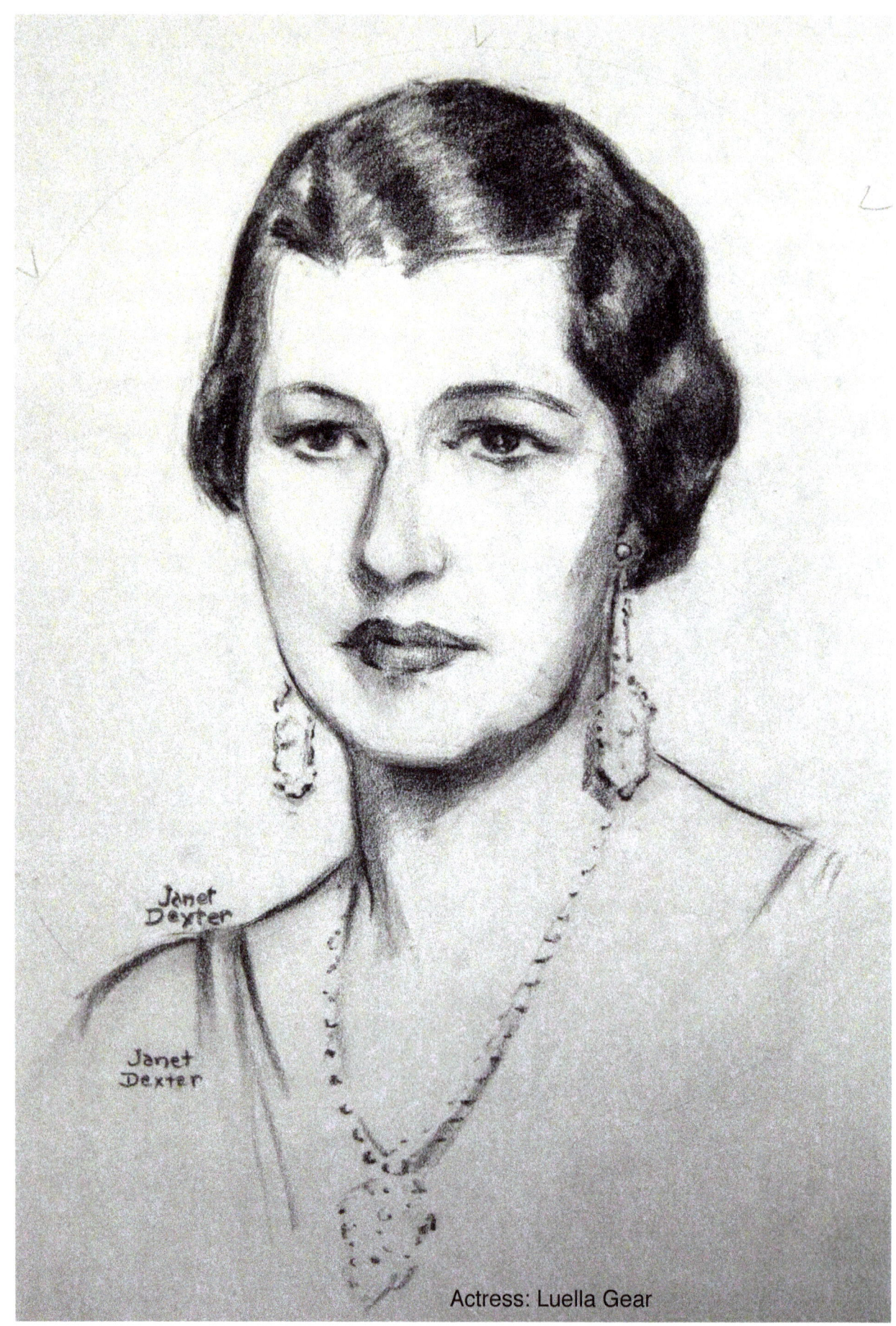

Actress: Luella Gear

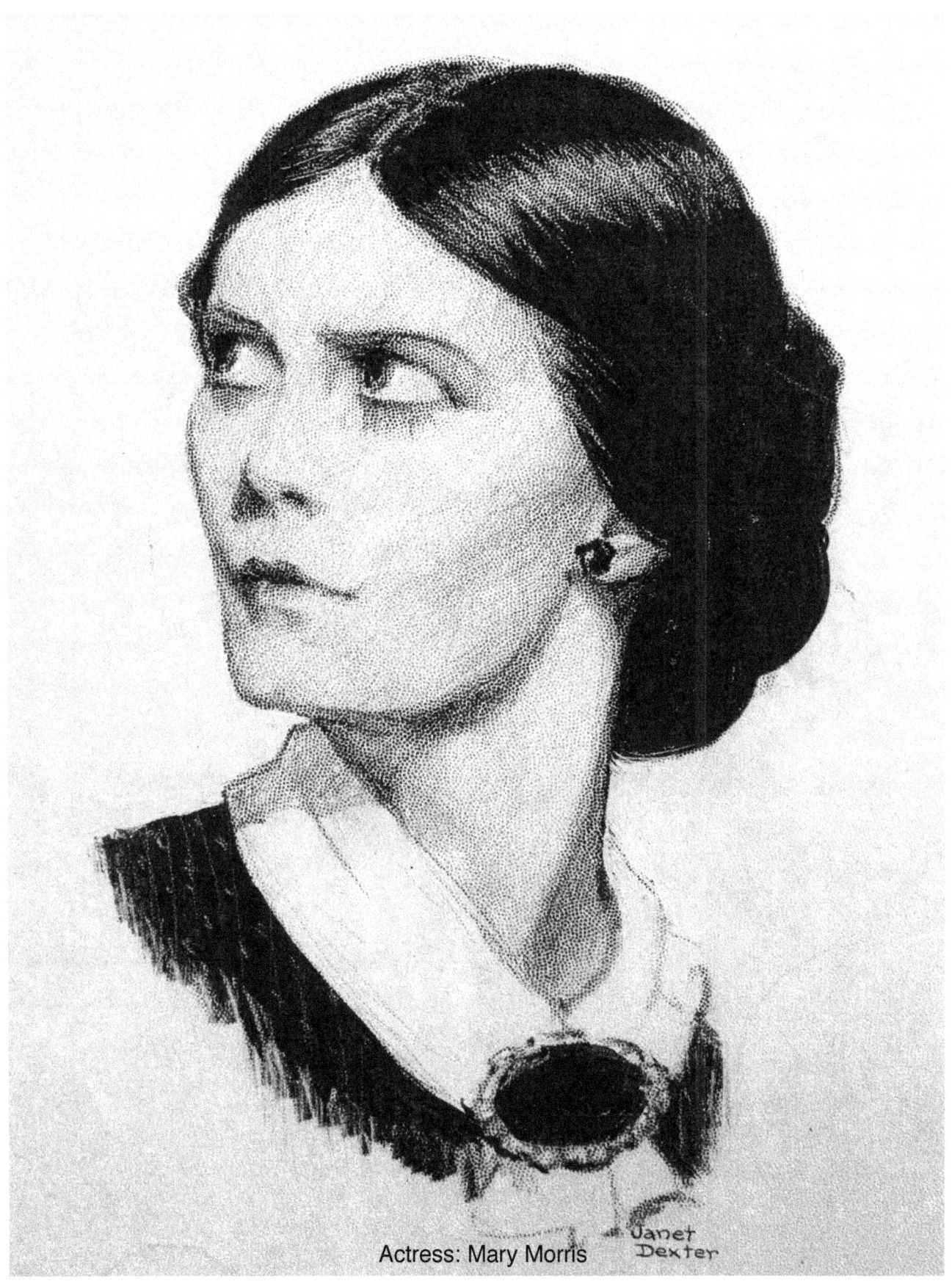

Actress: Mary Morris

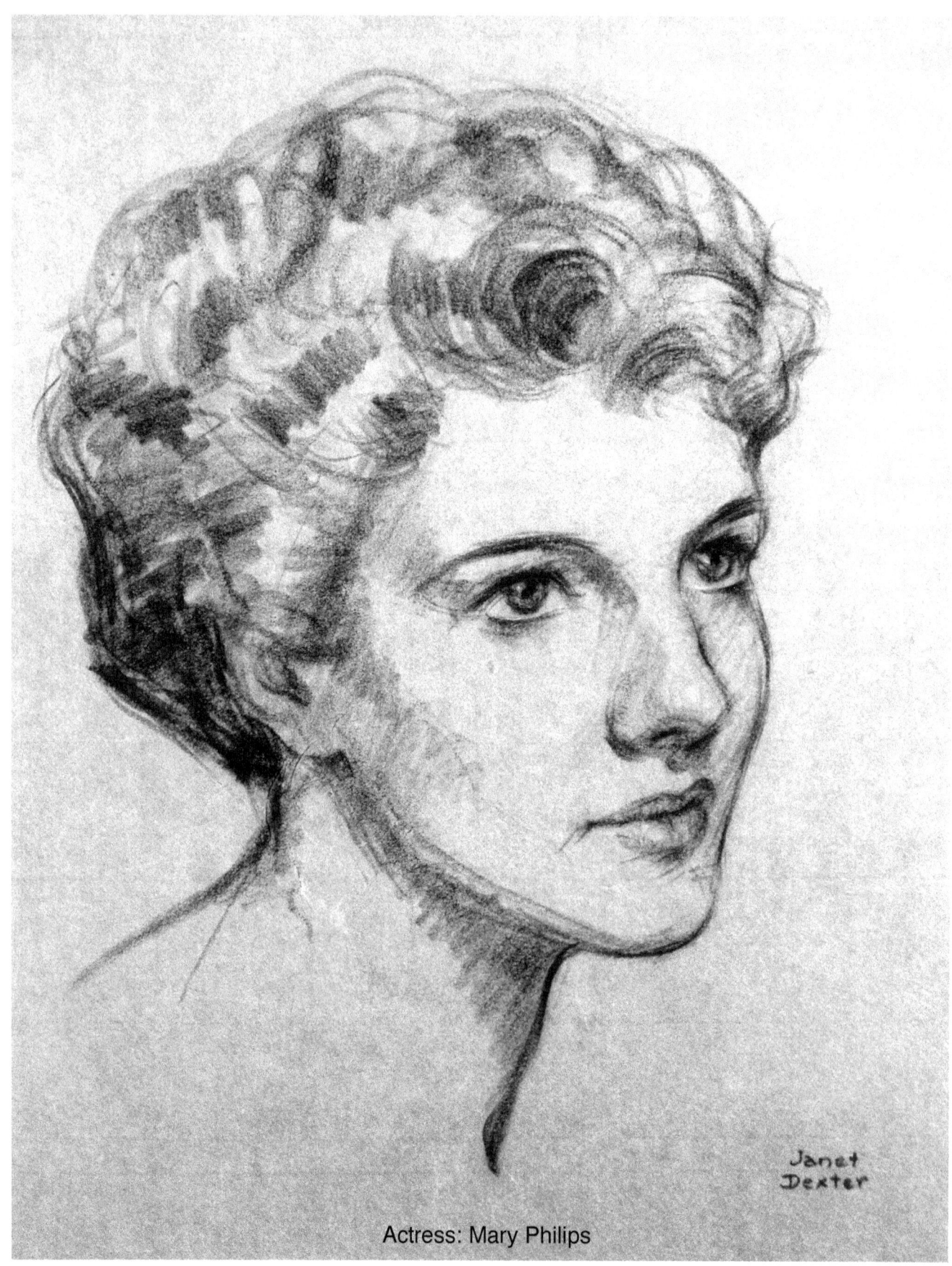

Actress: Mary Philips

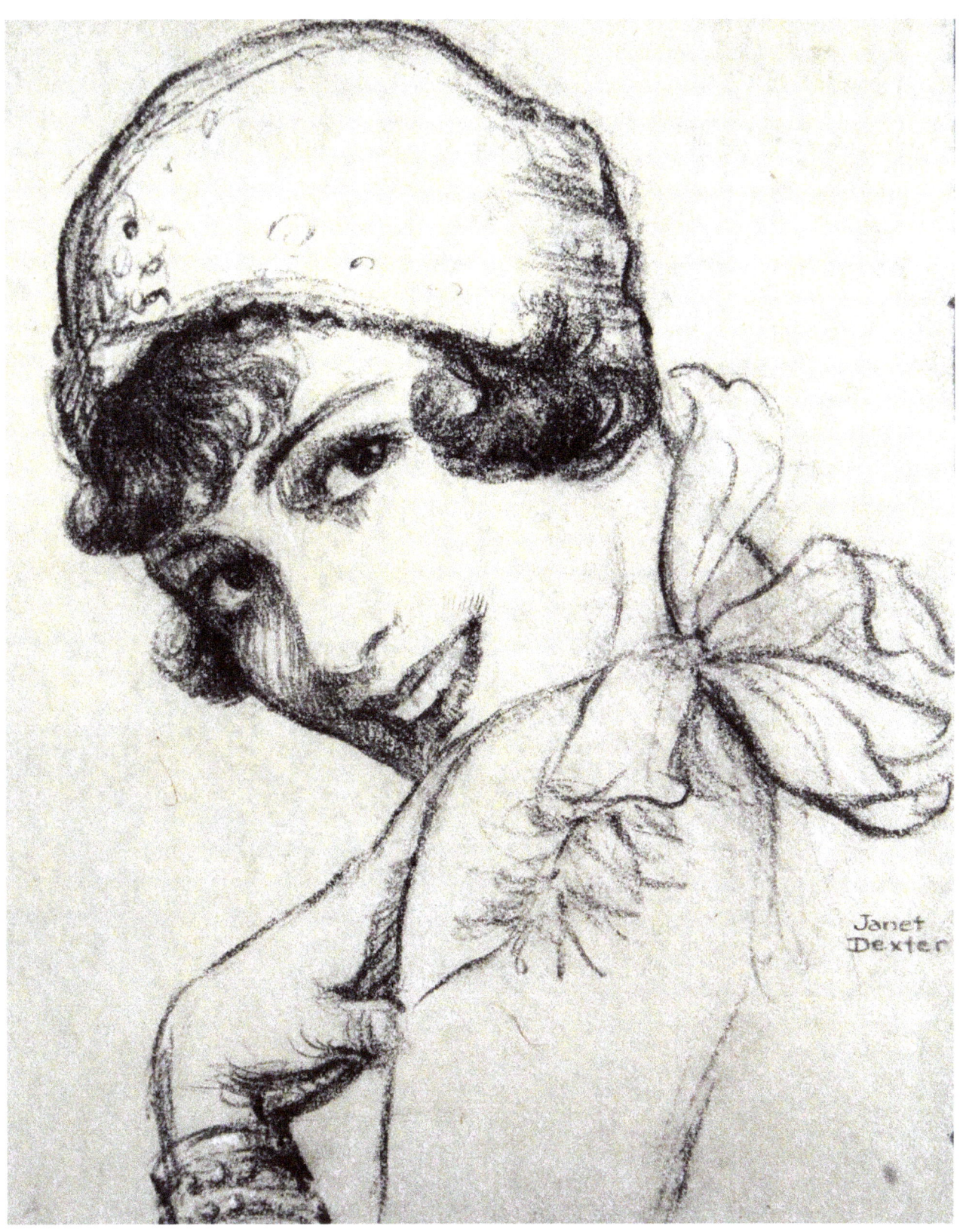

Actress: Fay Marbe

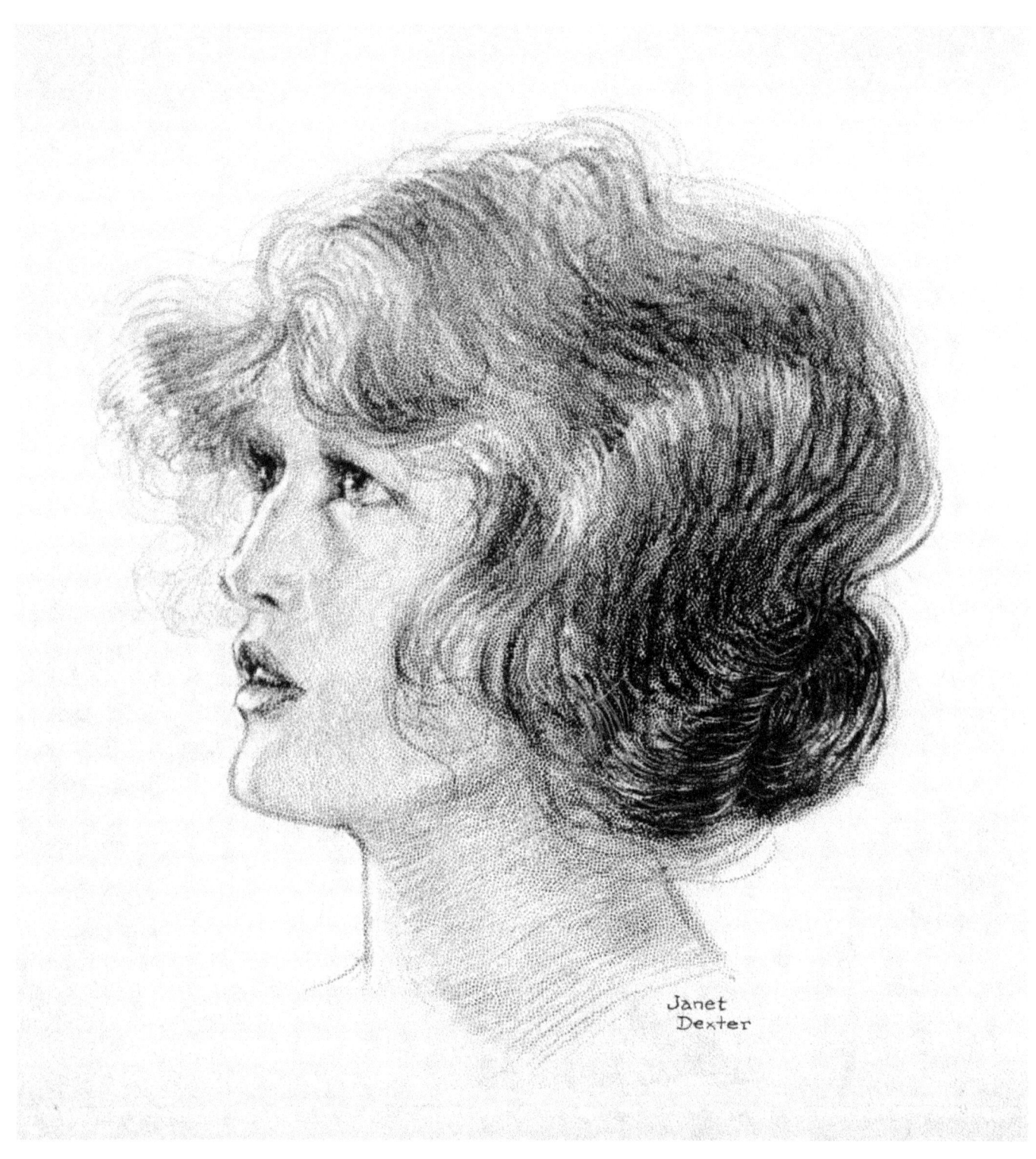

Actress: Francine Larrimore

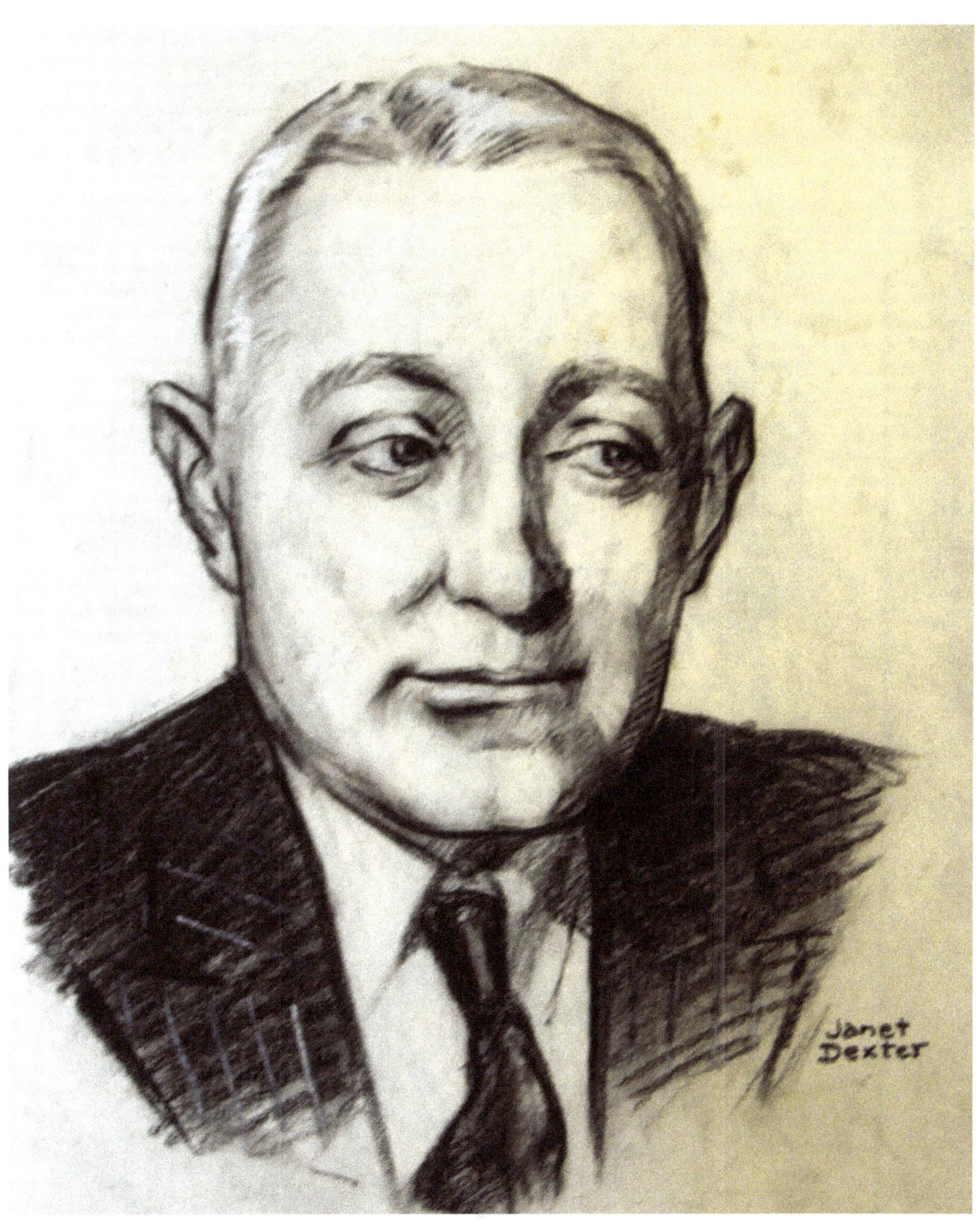

Composer: George M. Cohen

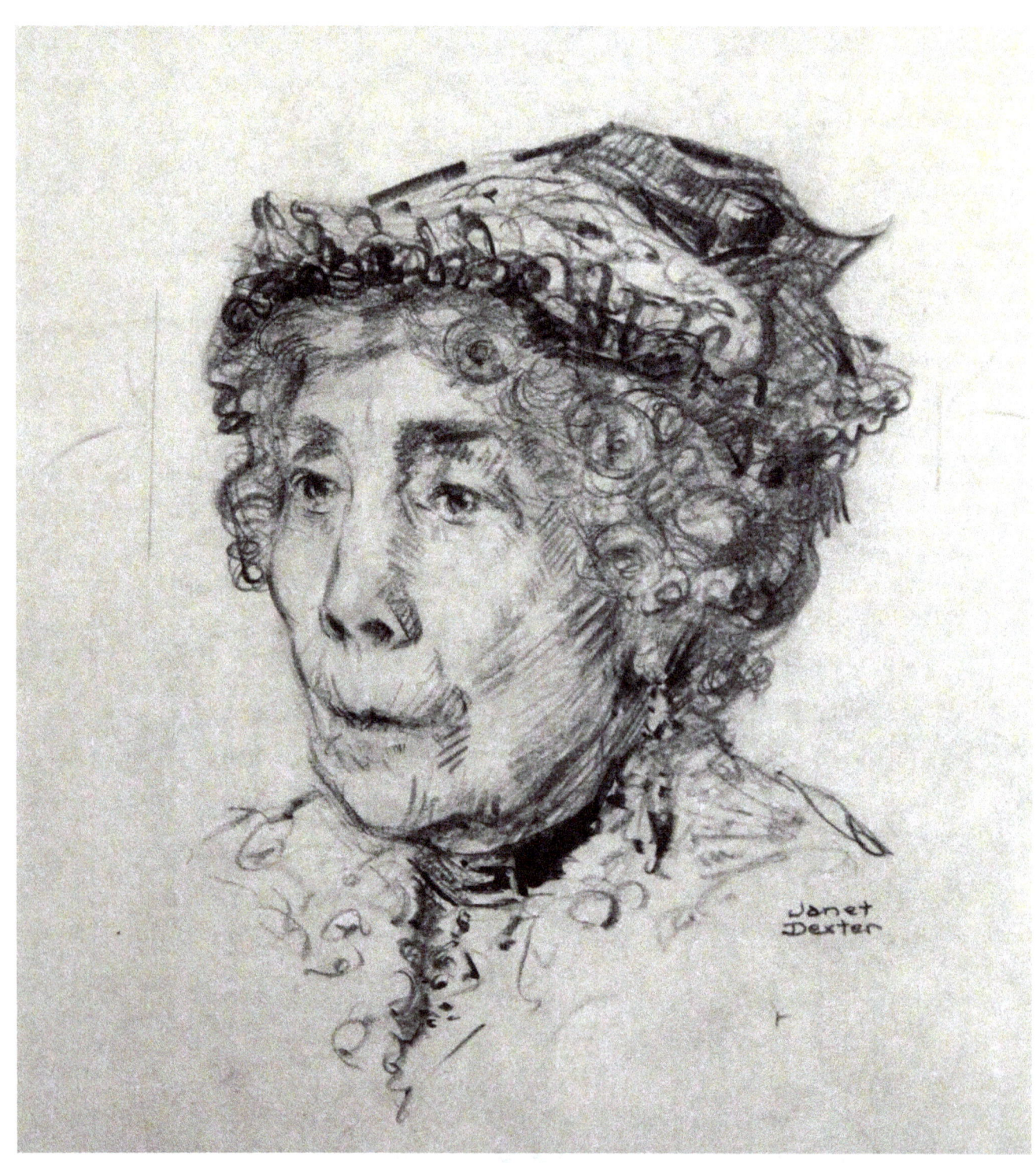

Actress: Mrs. Thomas Wiffen

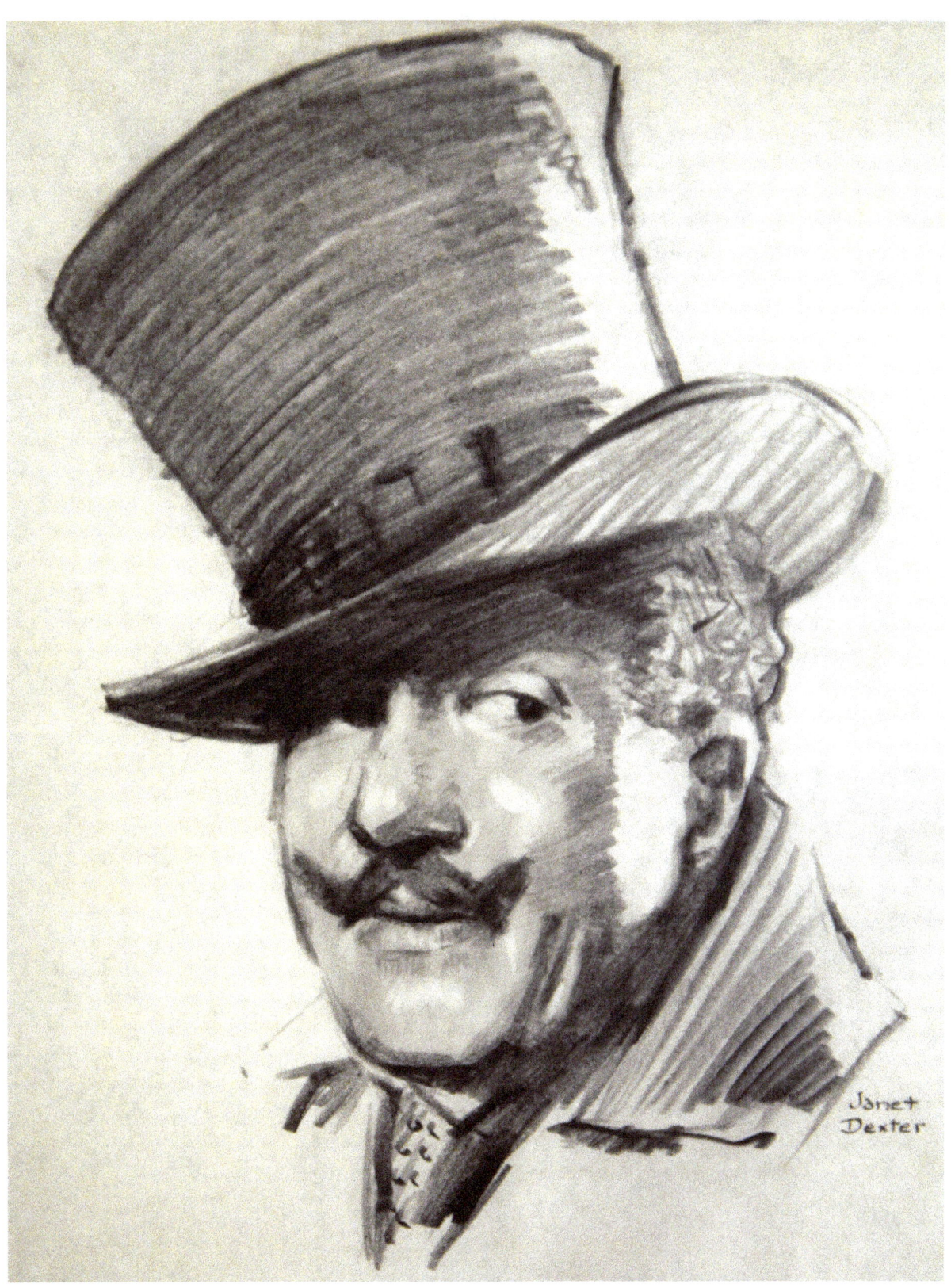

Actor: Otis Skinner

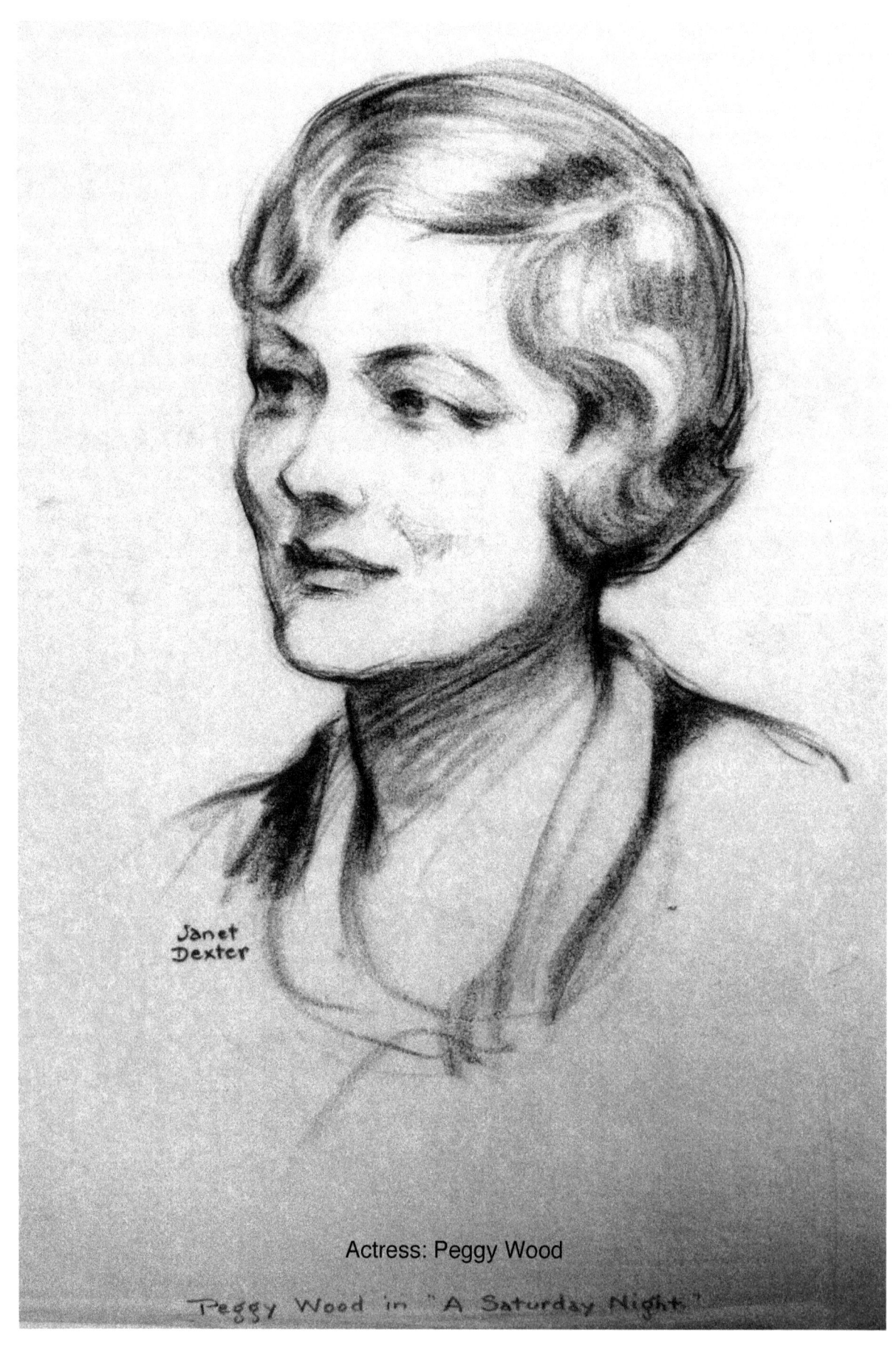

Janet
Dexter

Actress: Peggy Wood

Peggy Wood in "A Saturday Night"

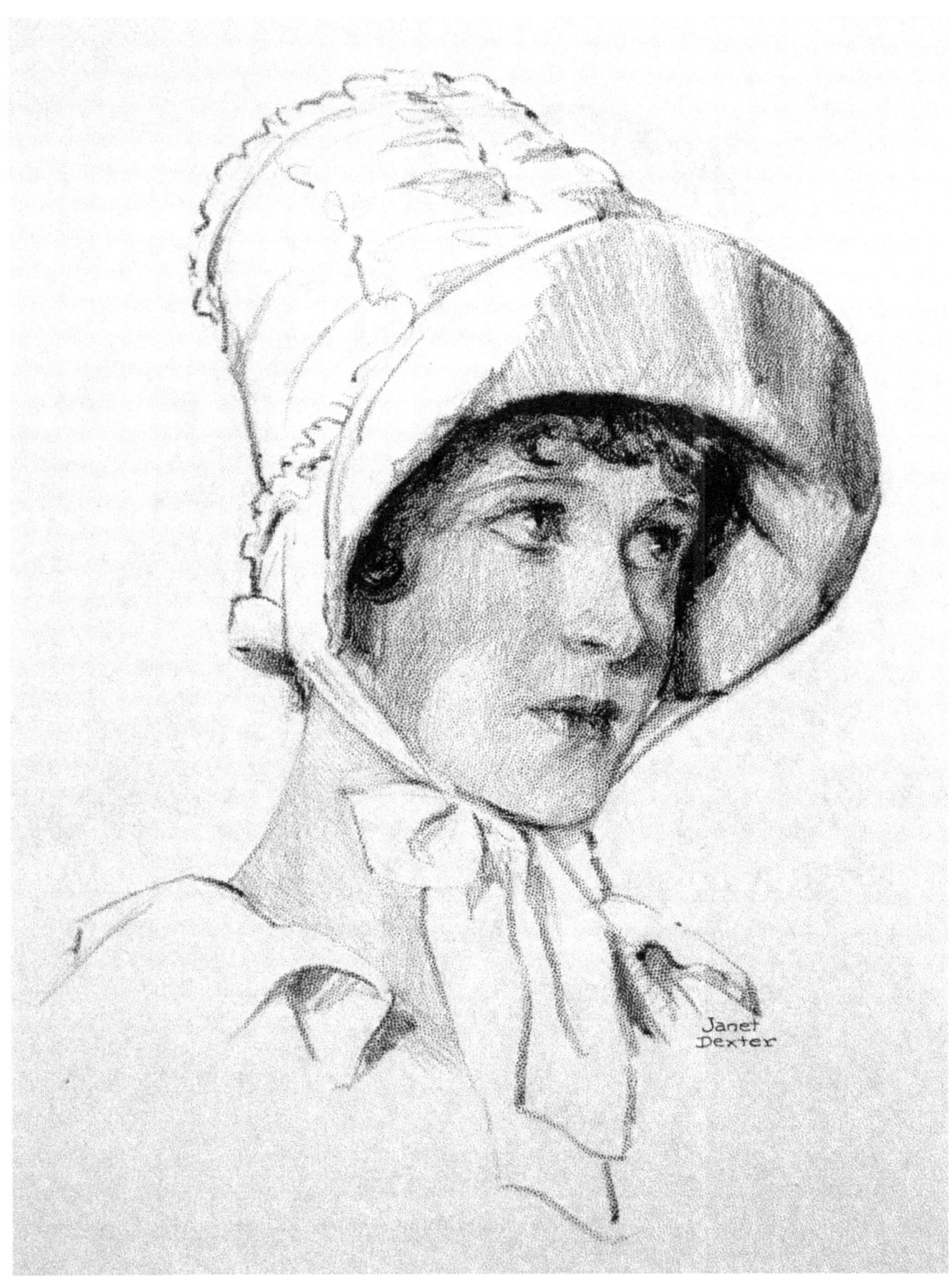

Actress: Ruth Chatterton

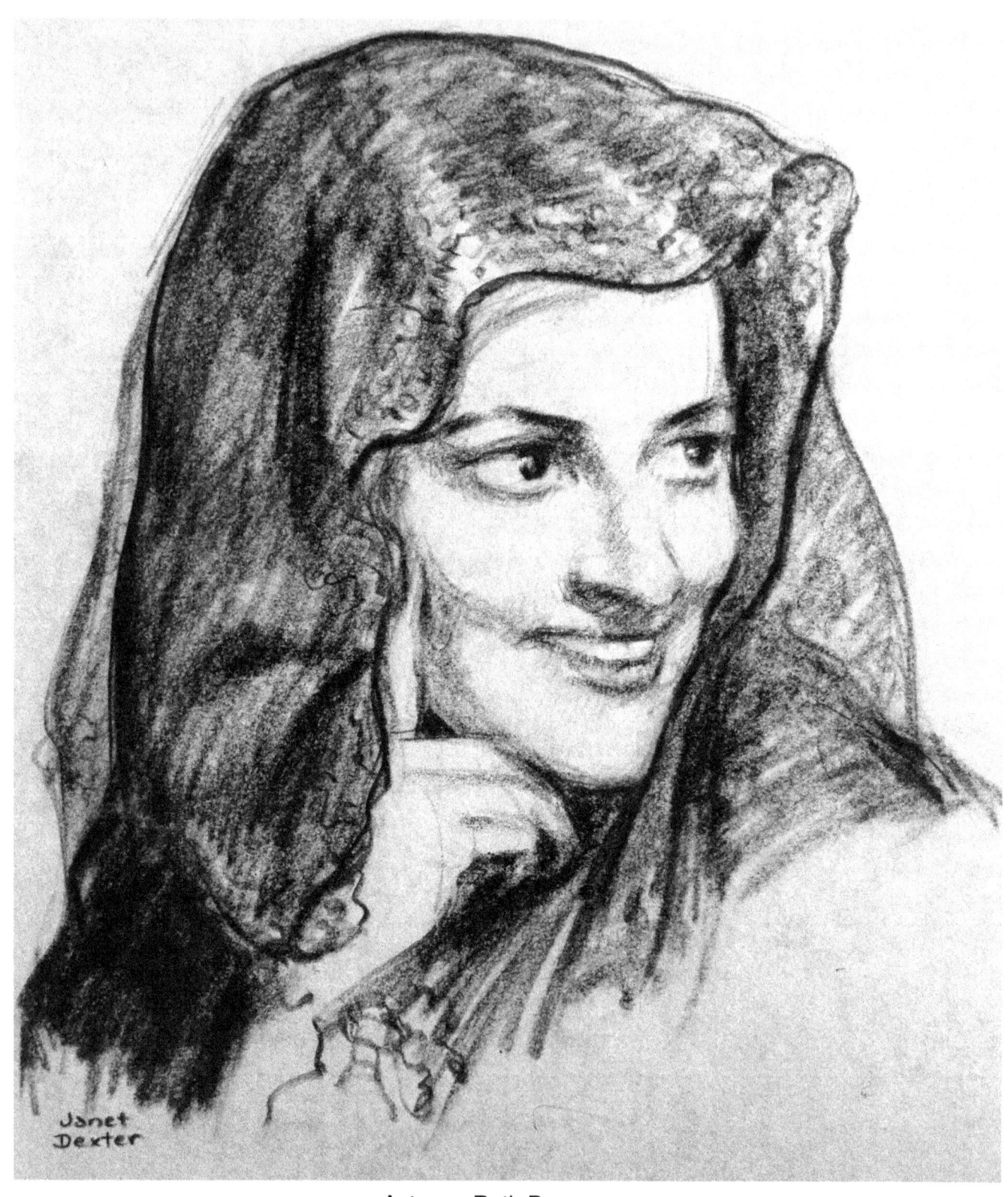

Actress: Ruth Draper

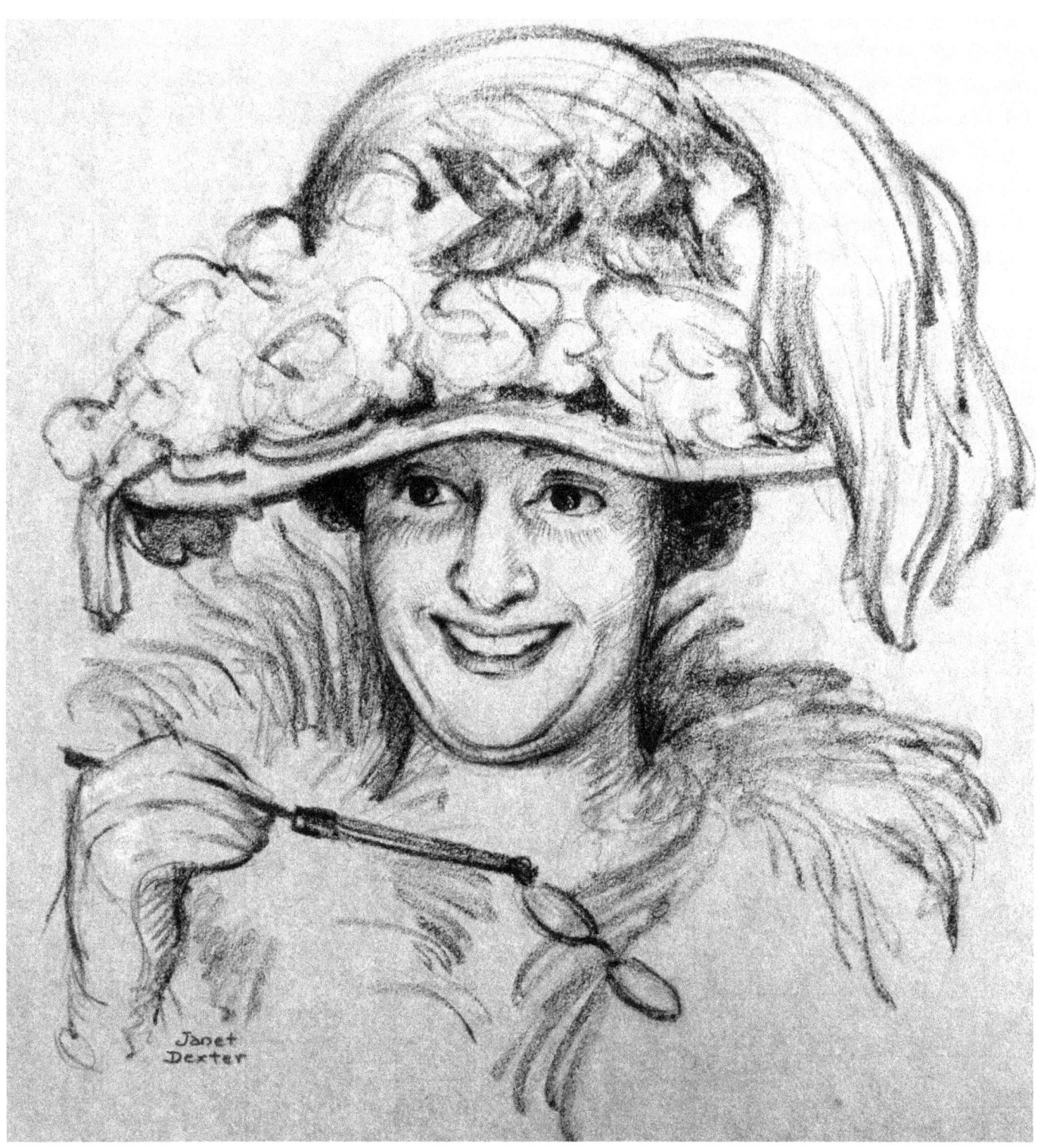

Actress: Ruth Draper

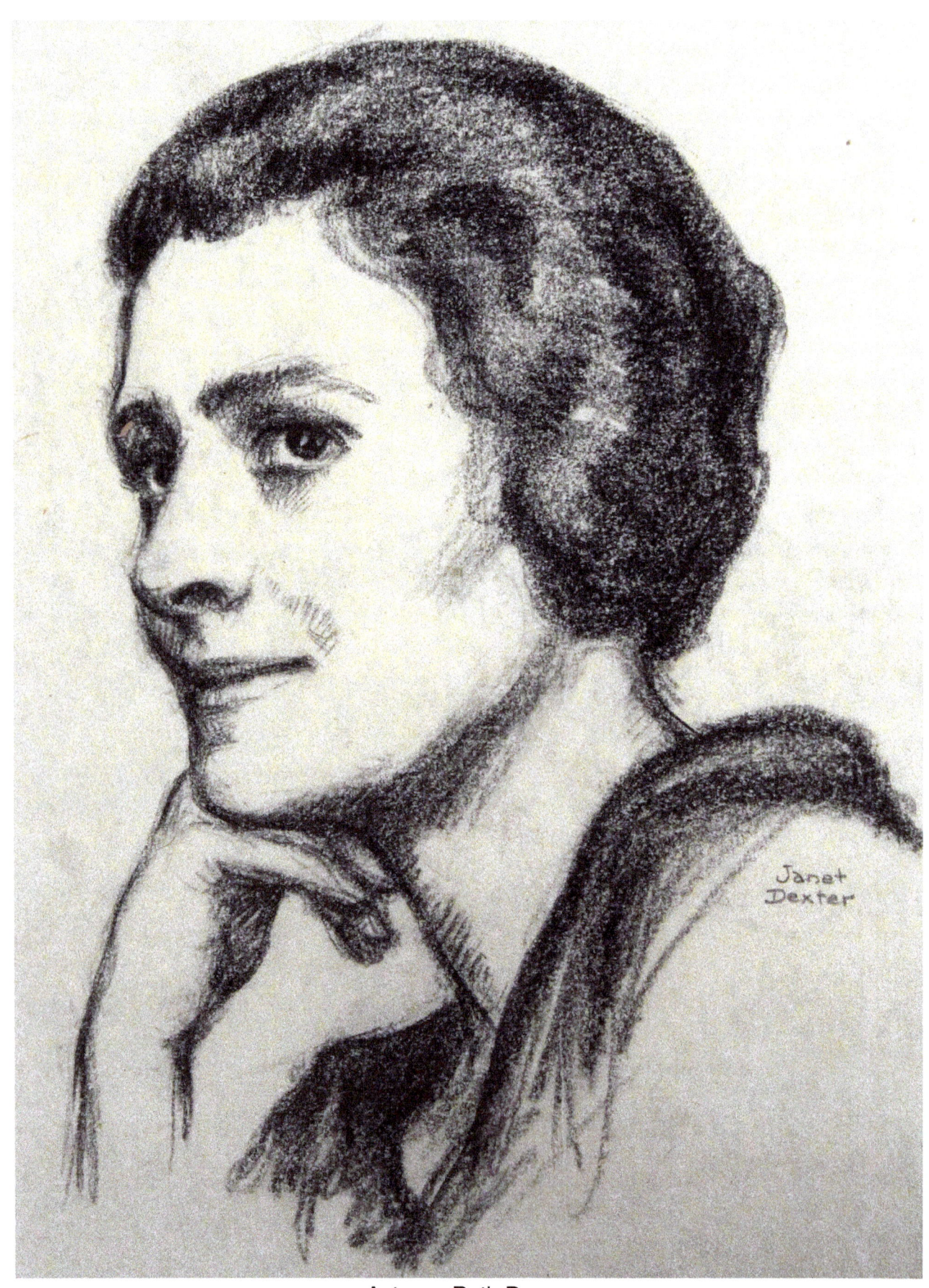

Actress: Ruth Draper

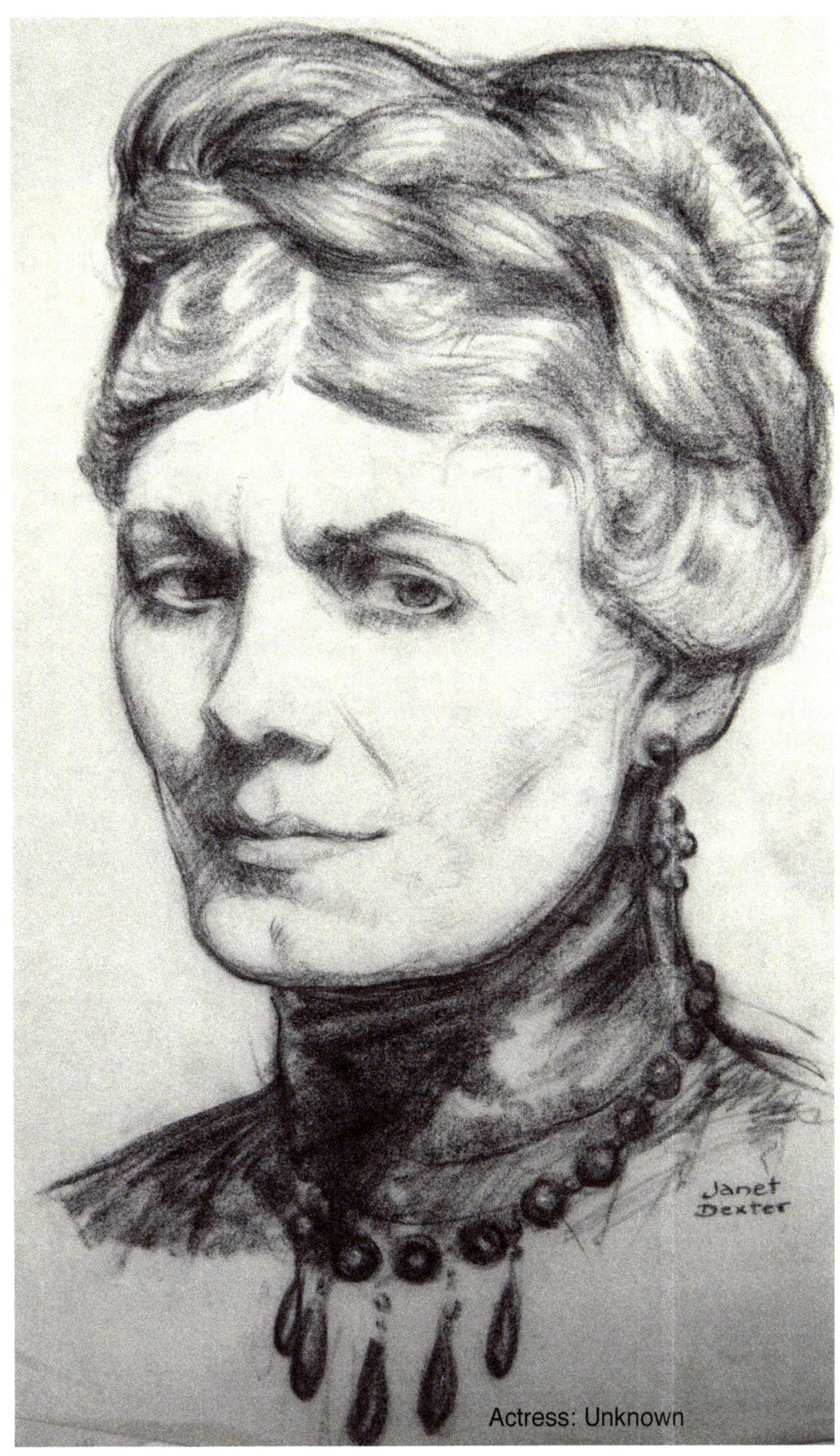

Actress: Unknown

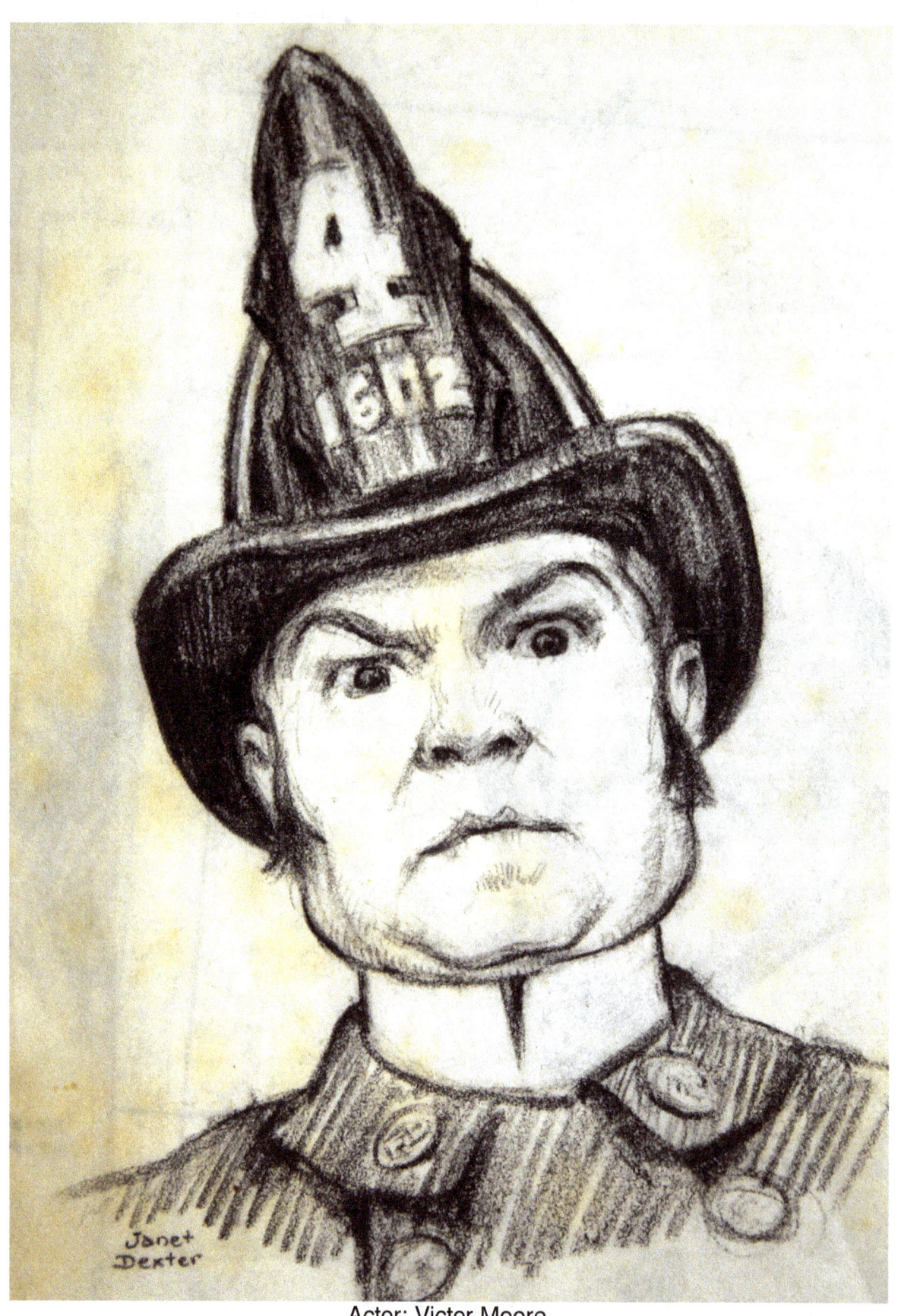

Actor: Victor Moore

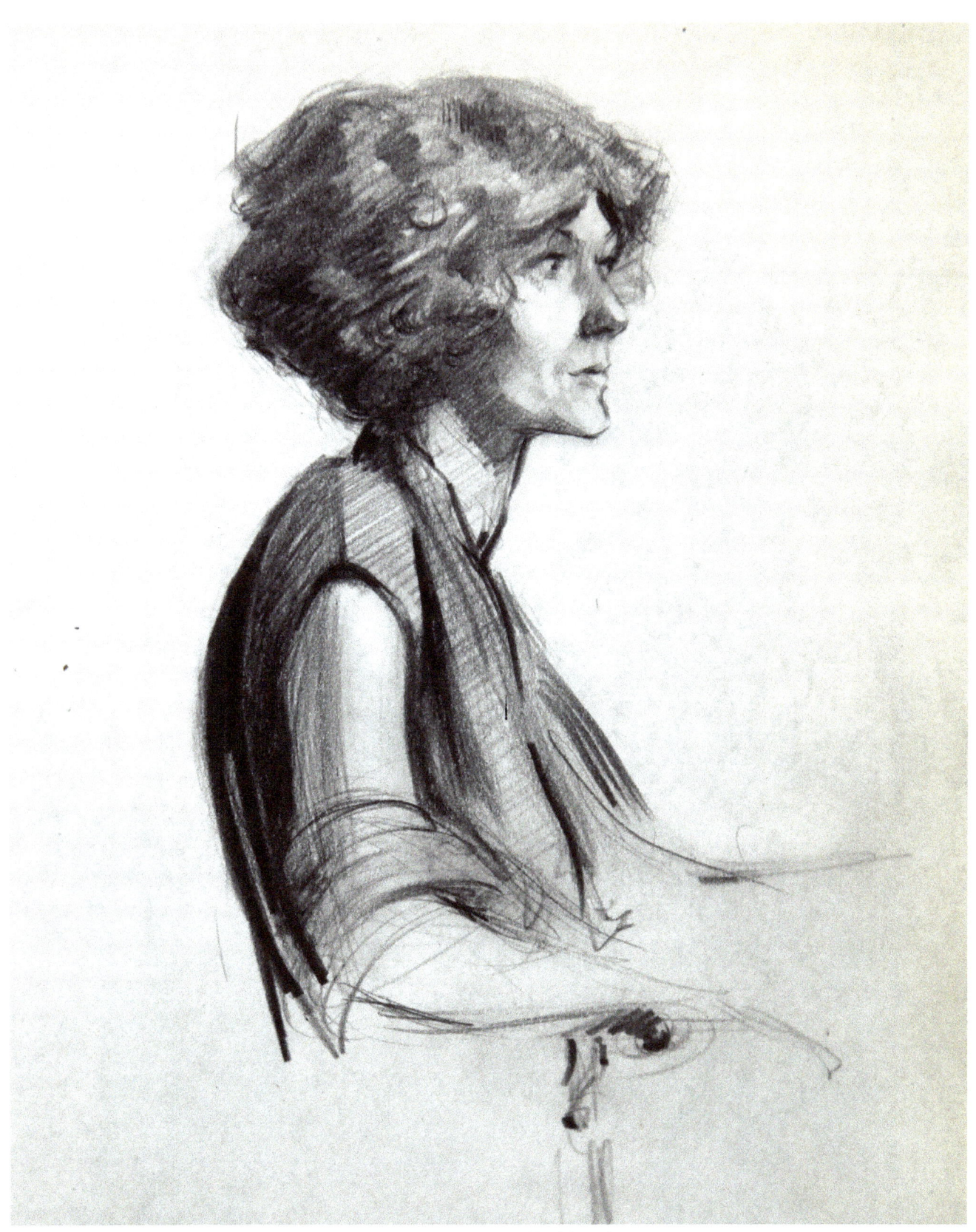

Unknown Family Member

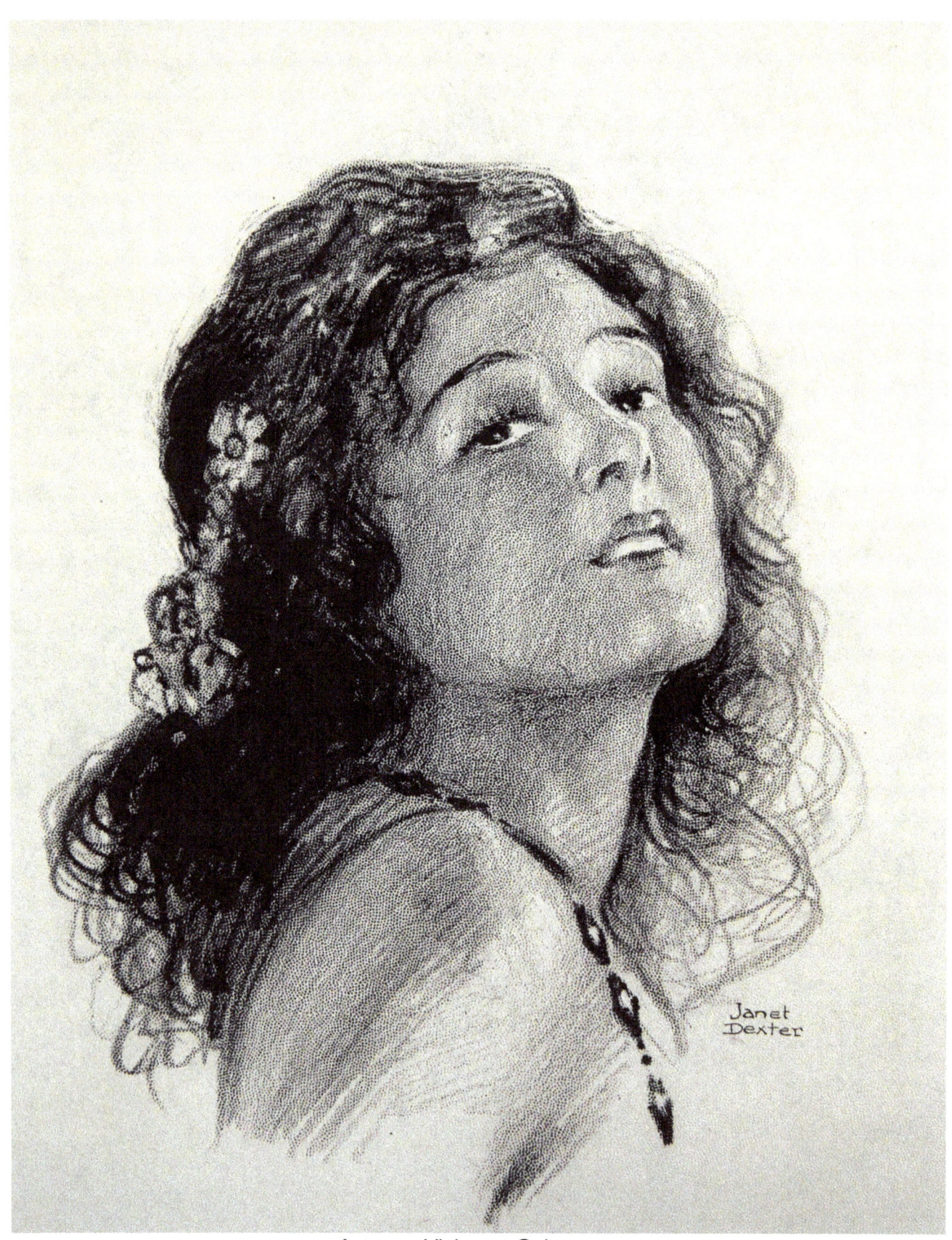

Actress: Vivienne Osborne

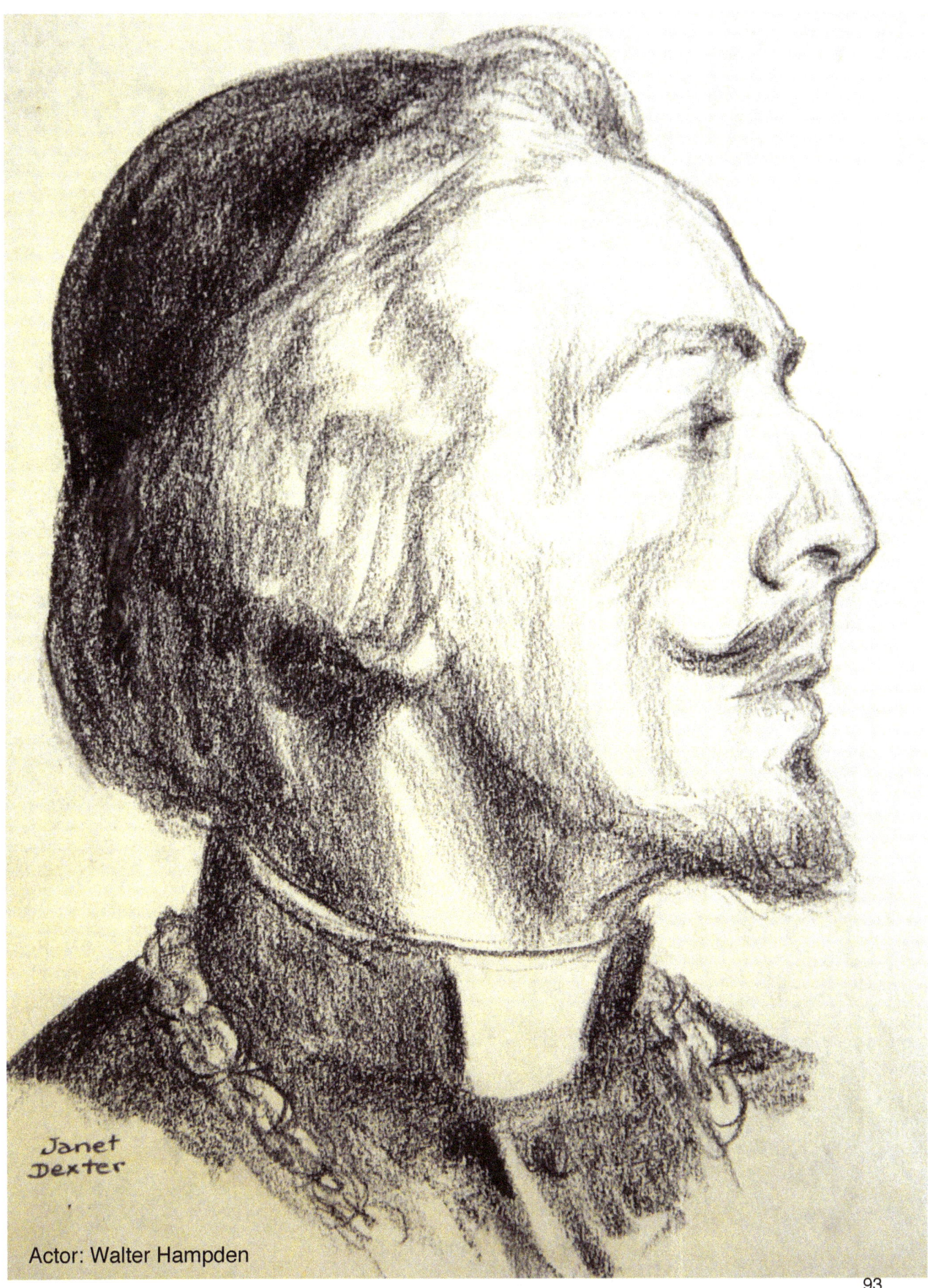

Janet
Dexter

Actor: Walter Hampden

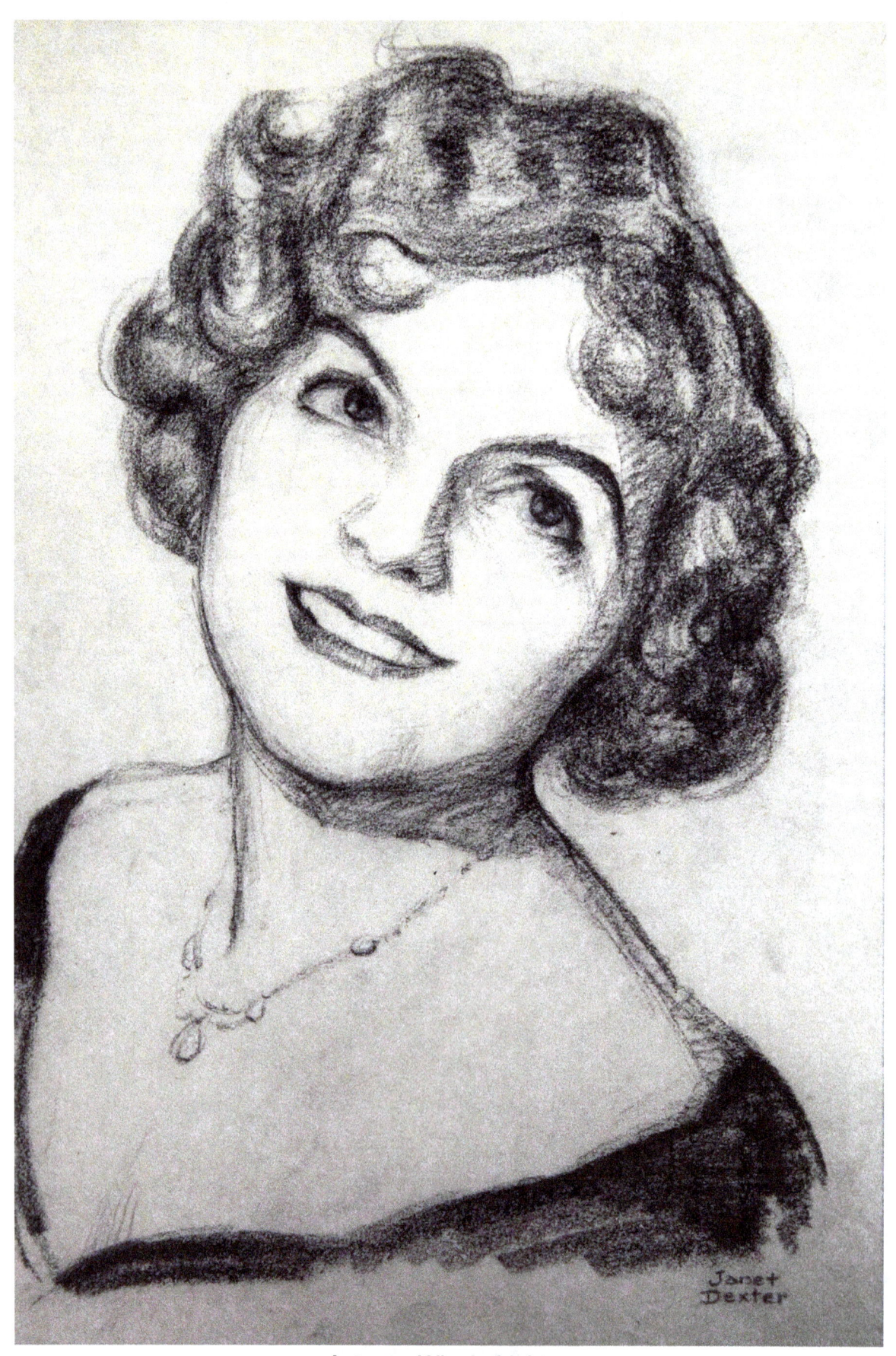

Actress: Winnie Lightner

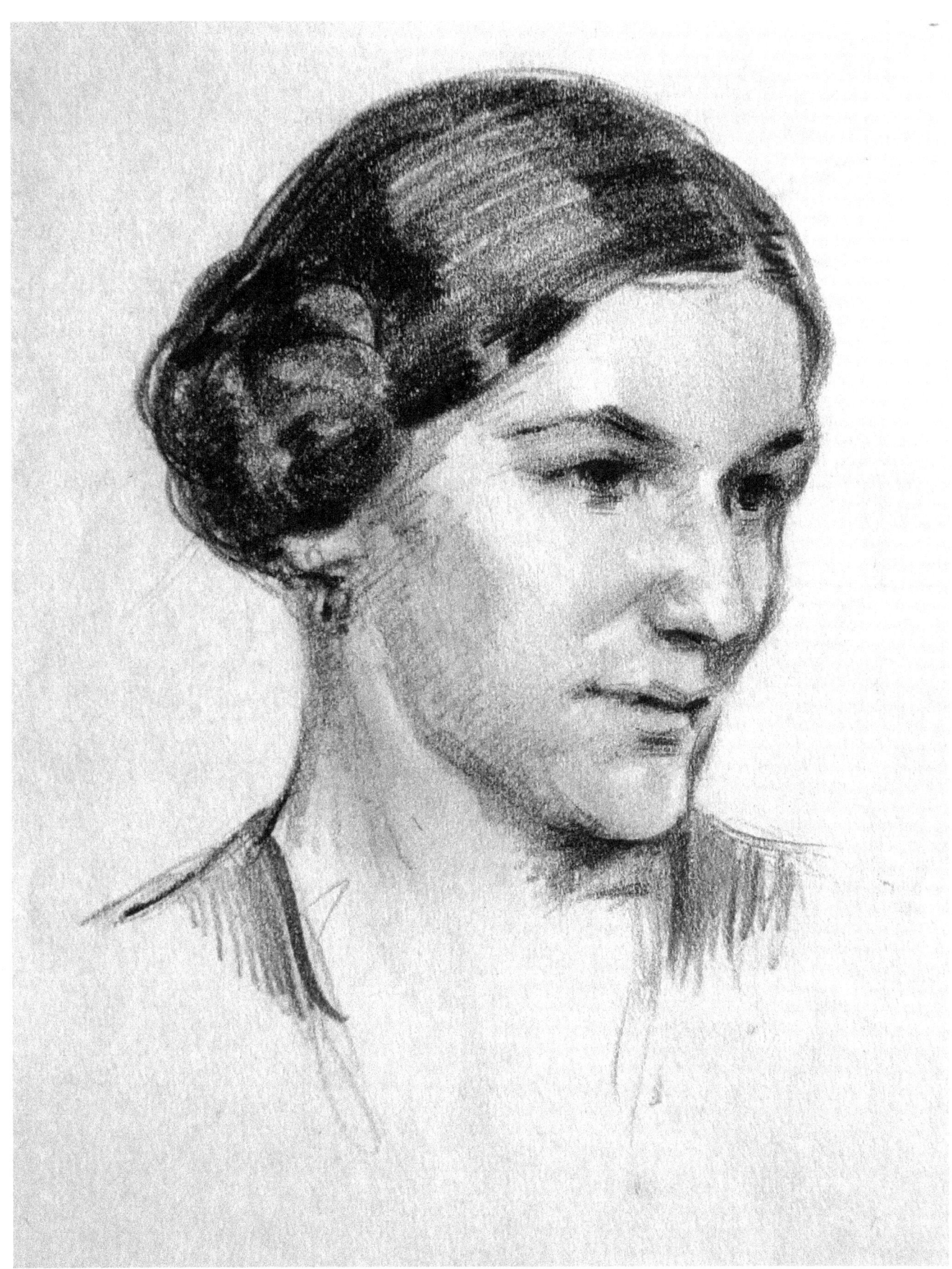

Unknown Model

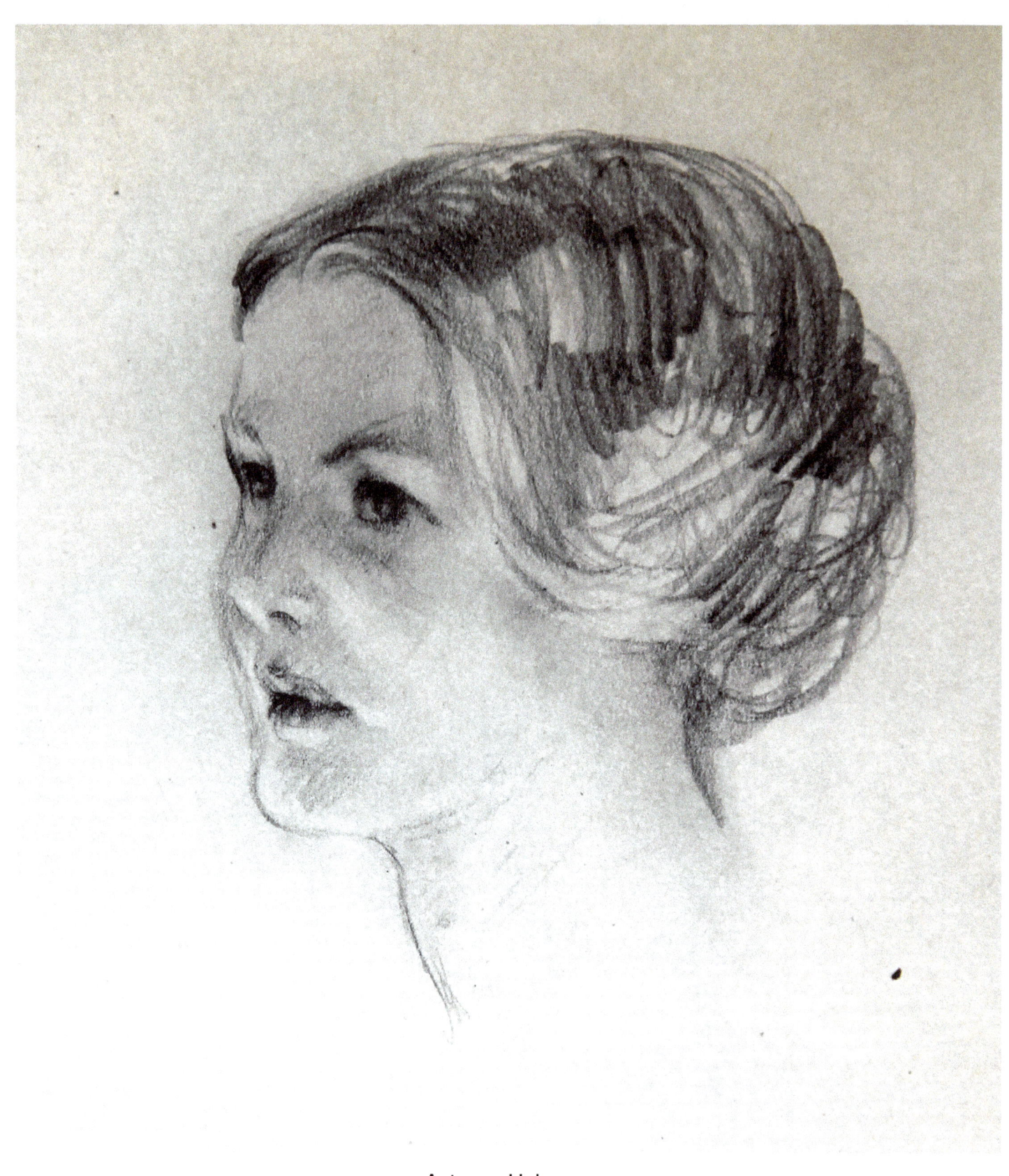

Actress: Unknown

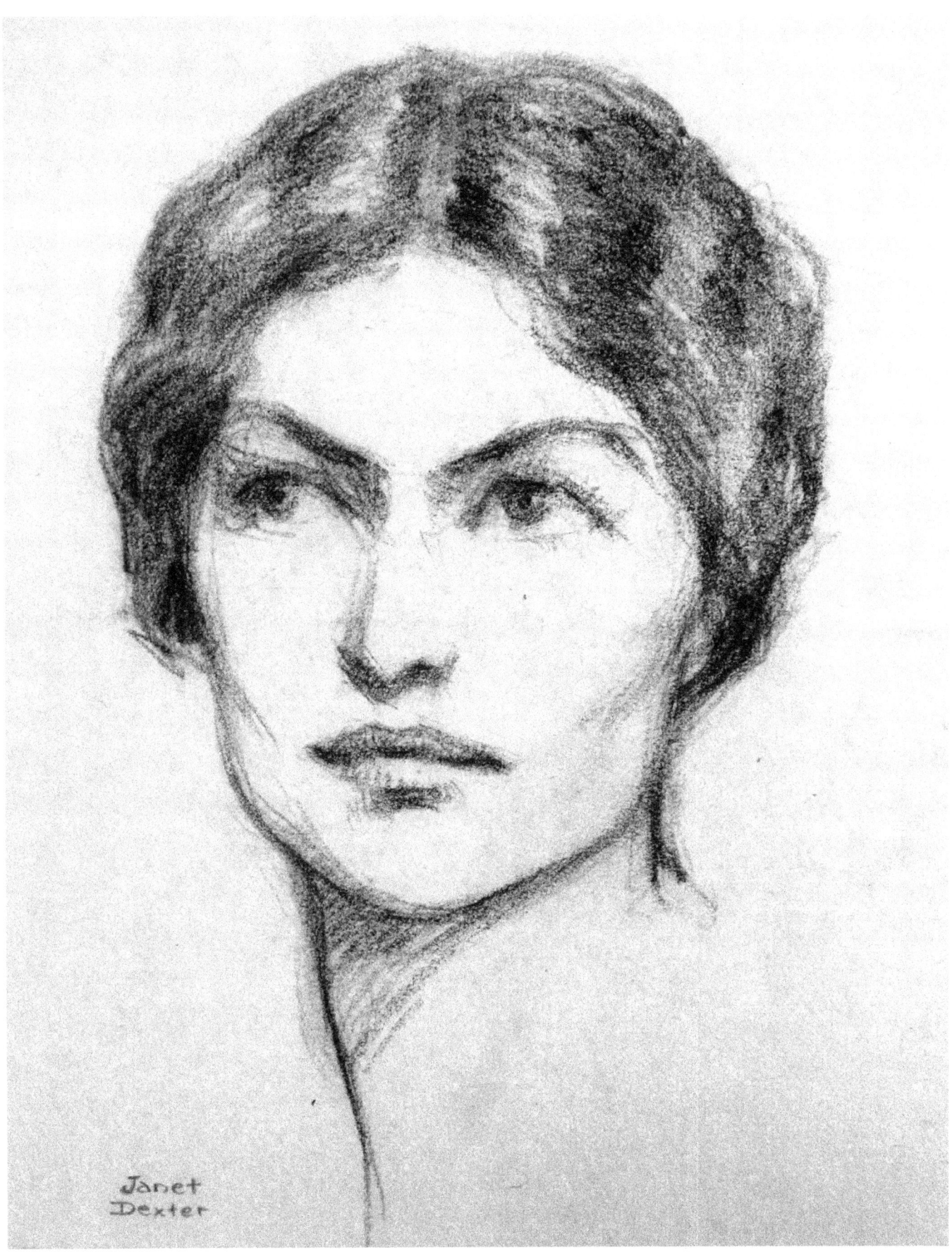

Actress: Winfred Leneher

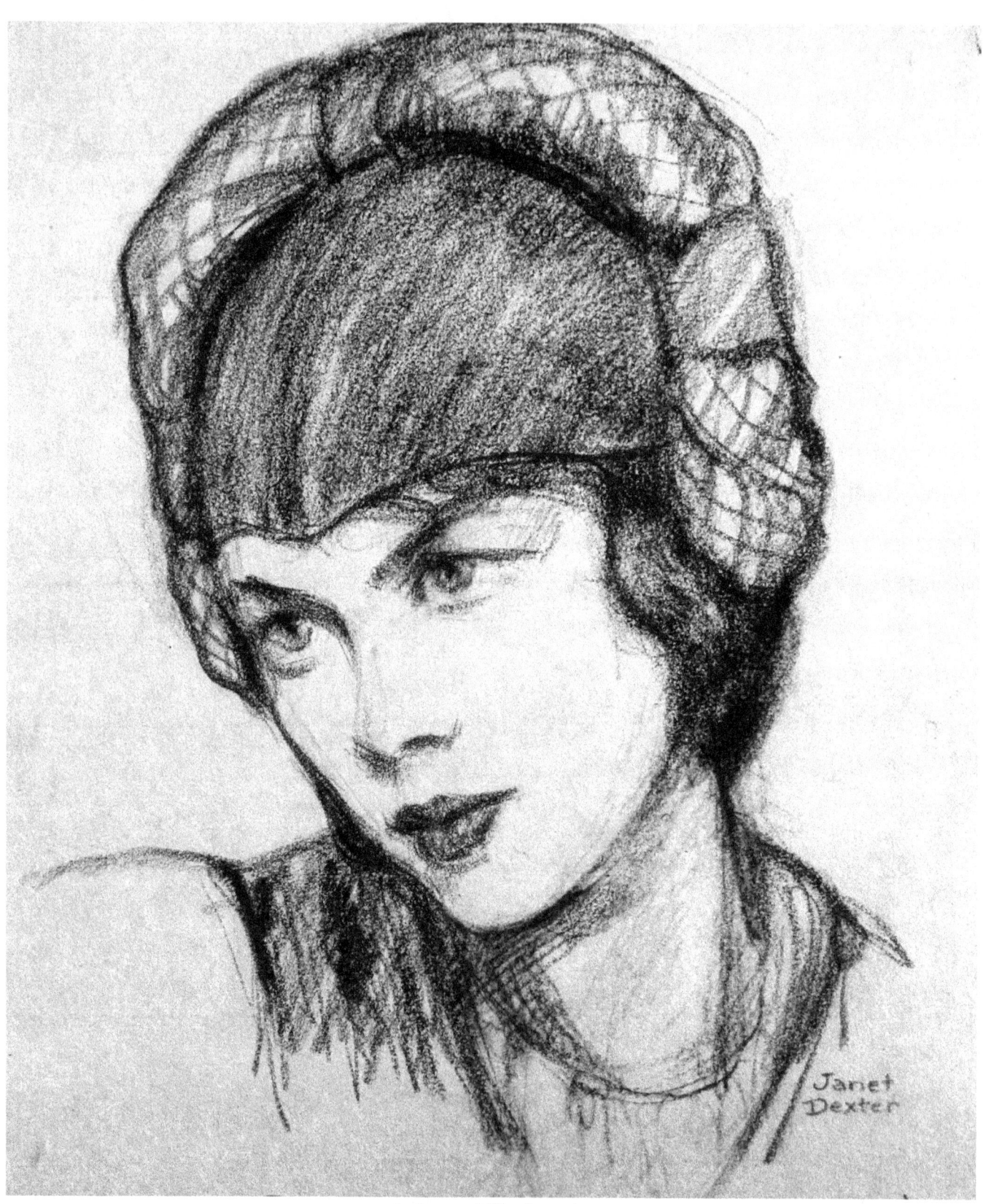

Actress: Yilly Losch

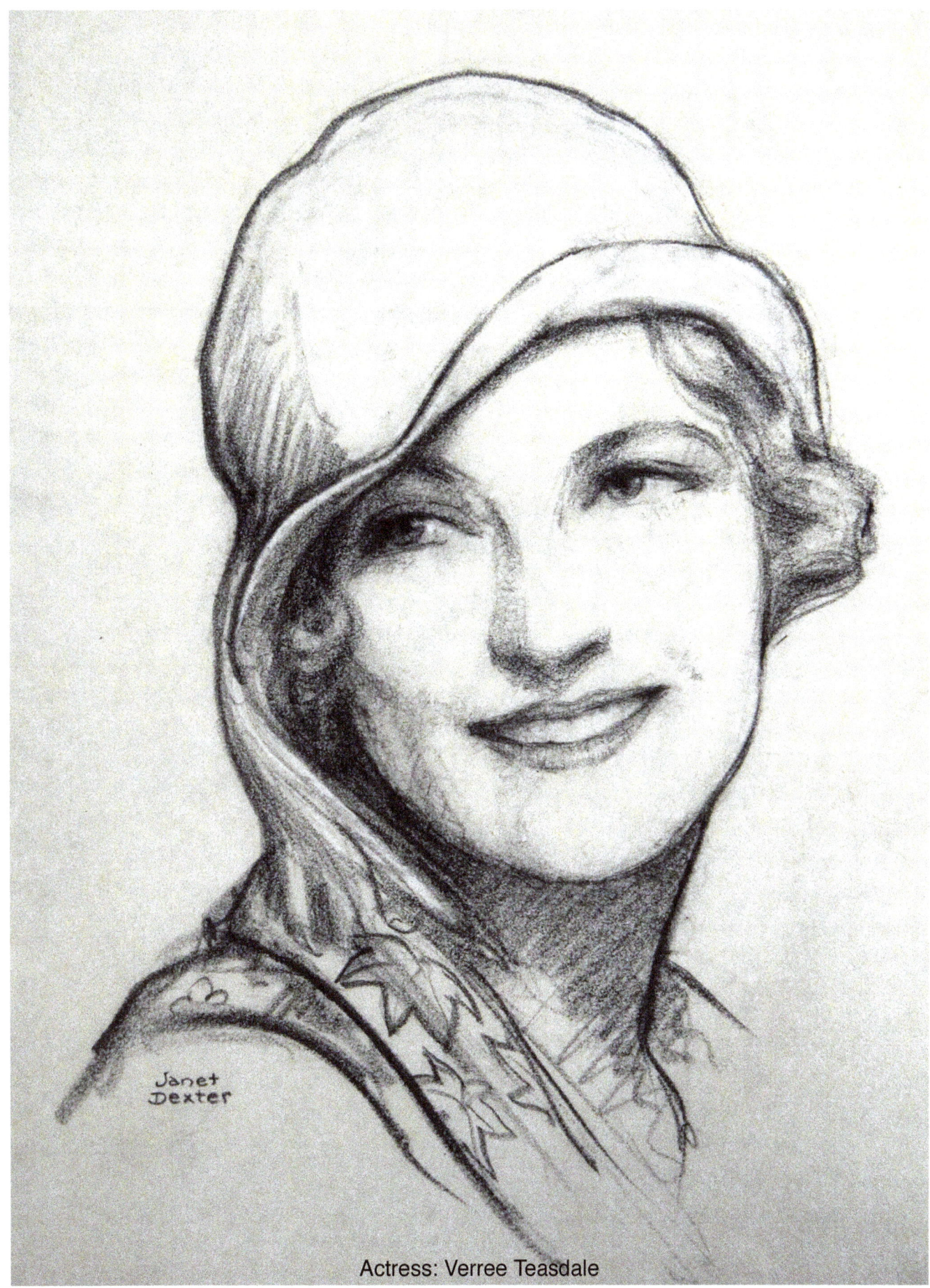

Actress: Verree Teasdale

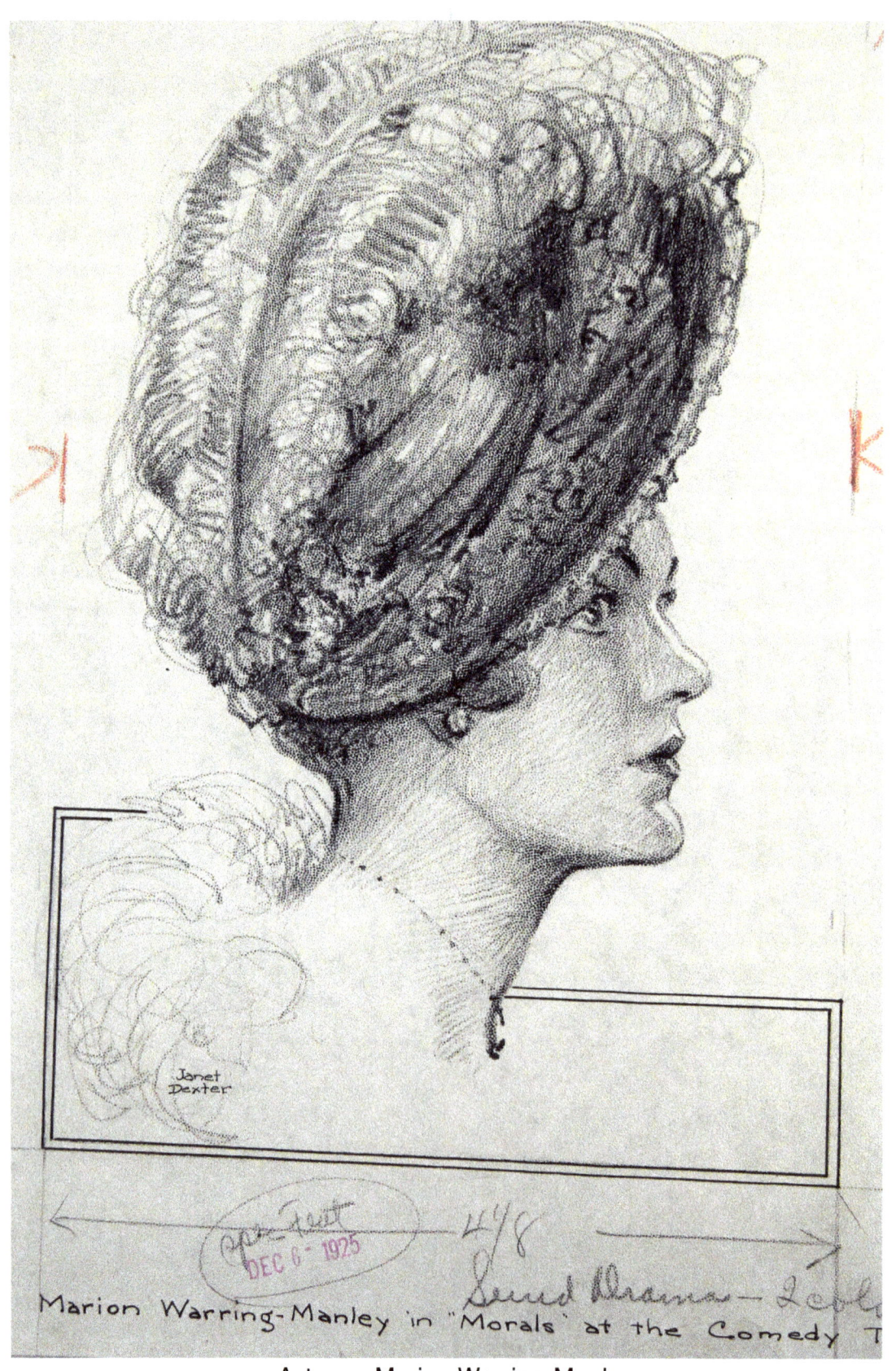

Actress: Marion Warring-Manley

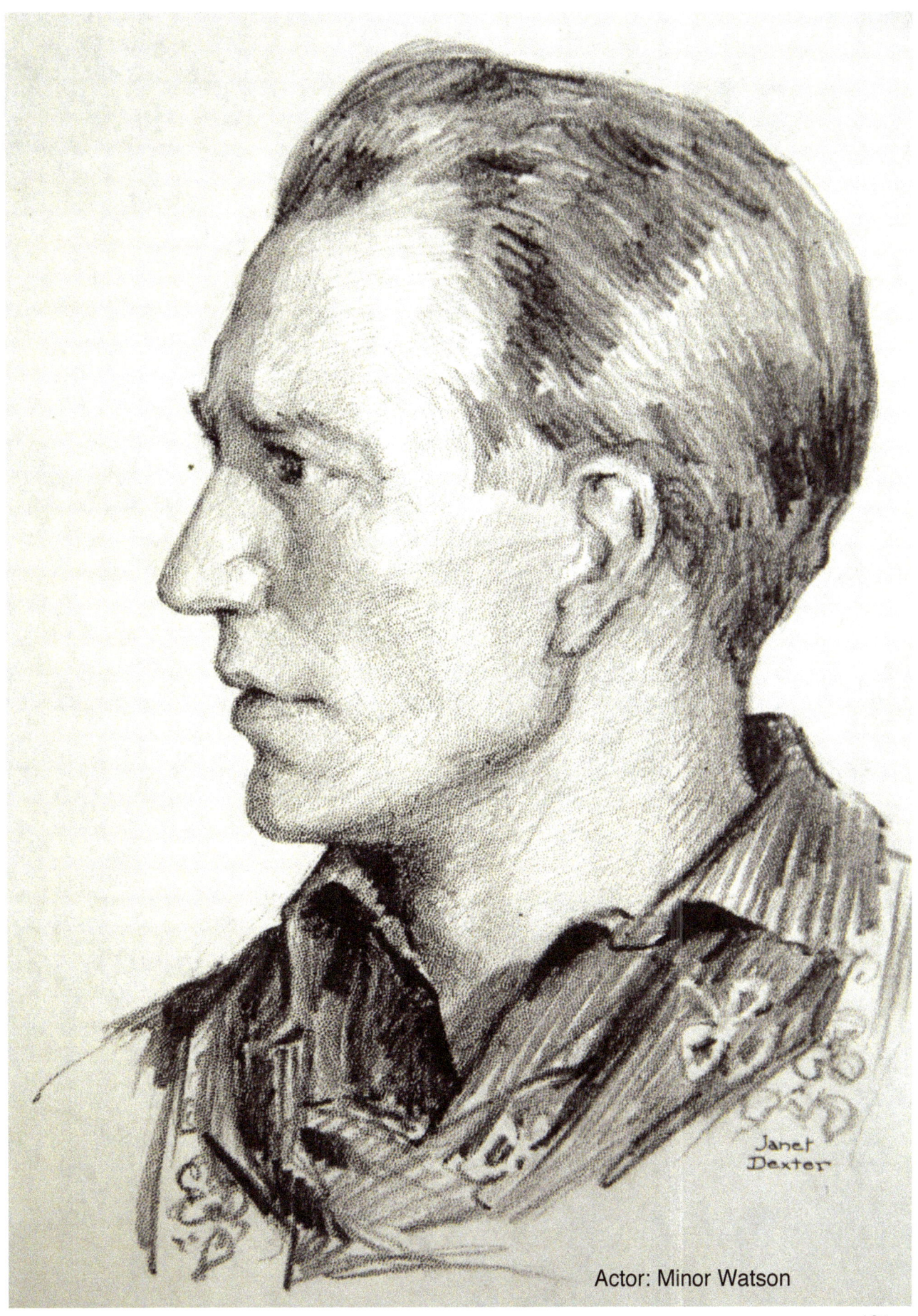

Actor: Minor Watson

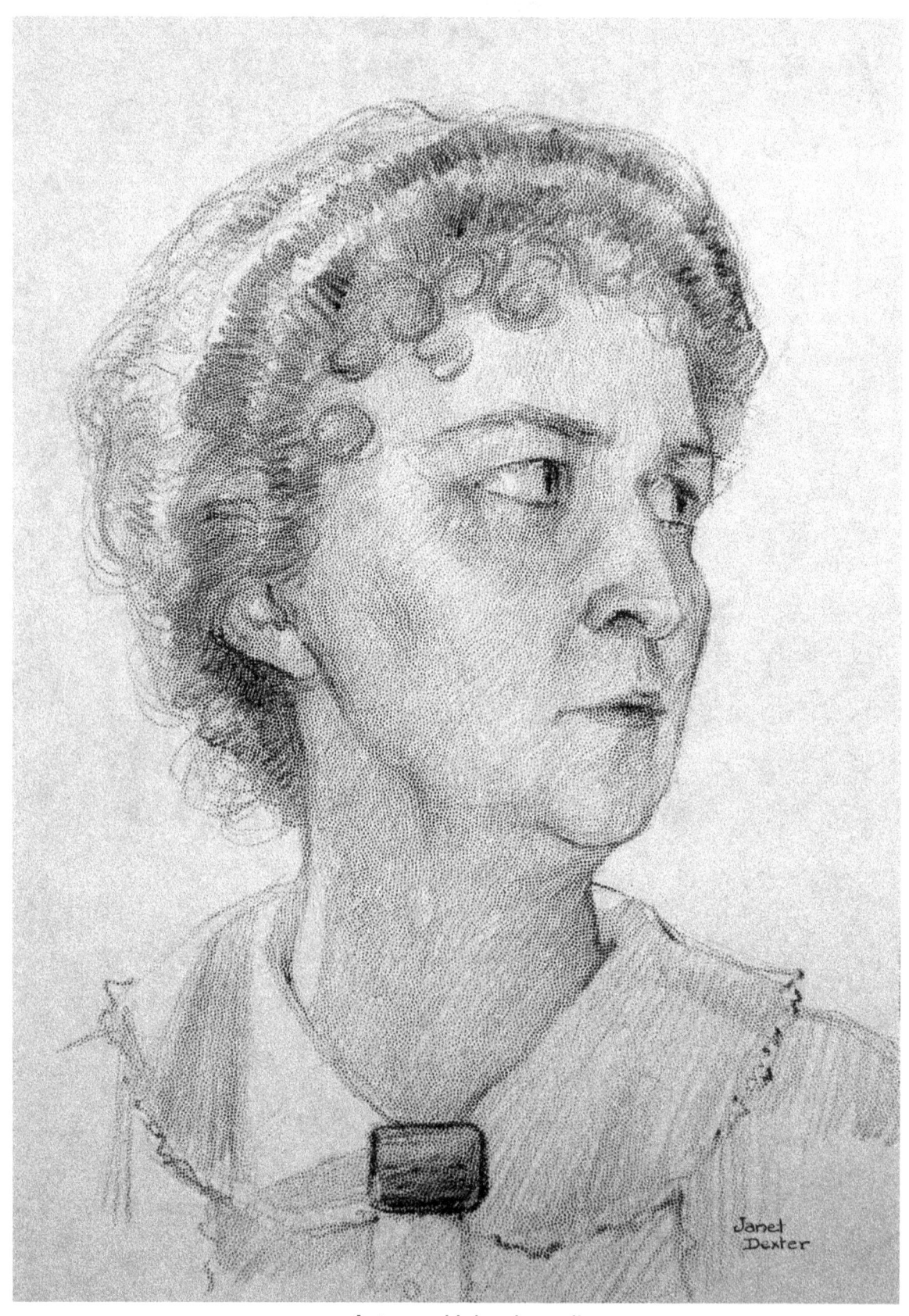

Actress: Helen Lowell

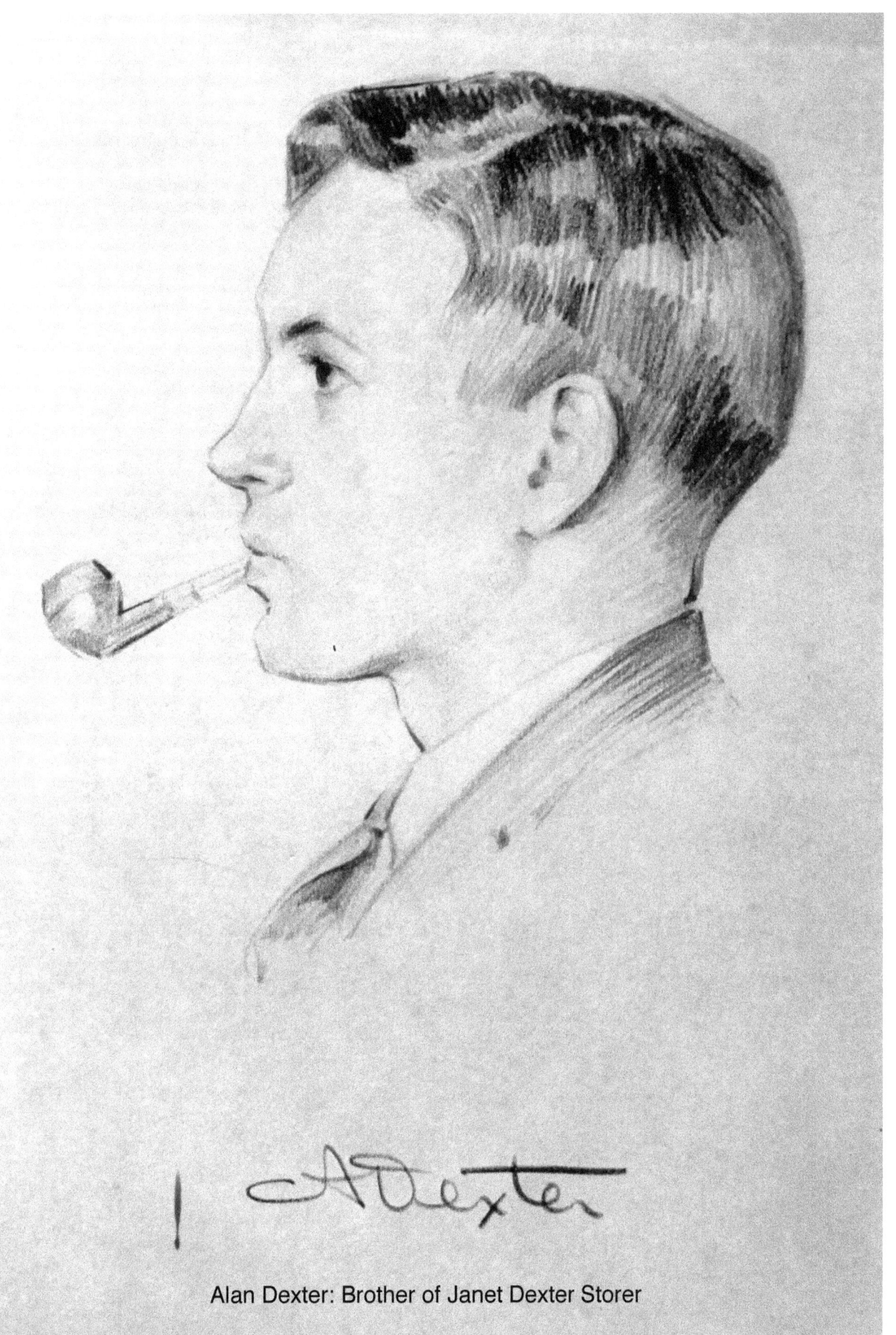

Alan Dexter: Brother of Janet Dexter Storer

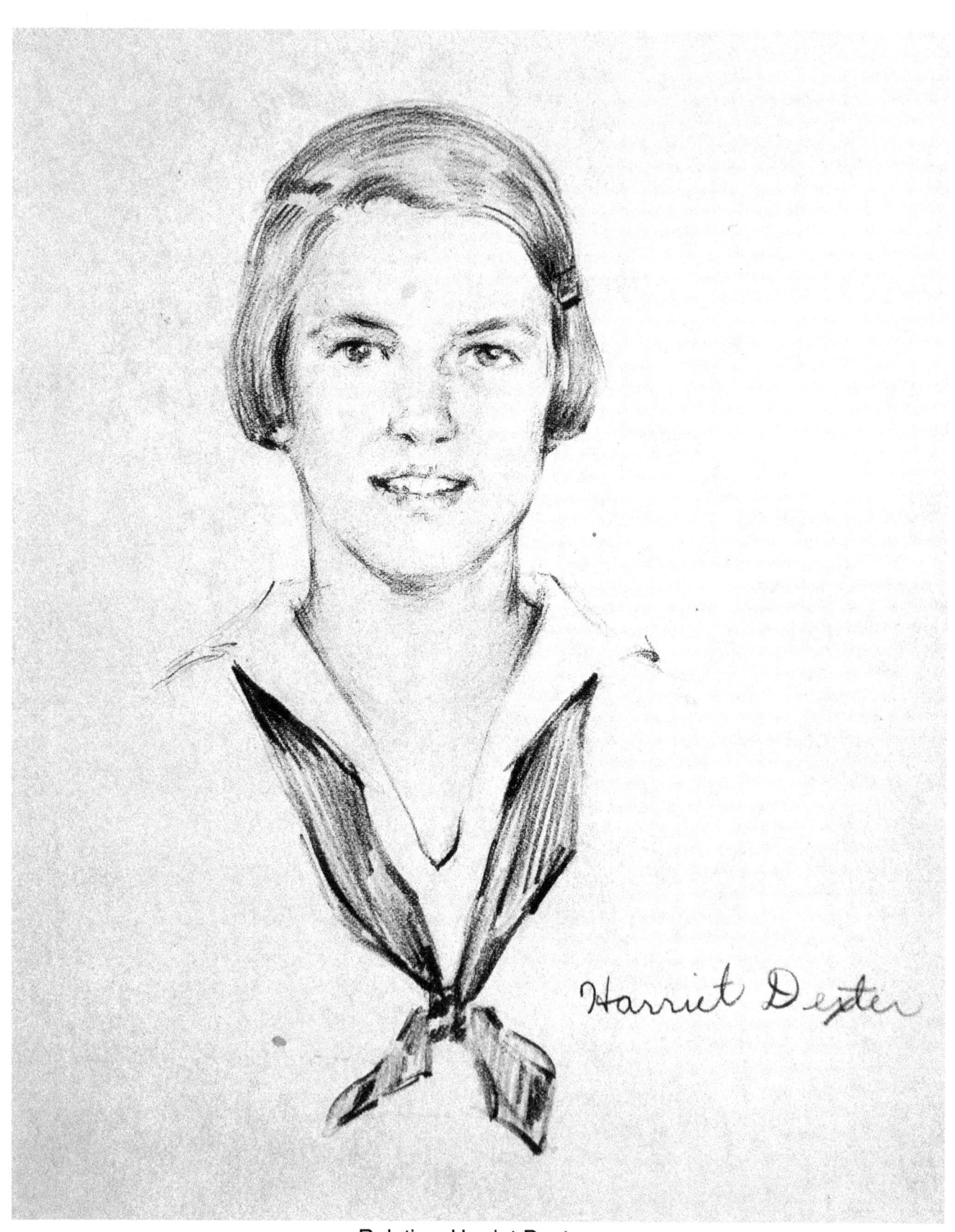

Relative: Harriet Dexter

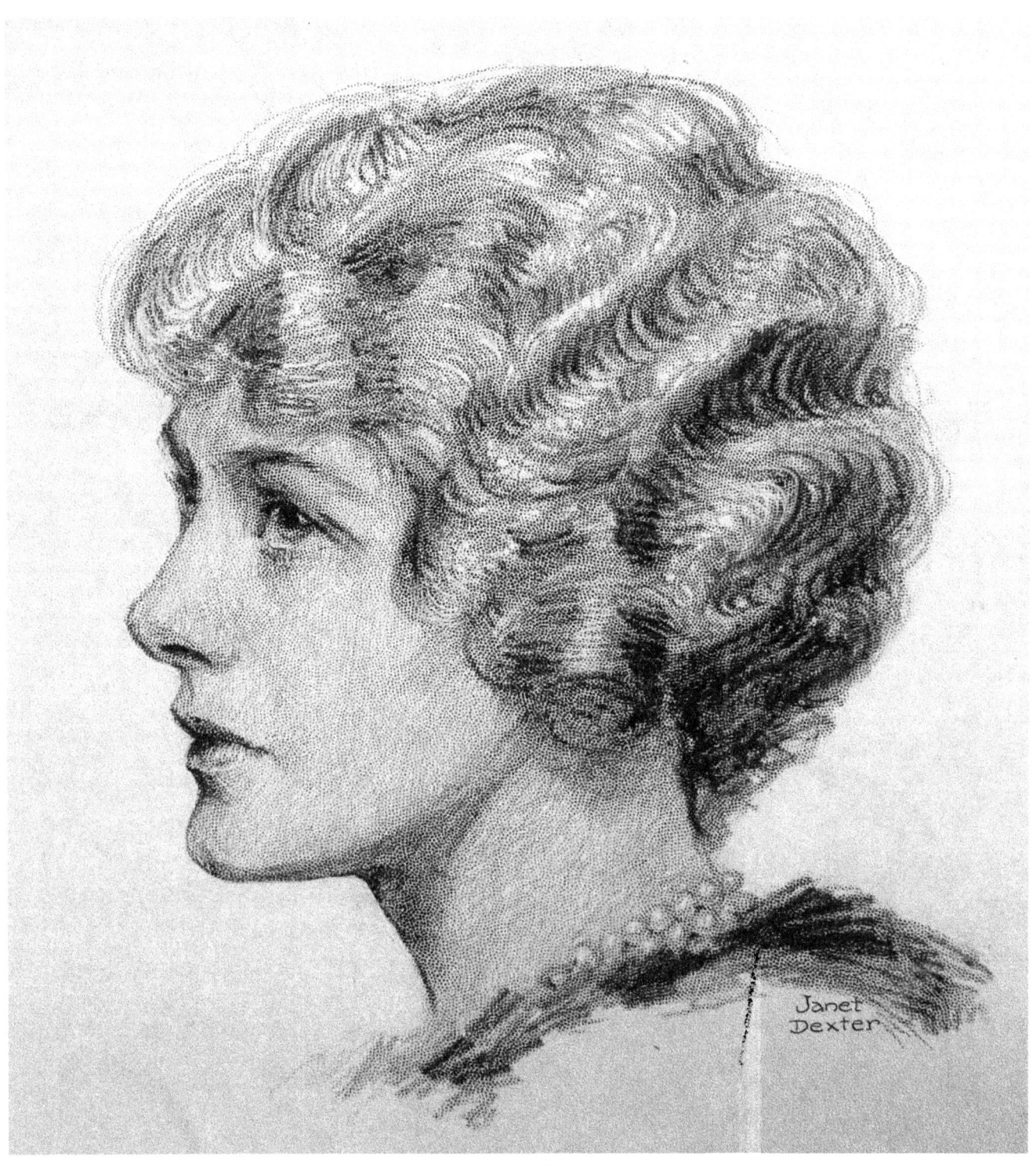

Actress: Elsie Ferguson

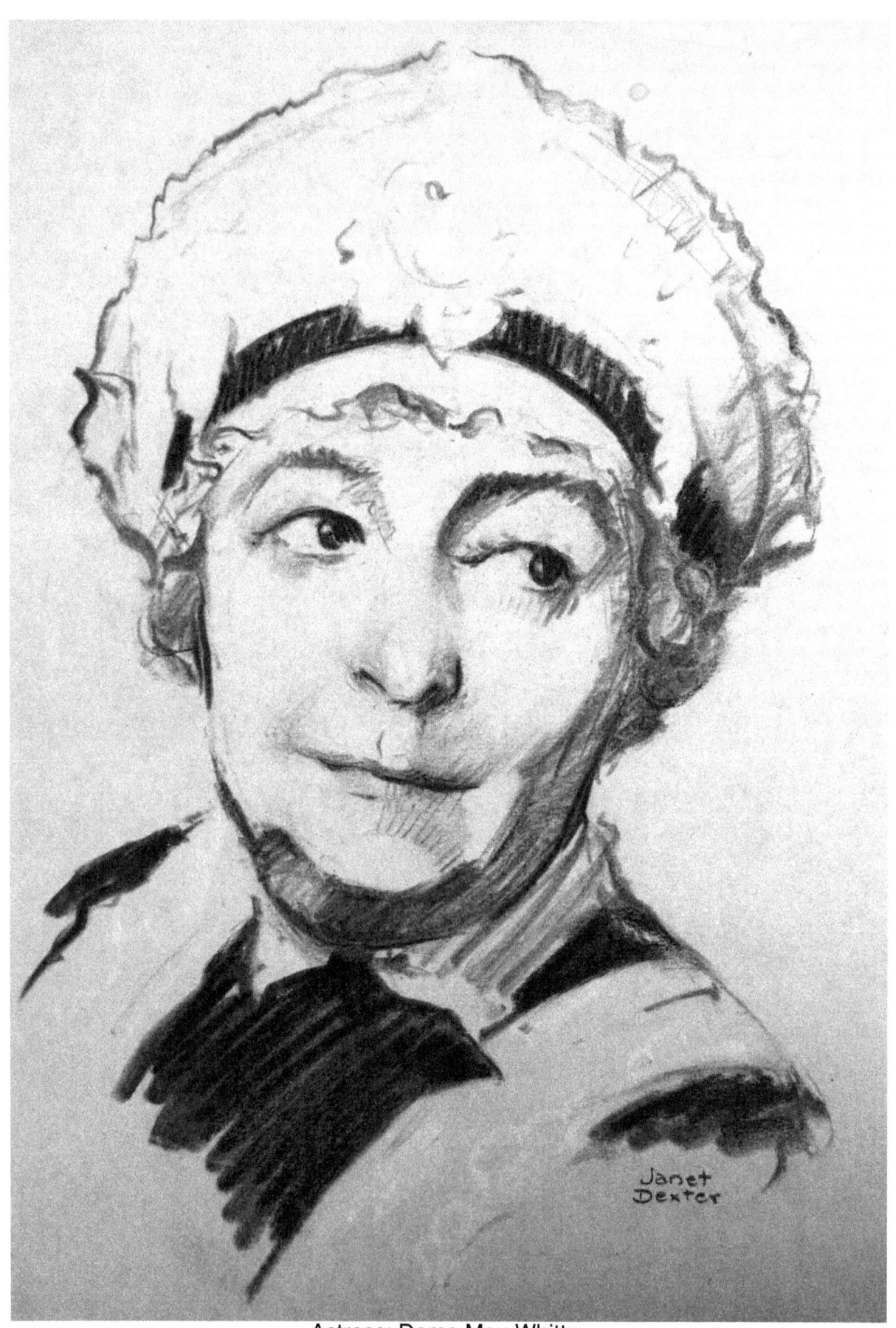

Actress: Dame May Whitty

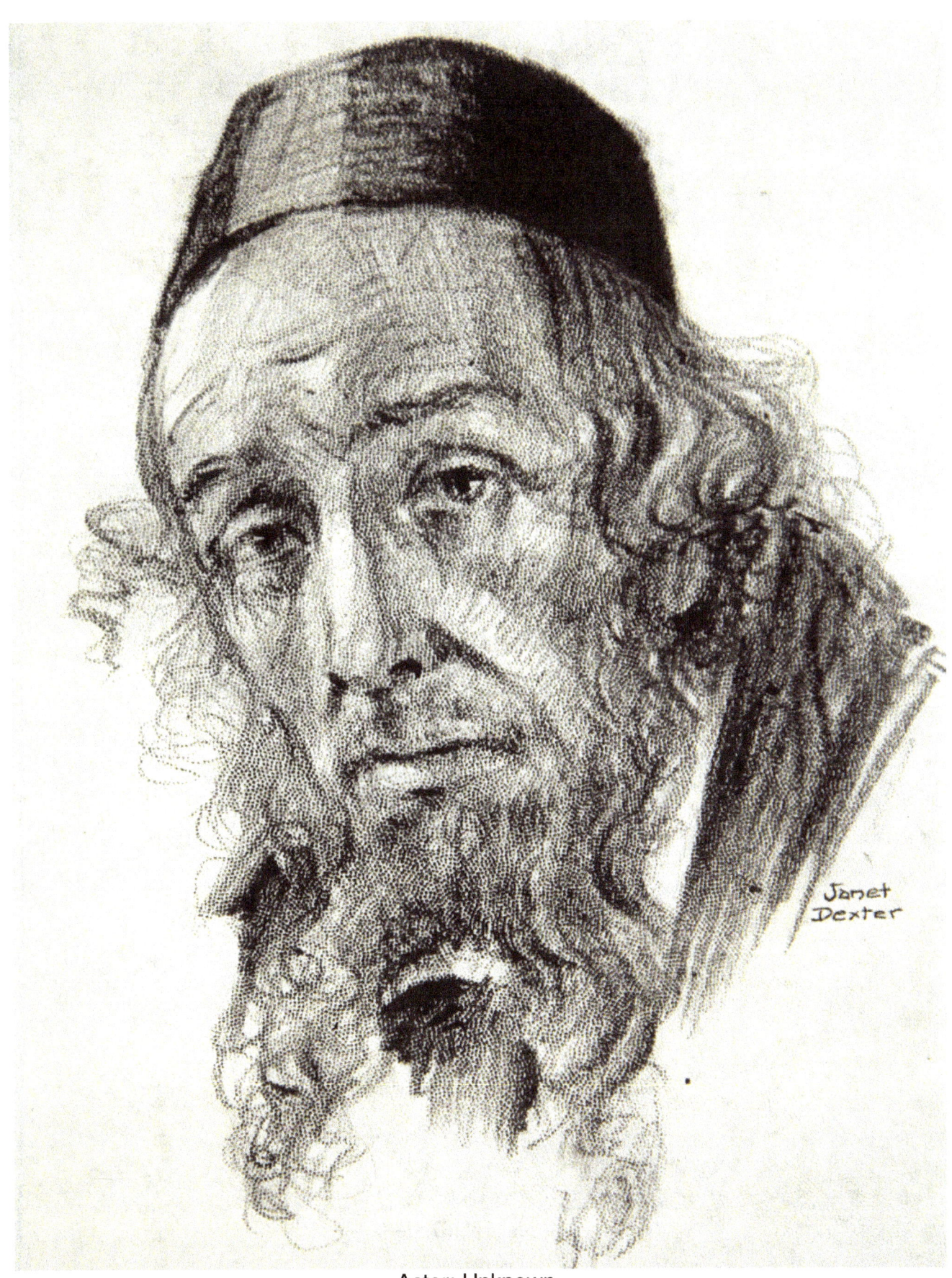

Actor: Unknown

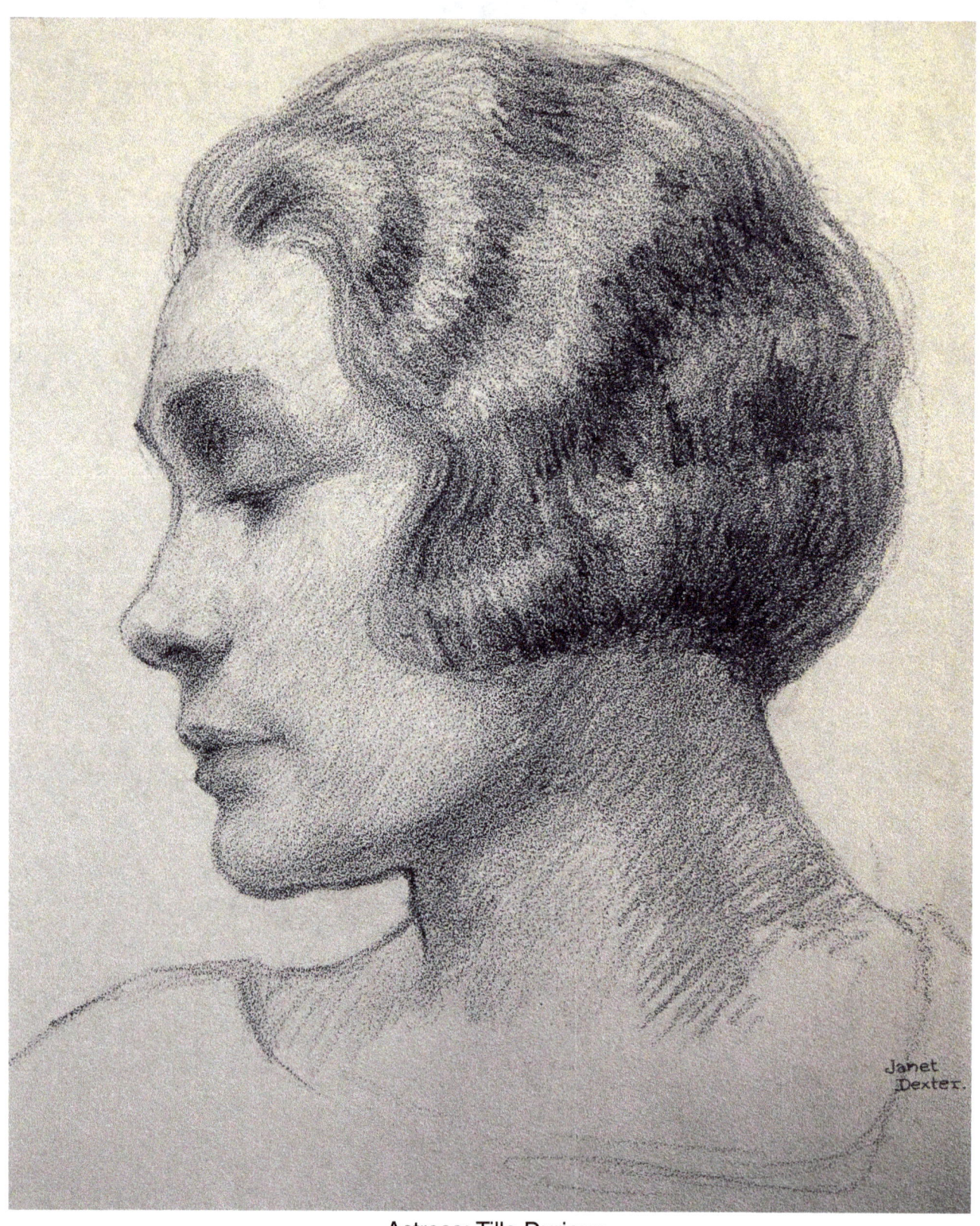

Actress: Tilla Durieux

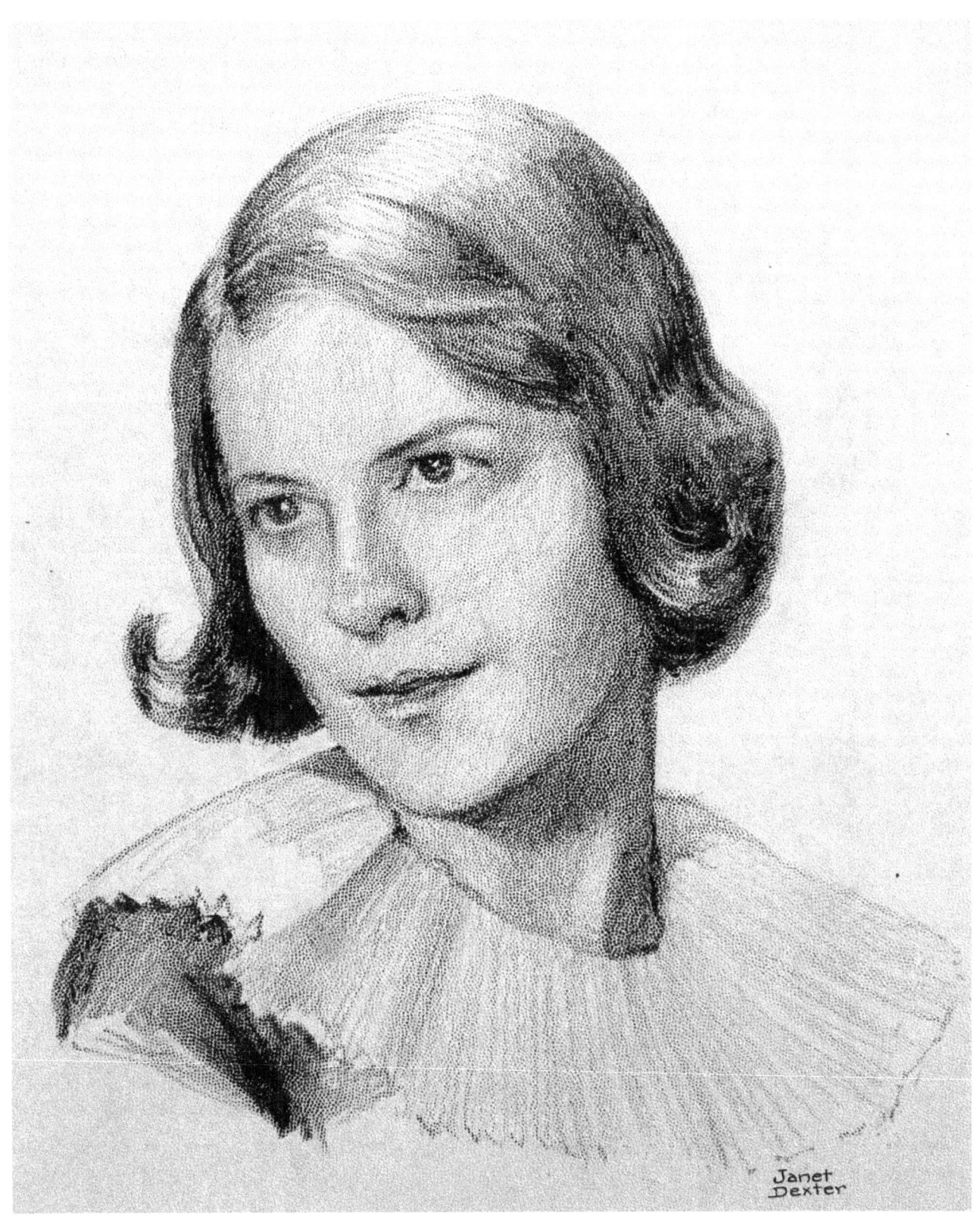

Actress: Ruth Gordon

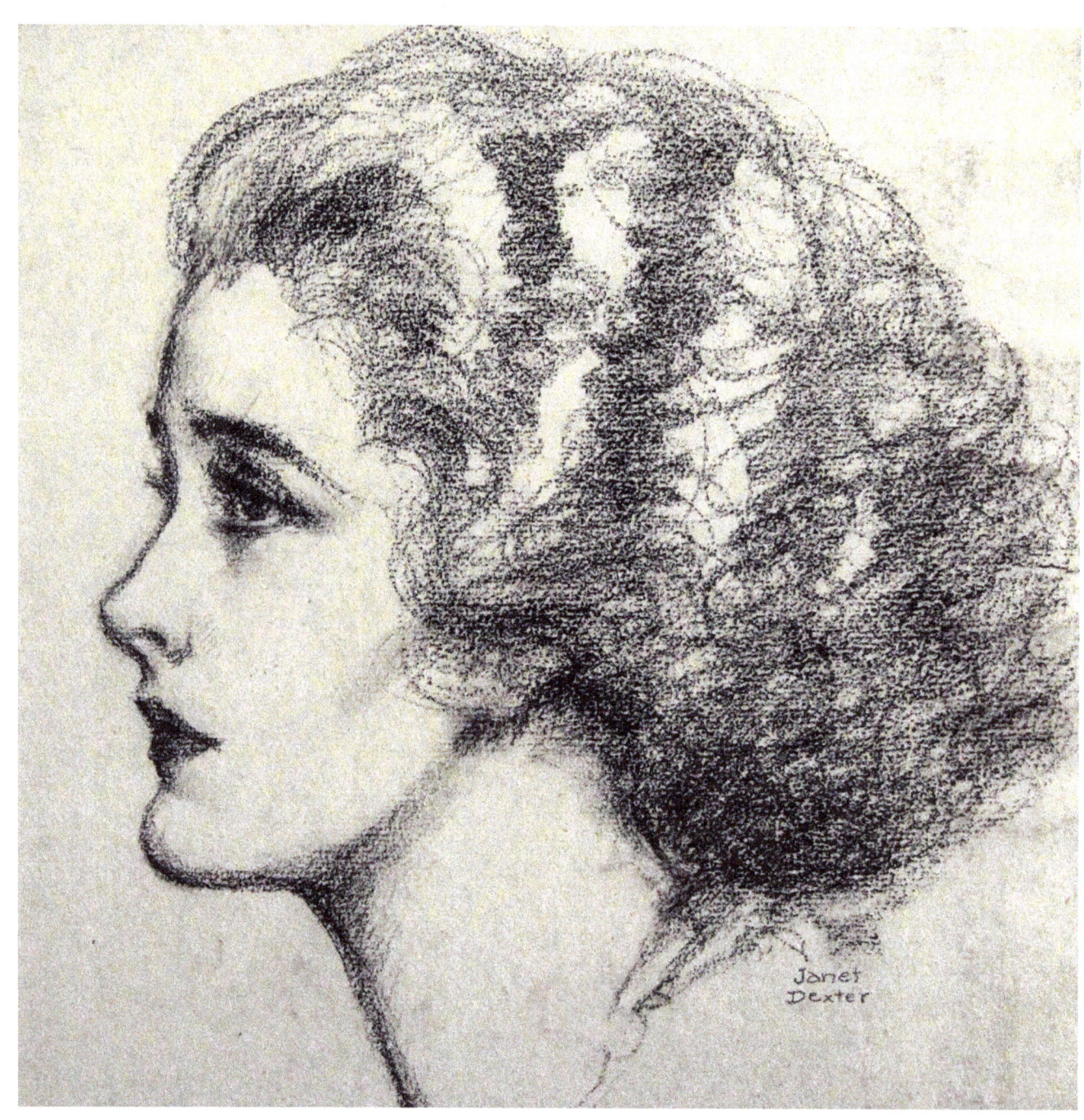

Actress: Margret Dale Owen

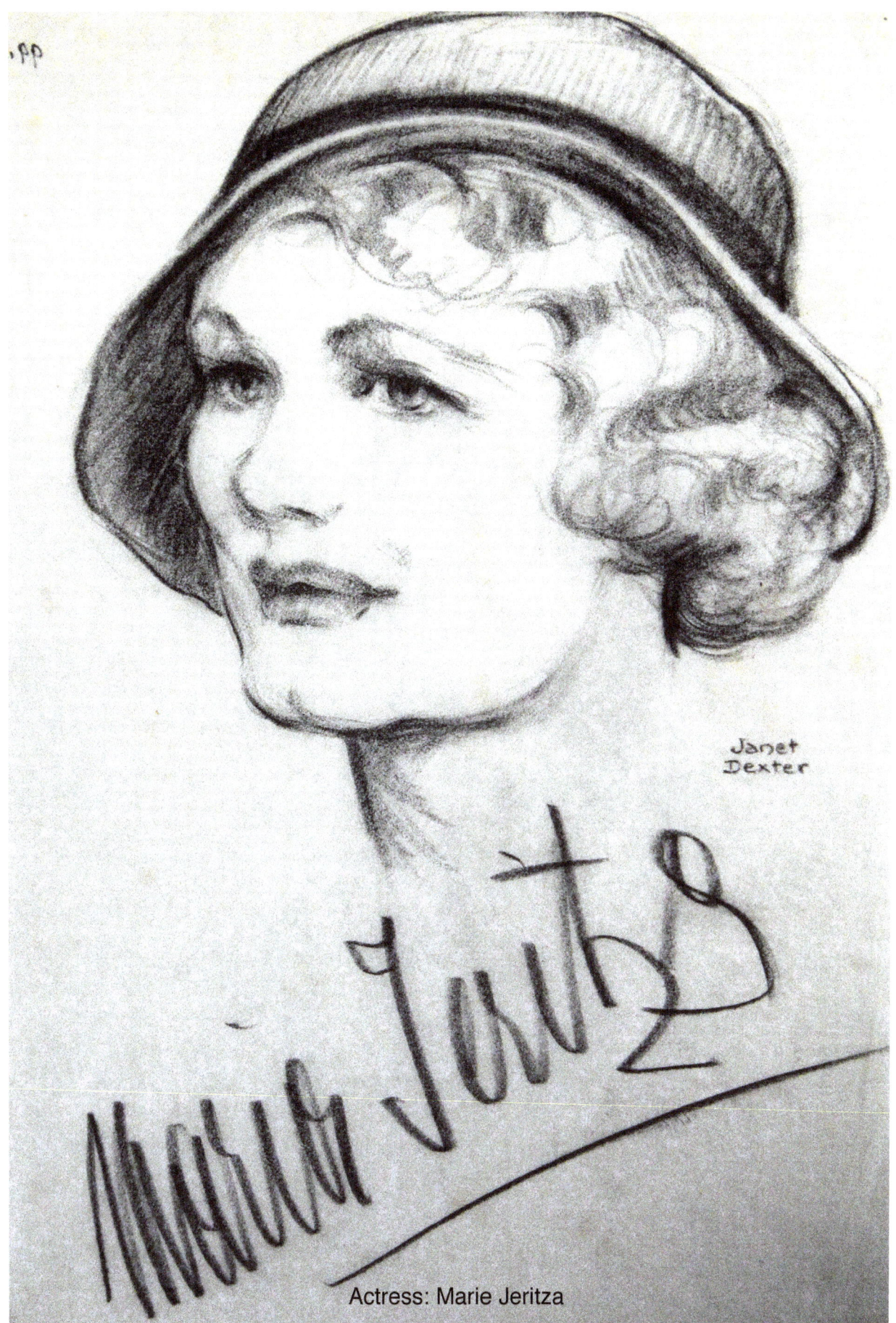

Janet
Dexter

Actress: Marie Jeritza

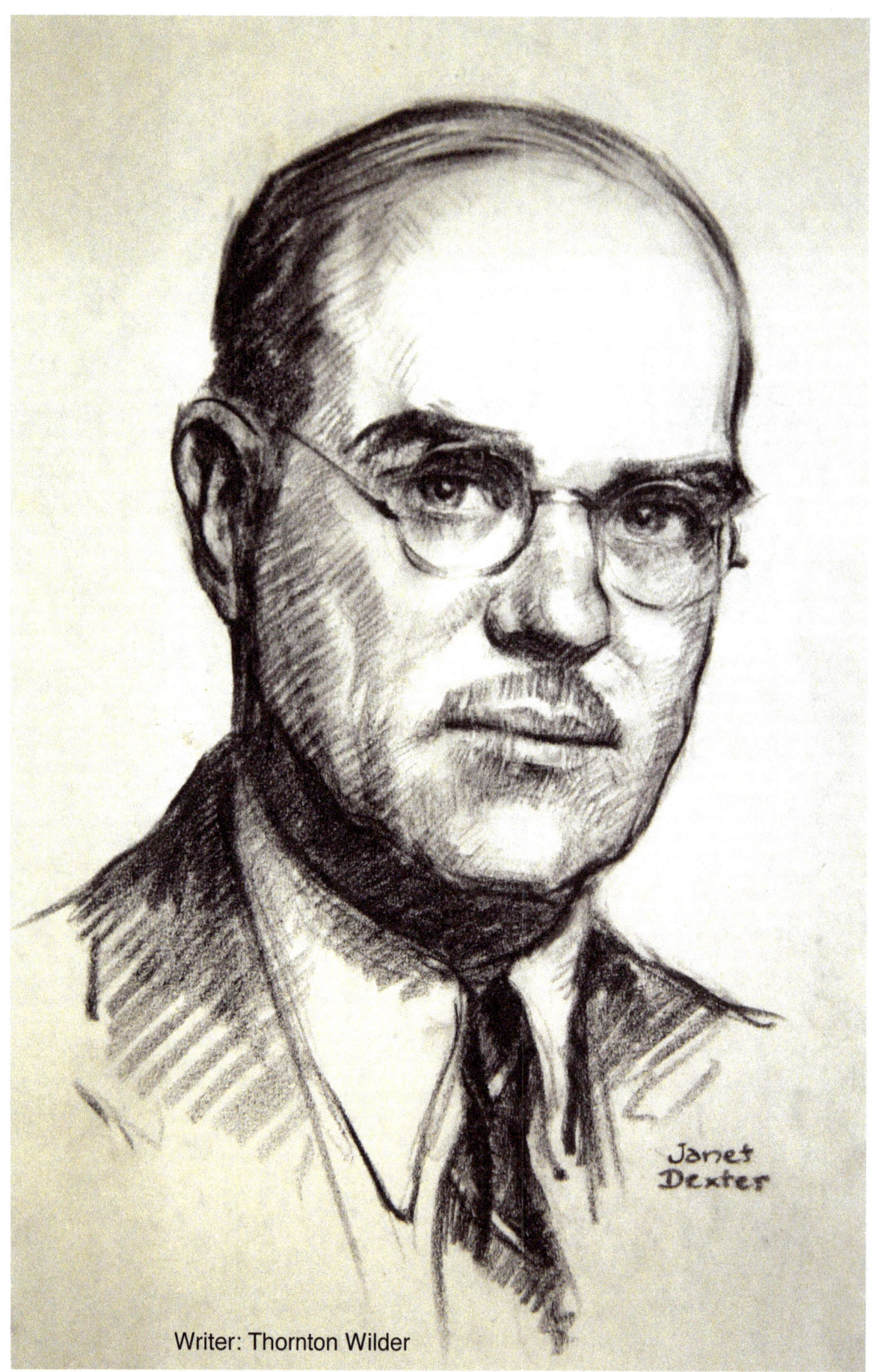

Writer: Thornton Wilder

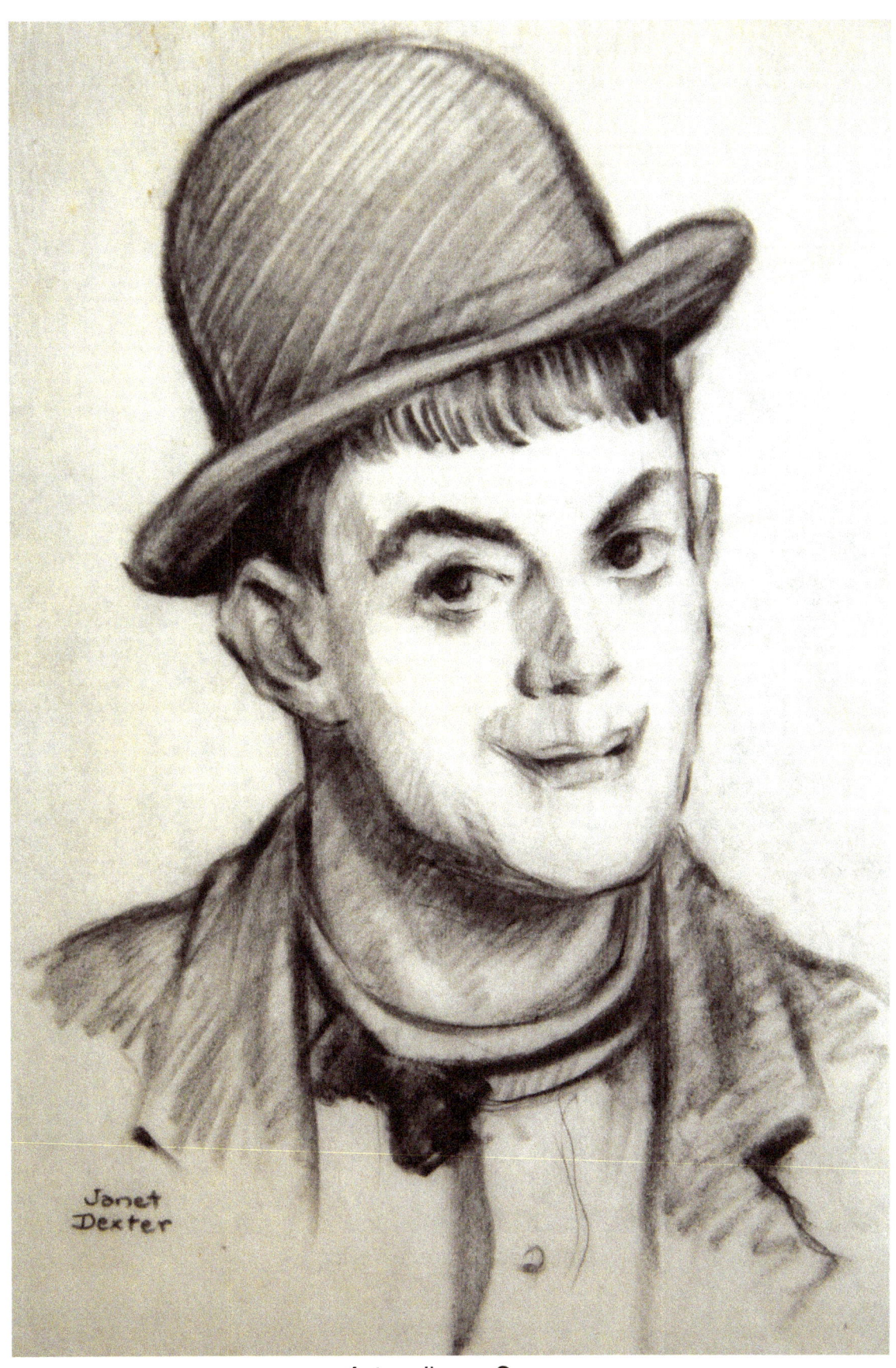

Actor: Jimmy Save

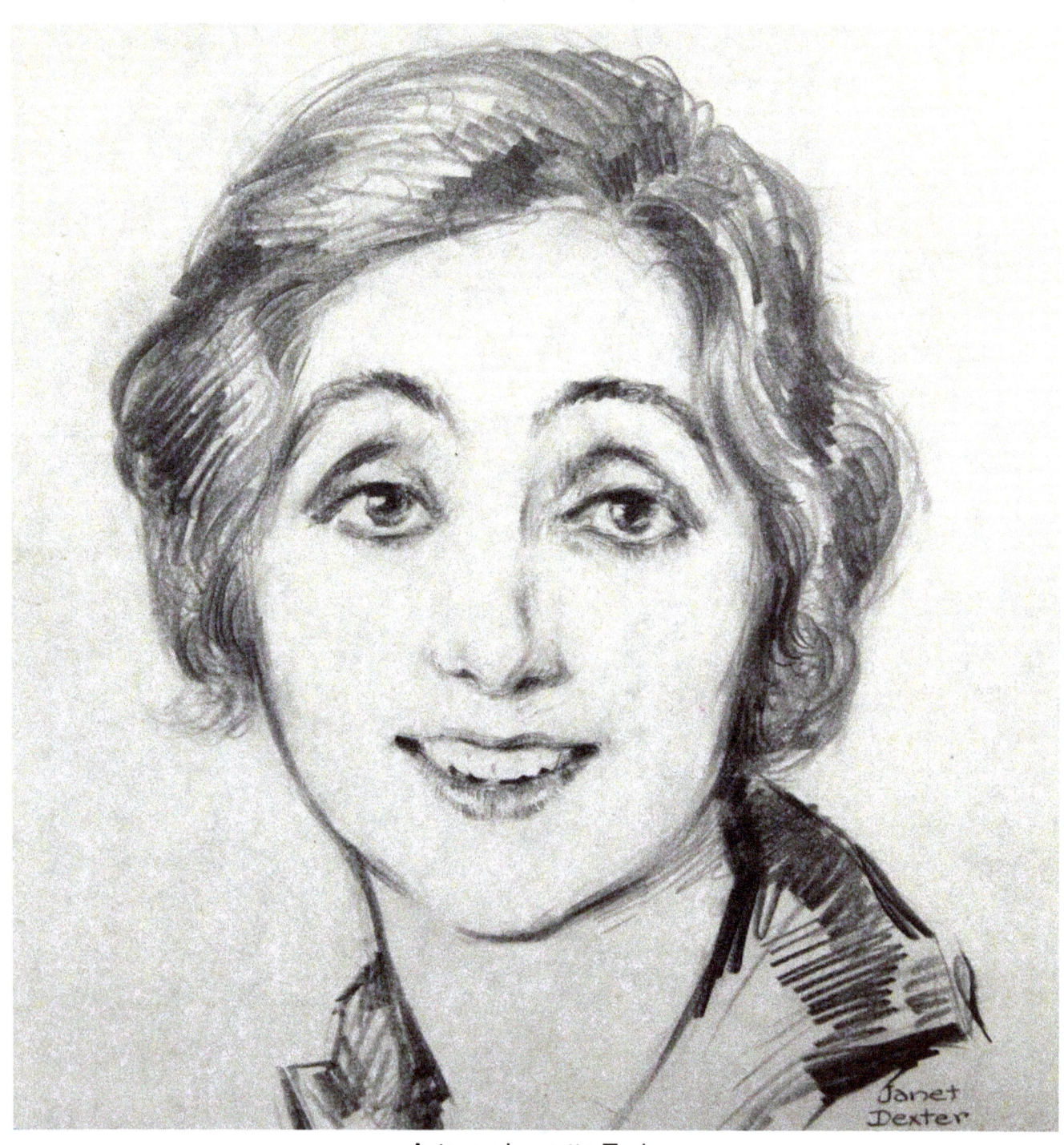

Actress: Laurette Taylor

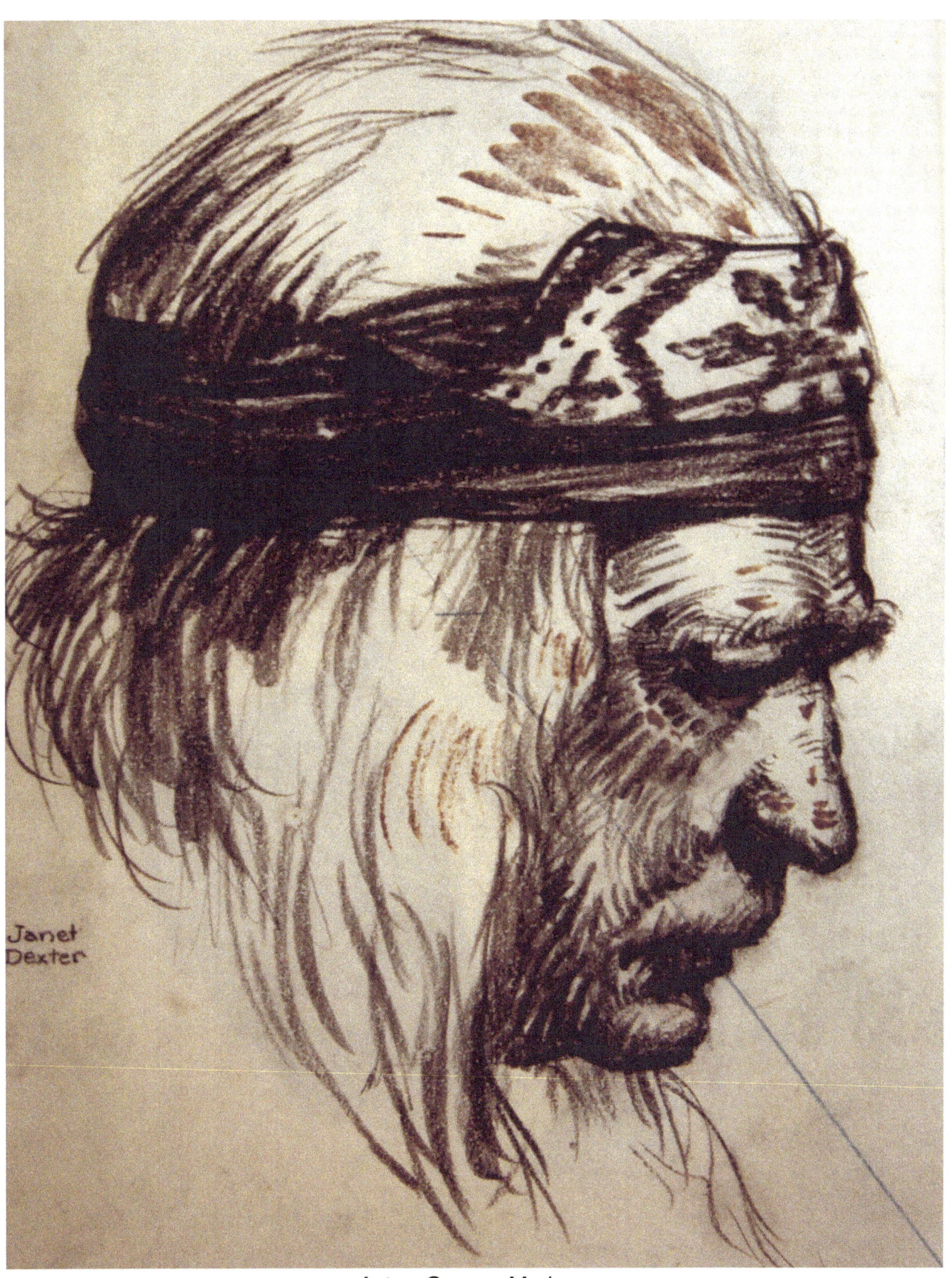

Actor: George Mariary

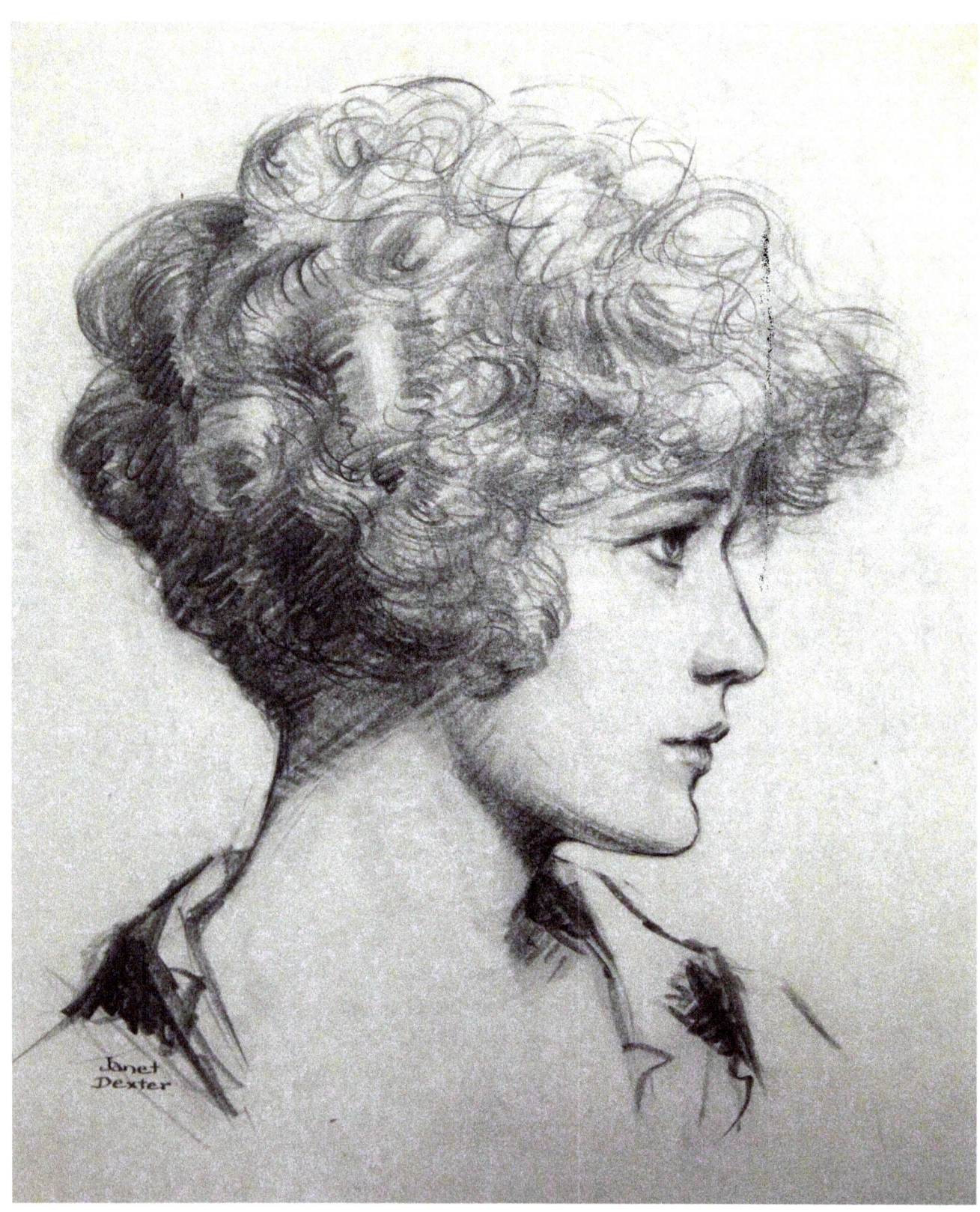

Actress: Miriam Hopkins

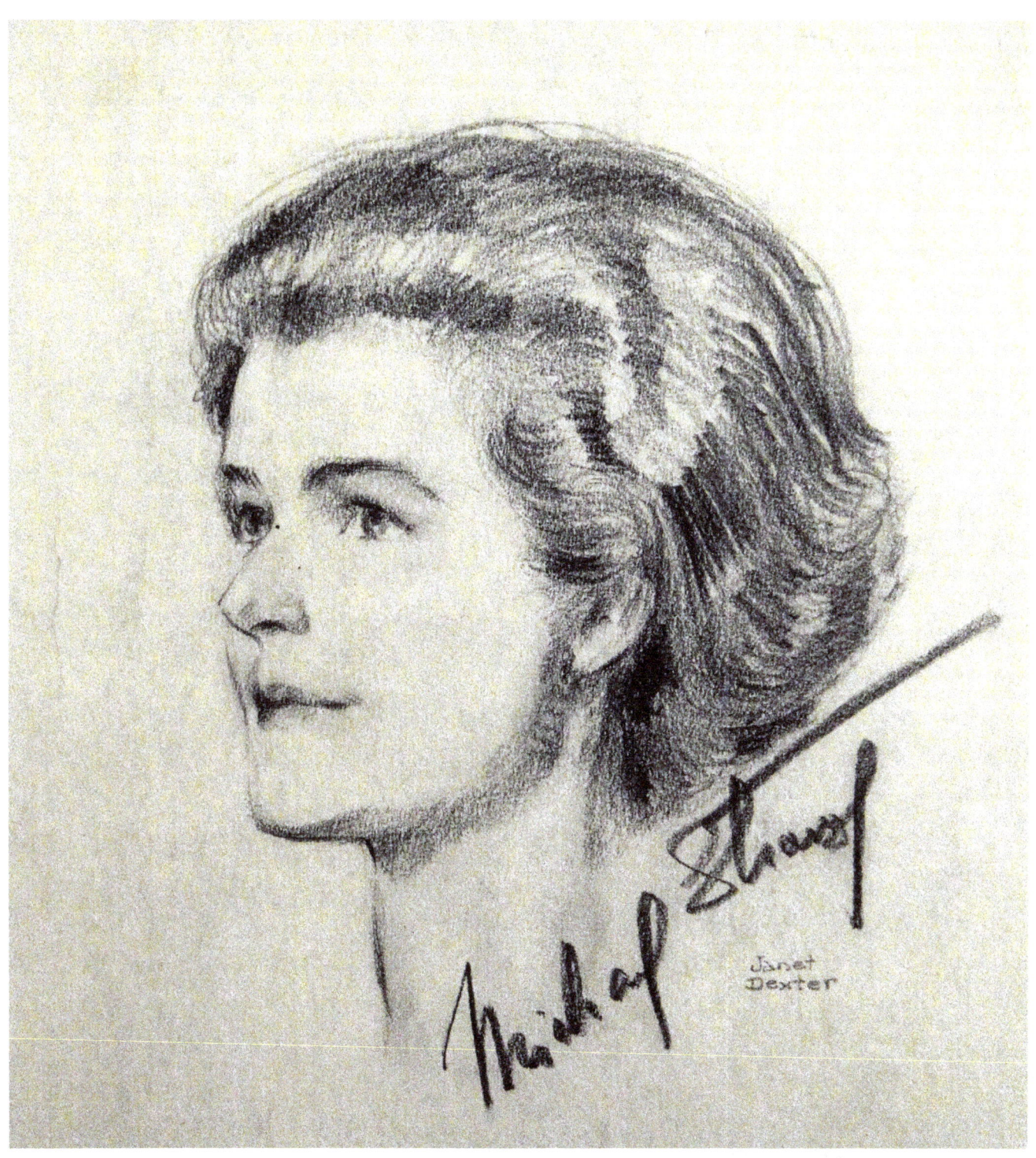

Actress: Michael Strauf

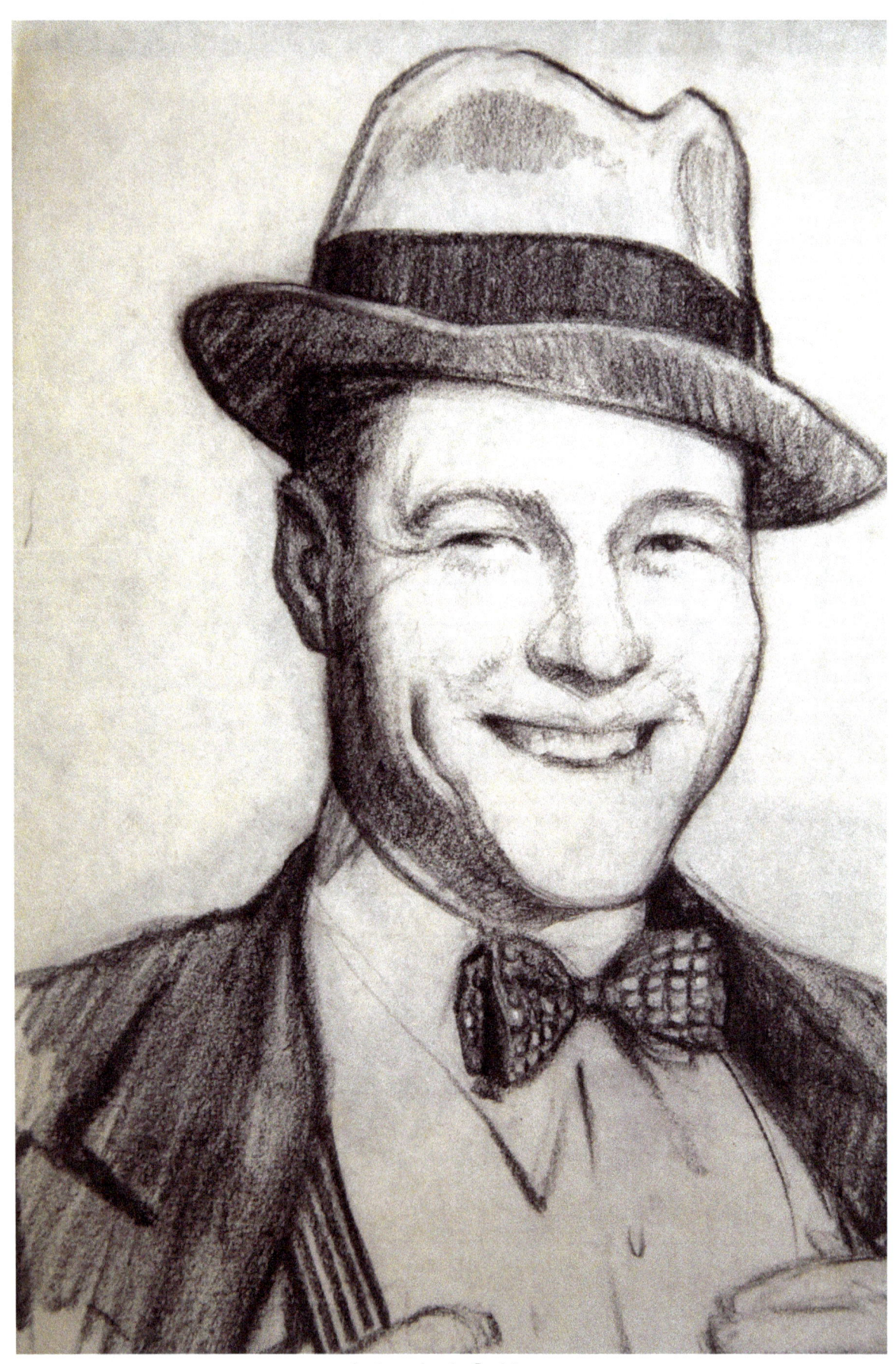

Actor: Jack Oakie

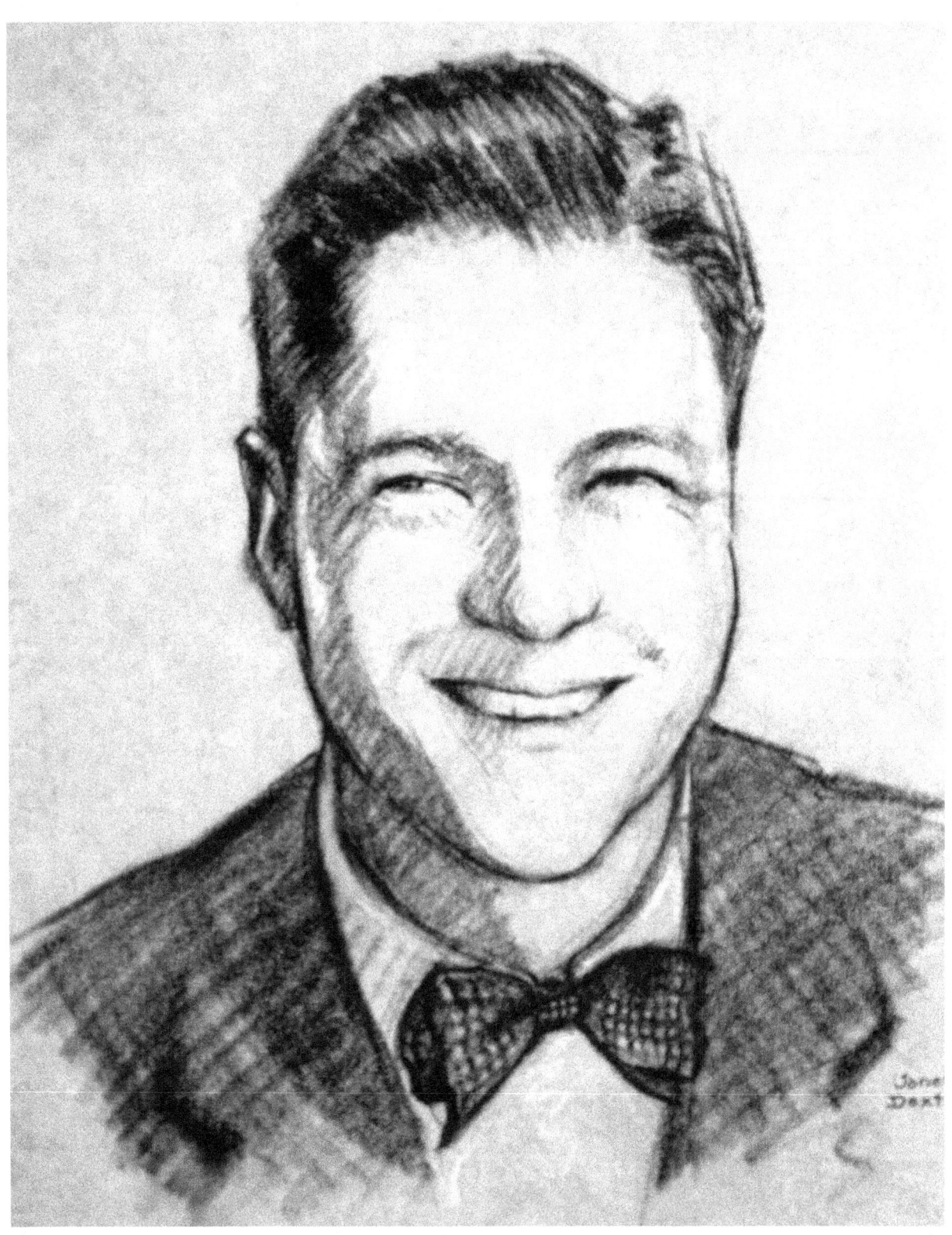

Actor: Jack Oakie

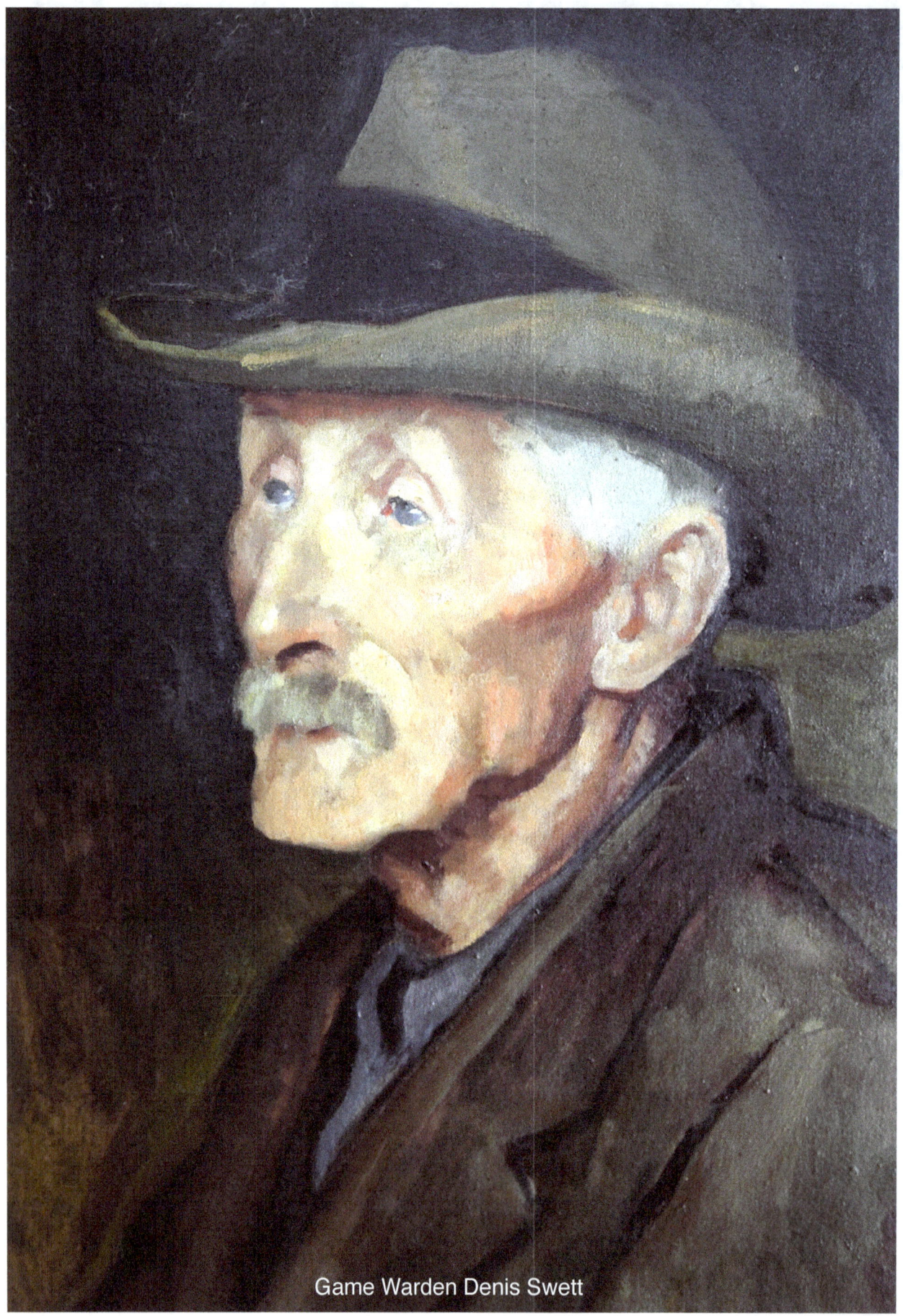

Game Warden Denis Swett

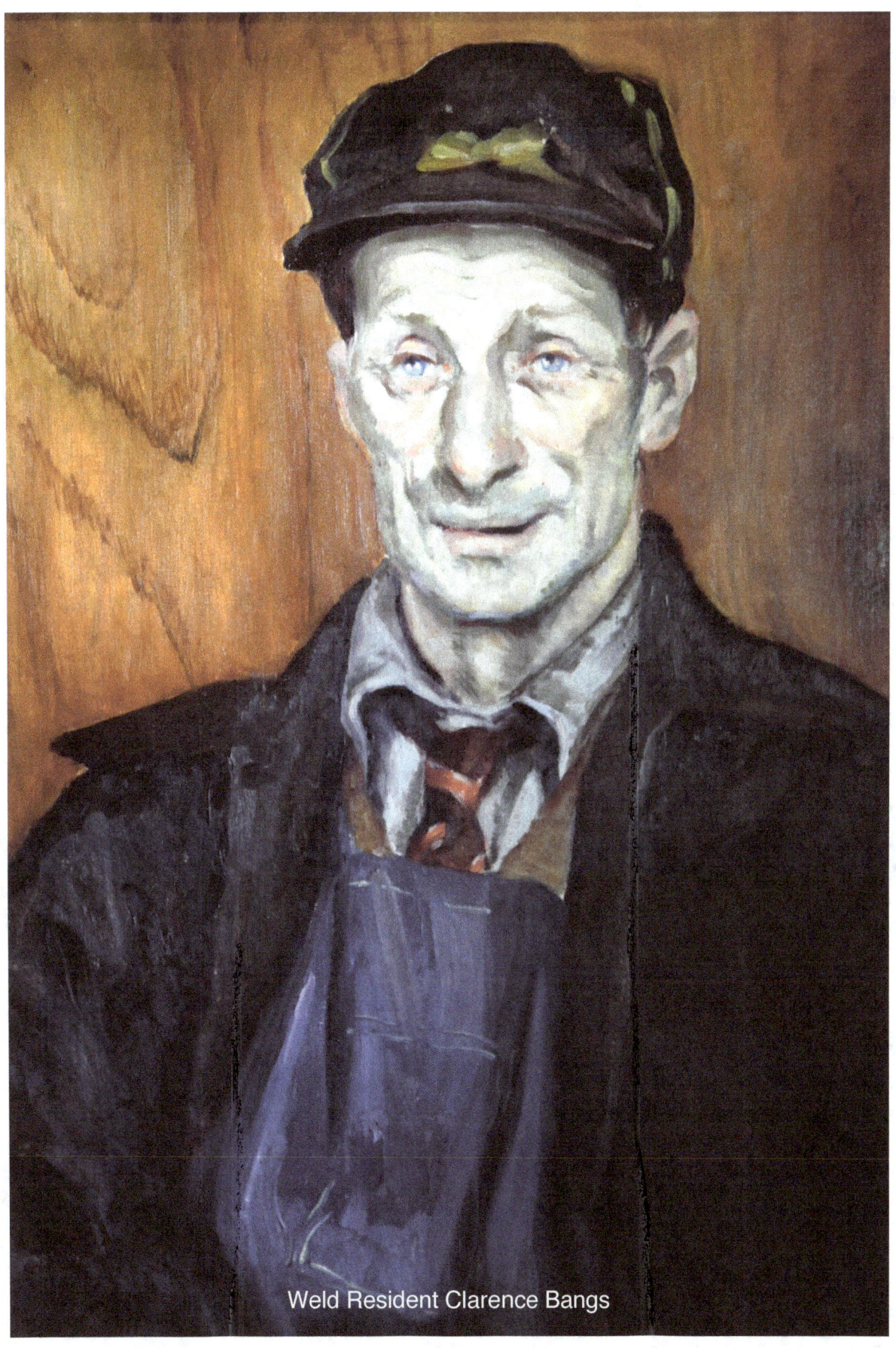

Weld Resident Clarence Bangs

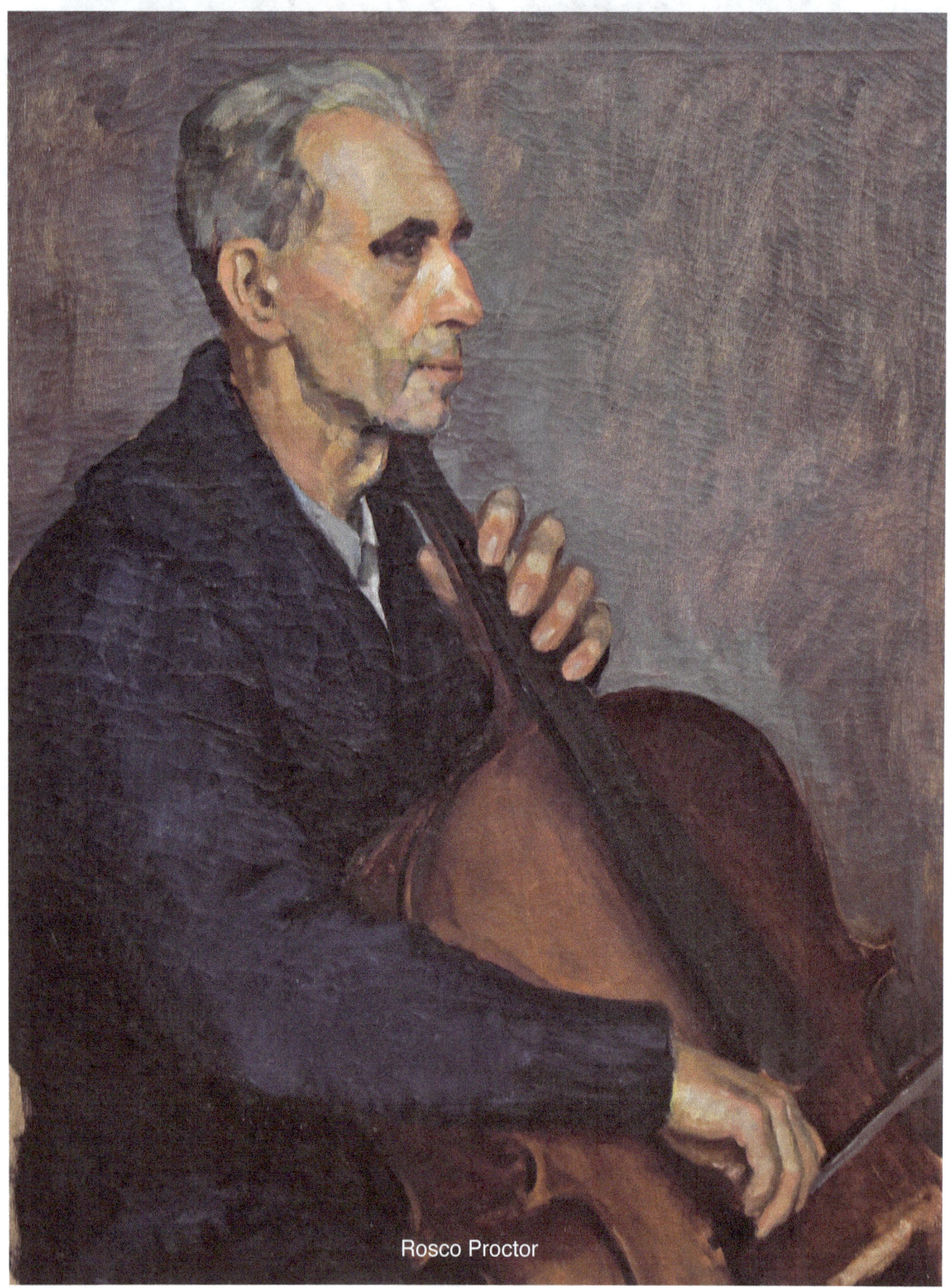

Rosco Proctor

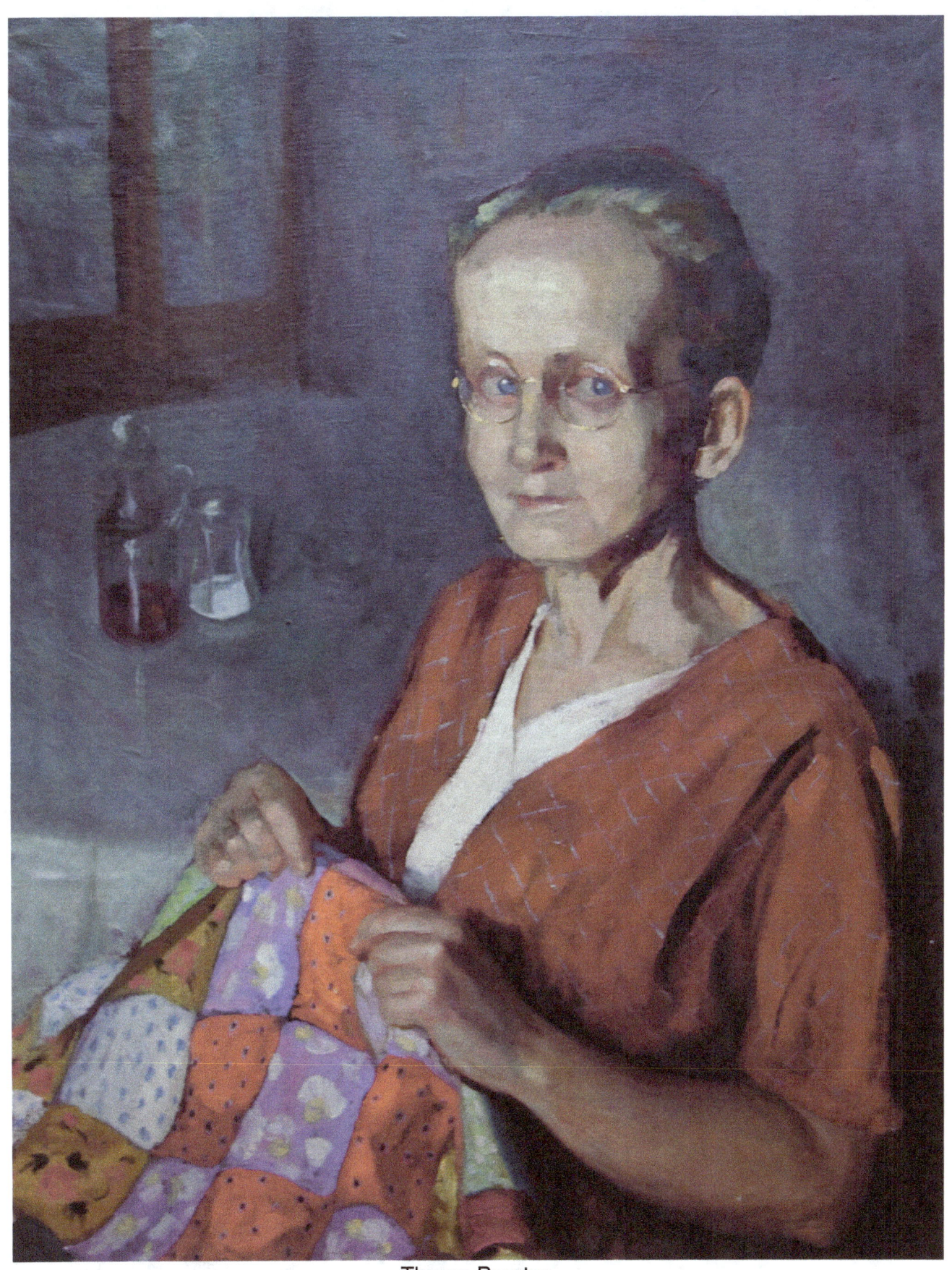

Thursa Proctor

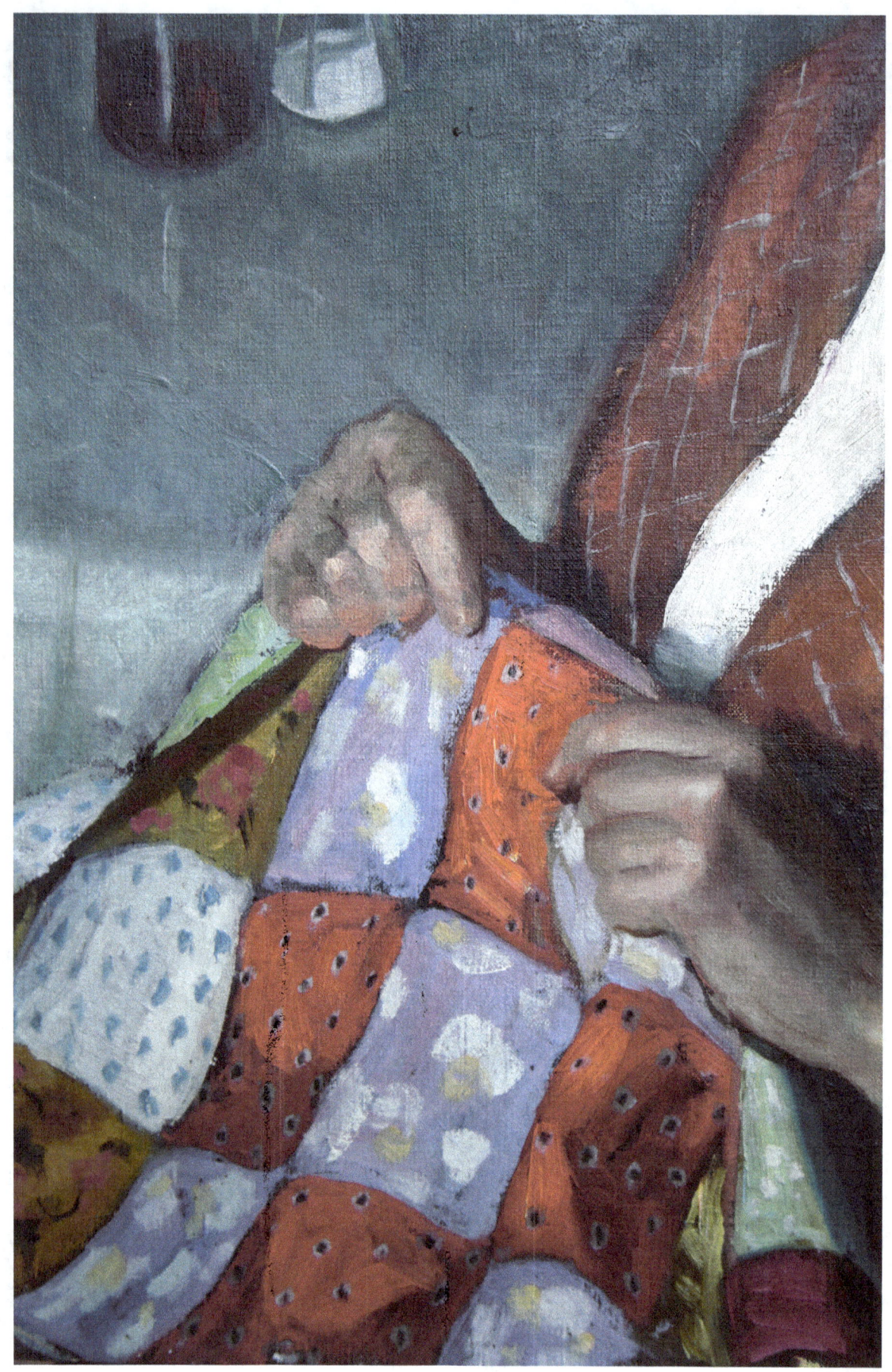

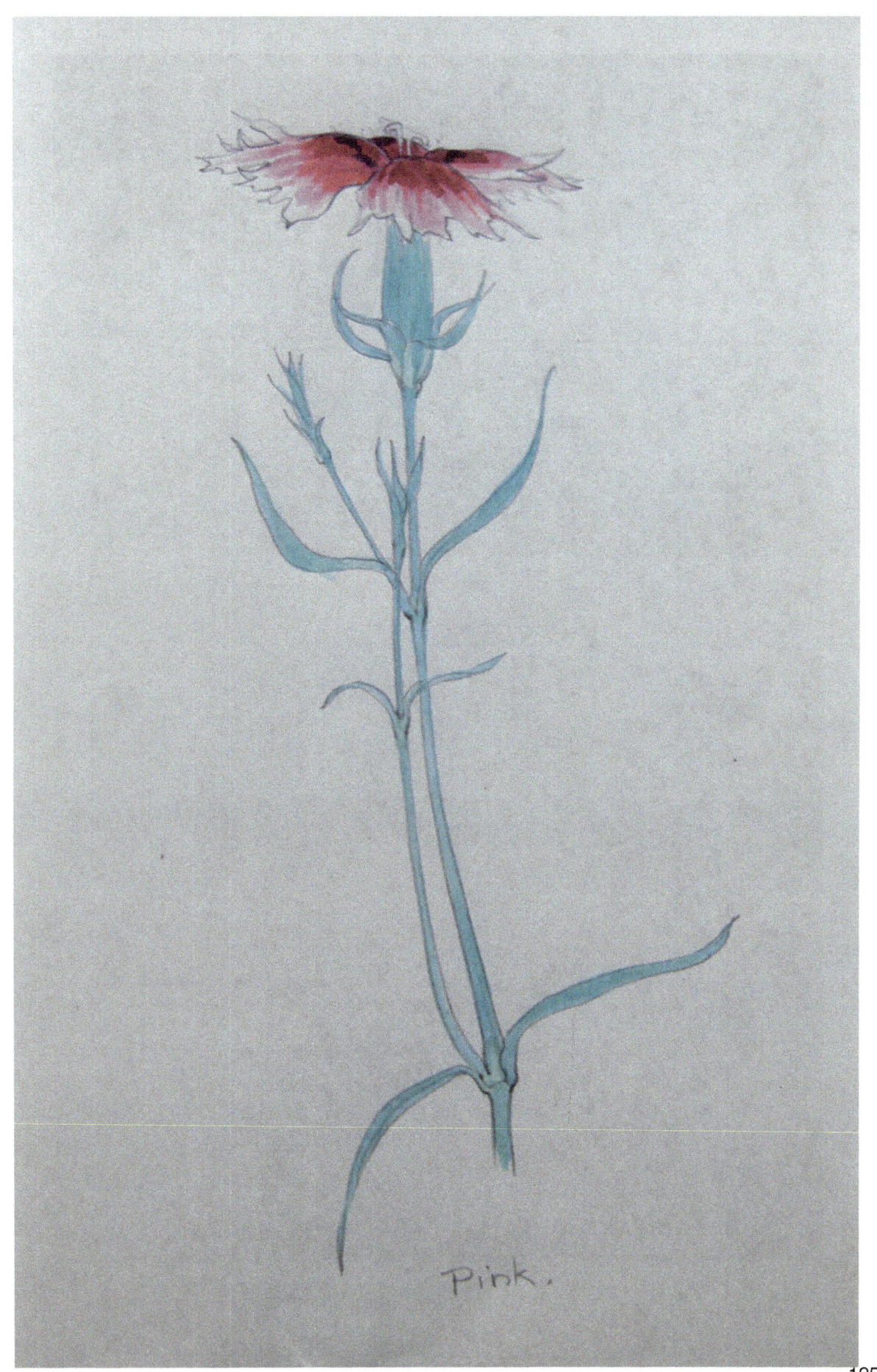

Pink.

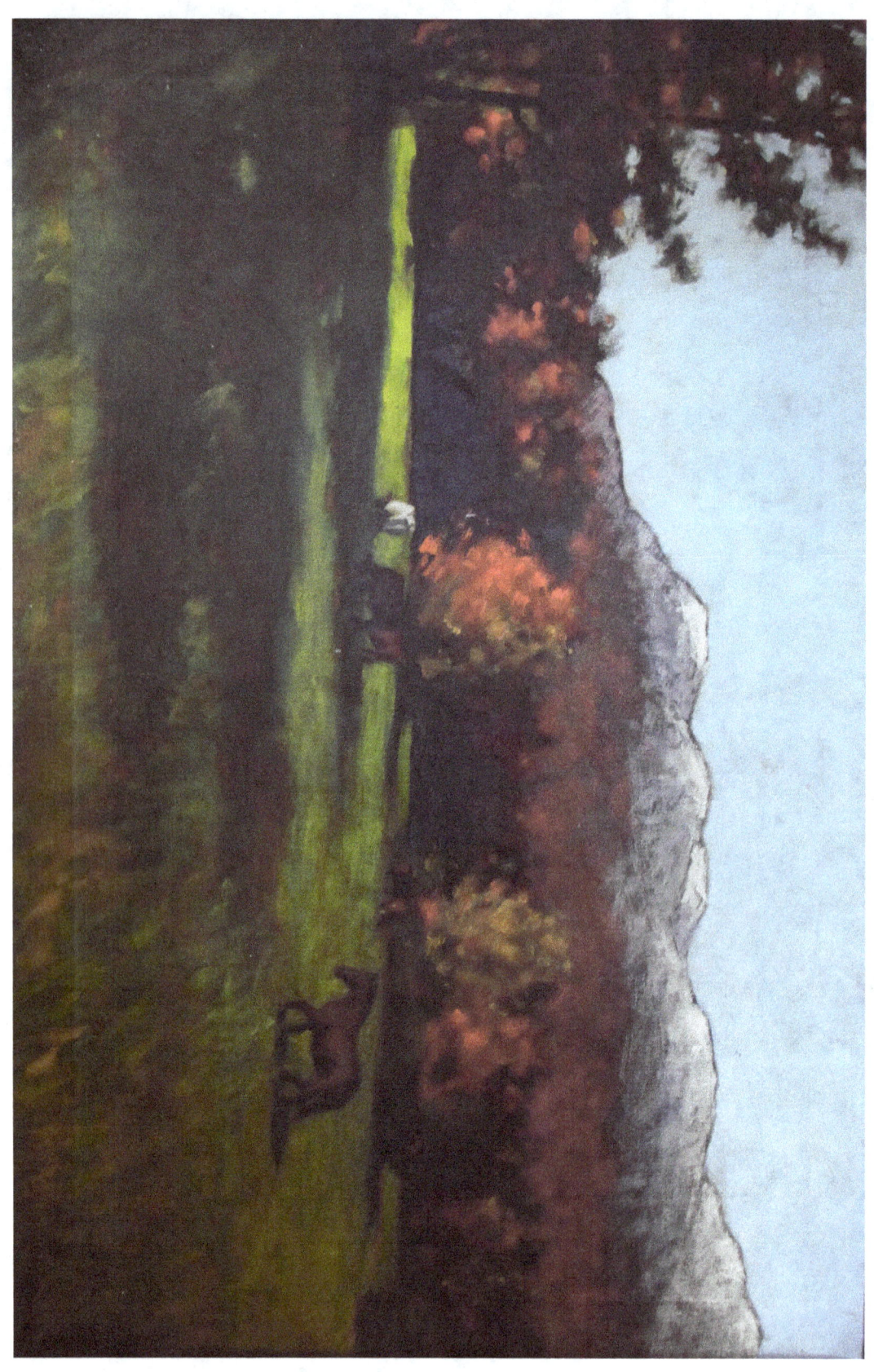

The Intervale, Weld, Maine

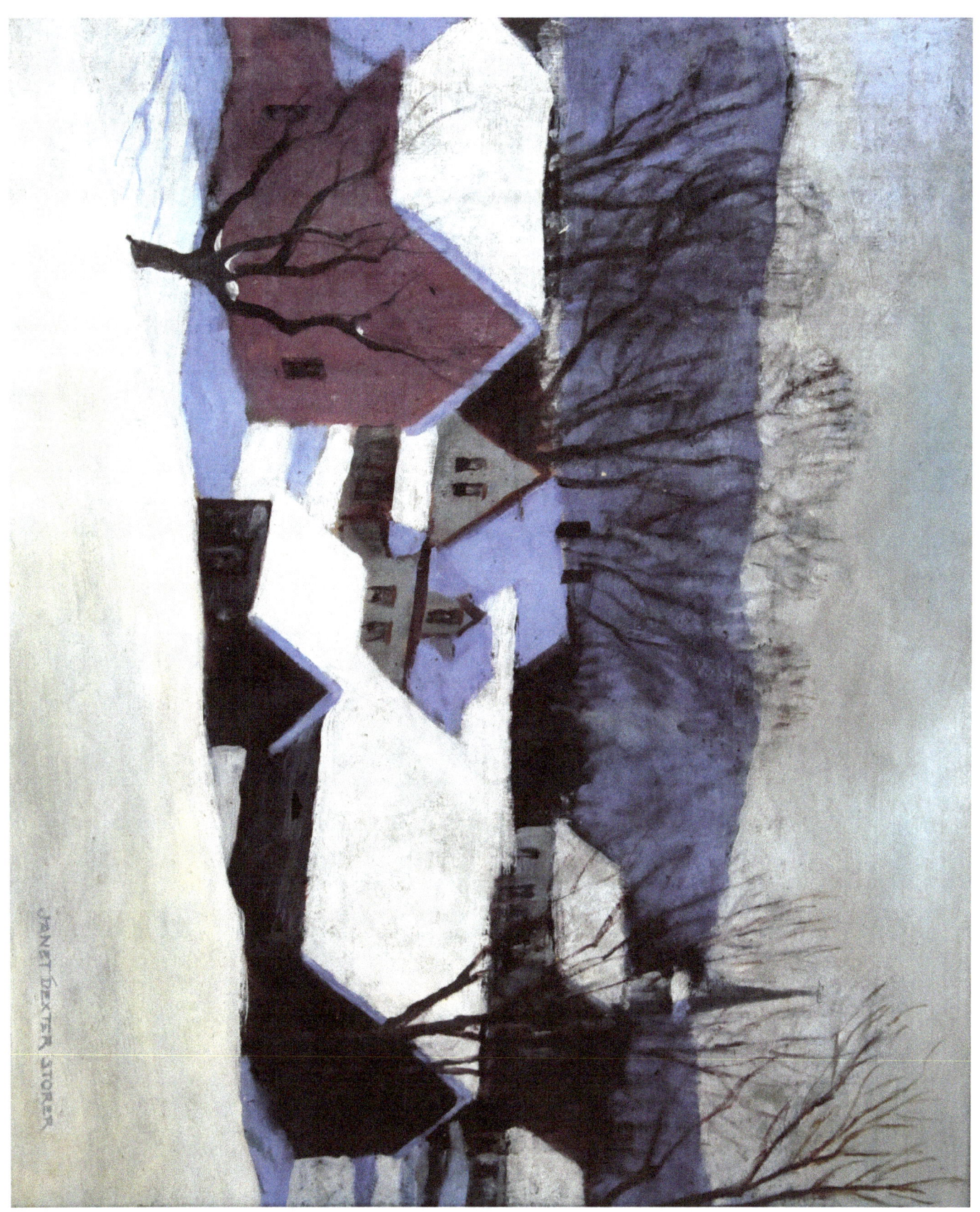

Winter: Weld, Maine

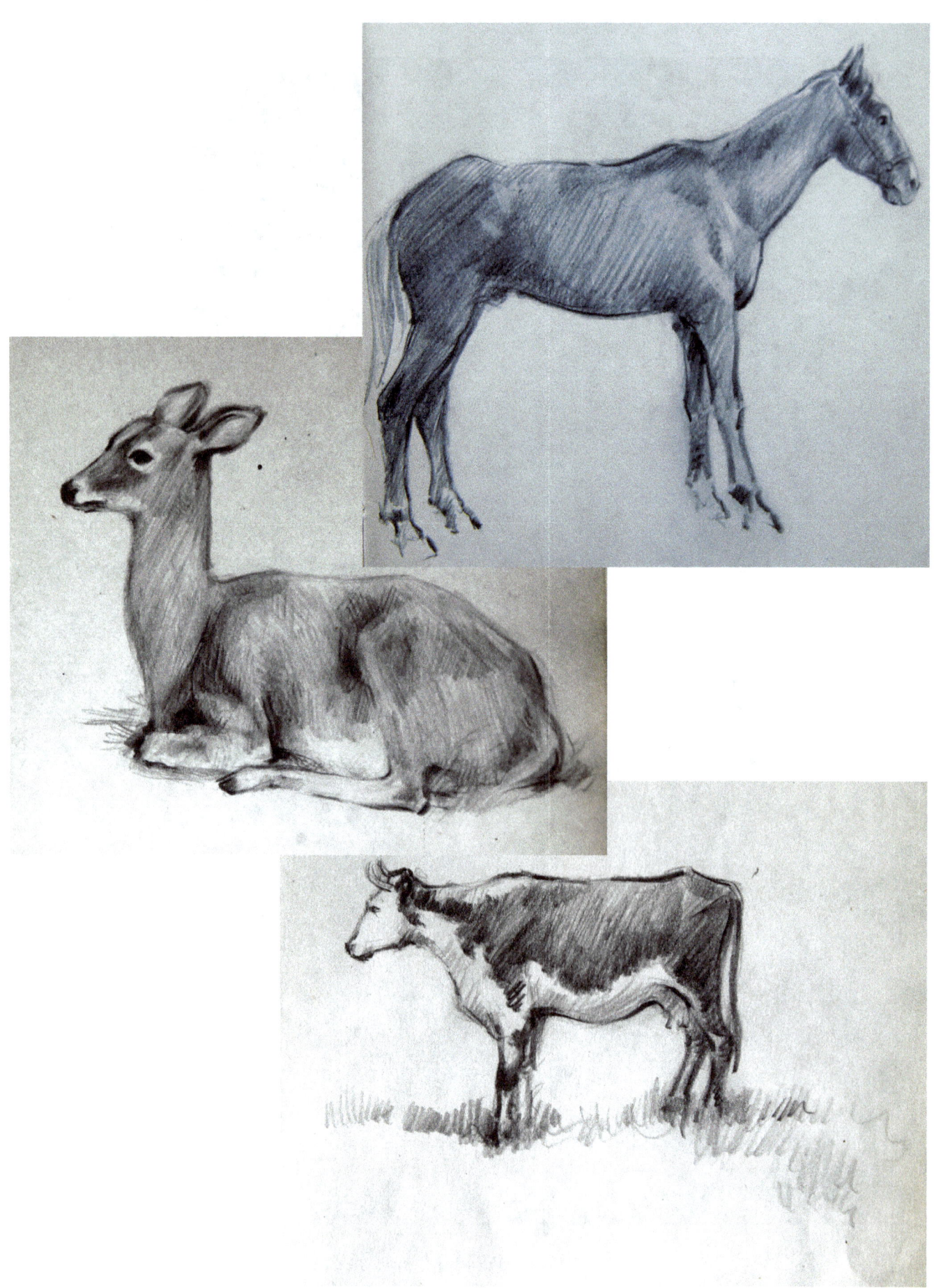

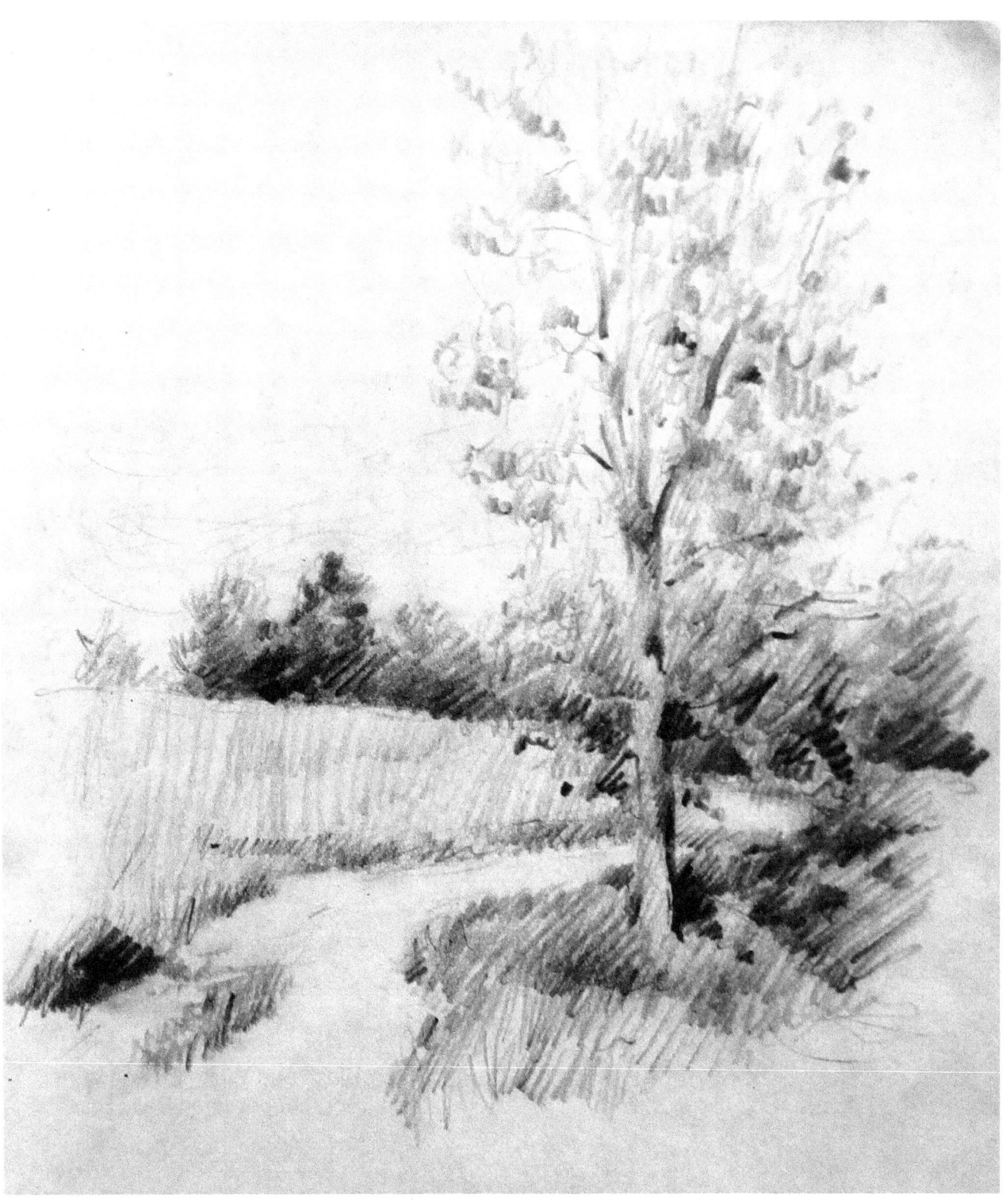

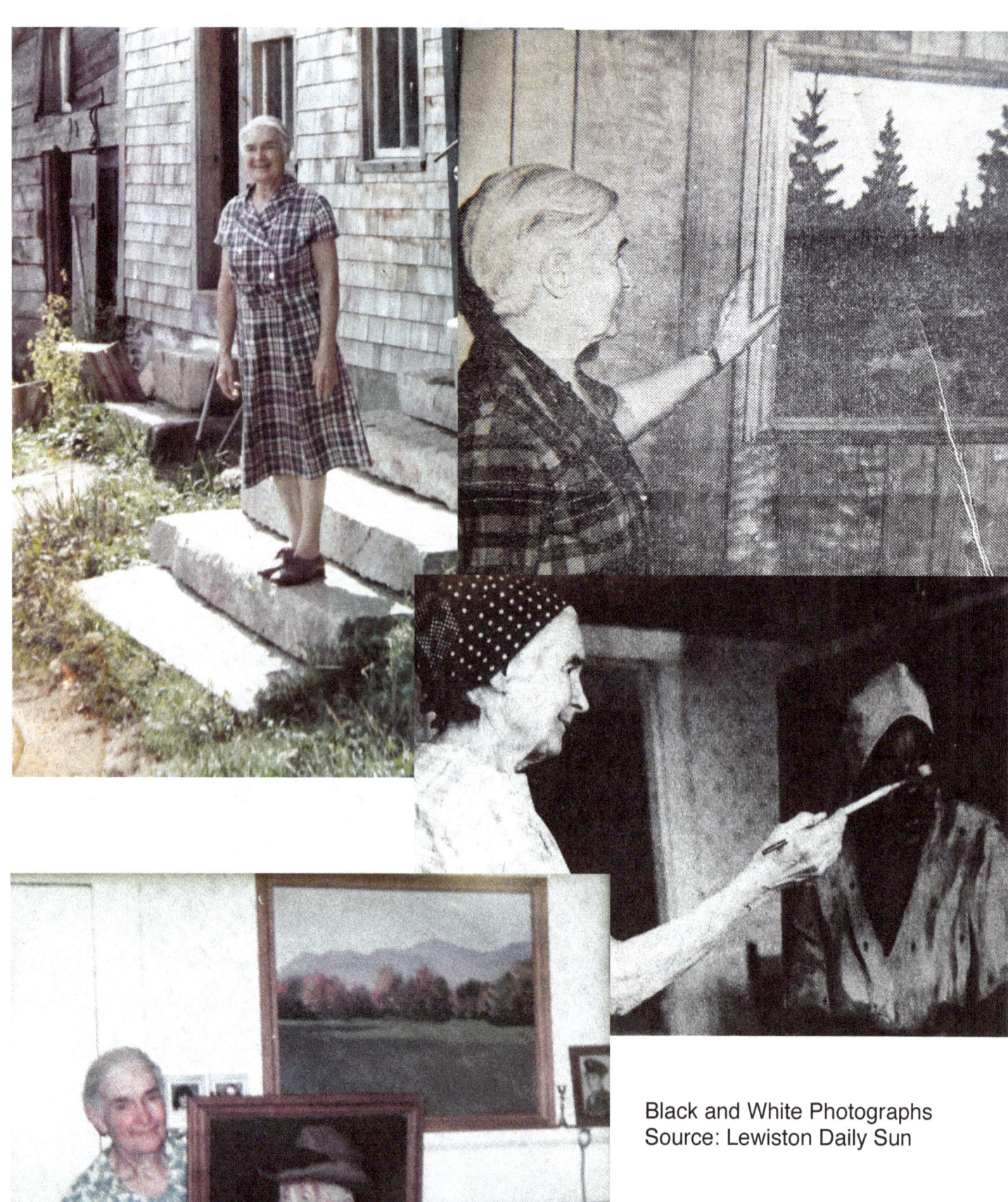

Black and White Photographs
Source: Lewiston Daily Sun

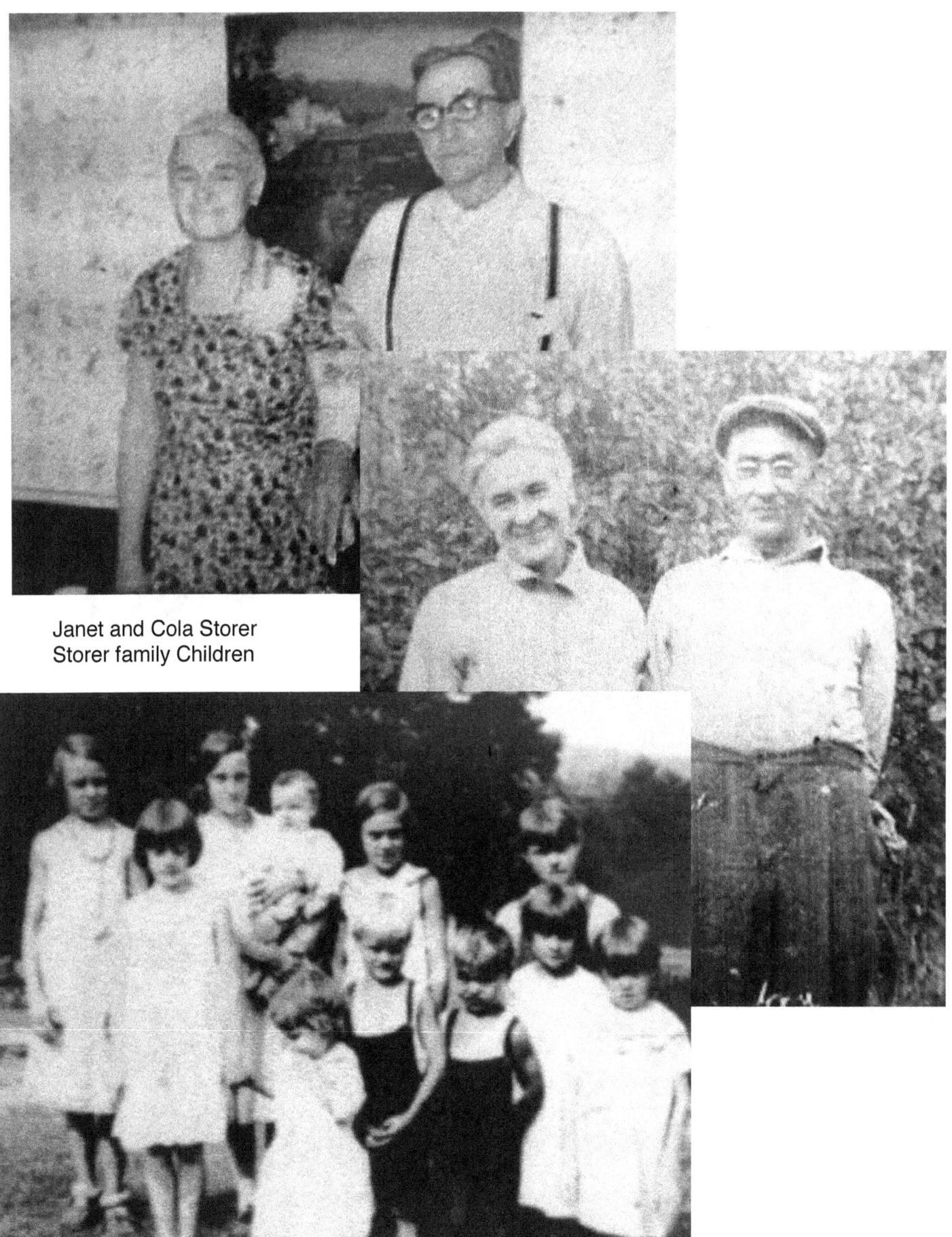

Janet and Cola Storer
Storer family Children

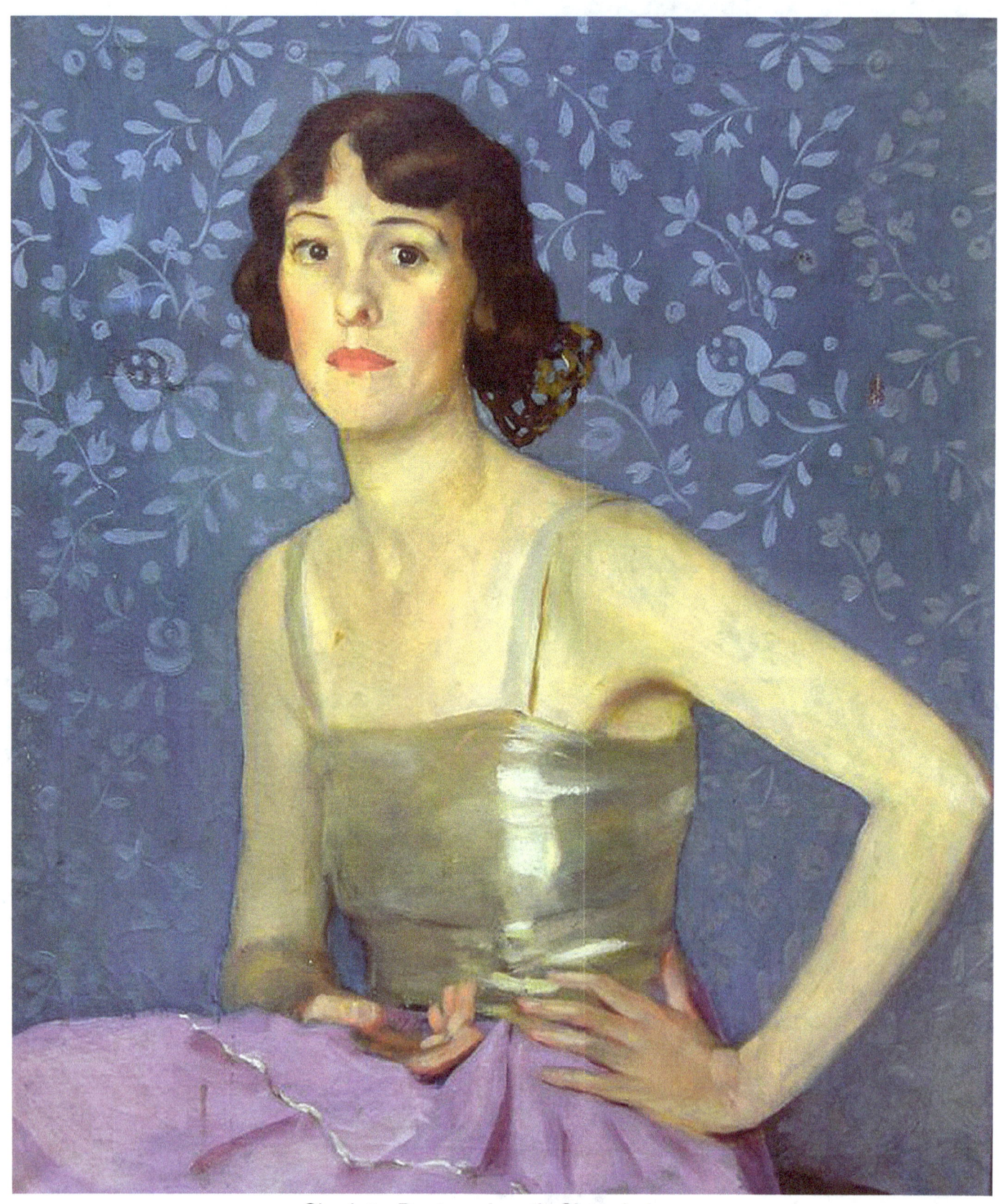

Charlotte Dexter - Janet's Sister in Law

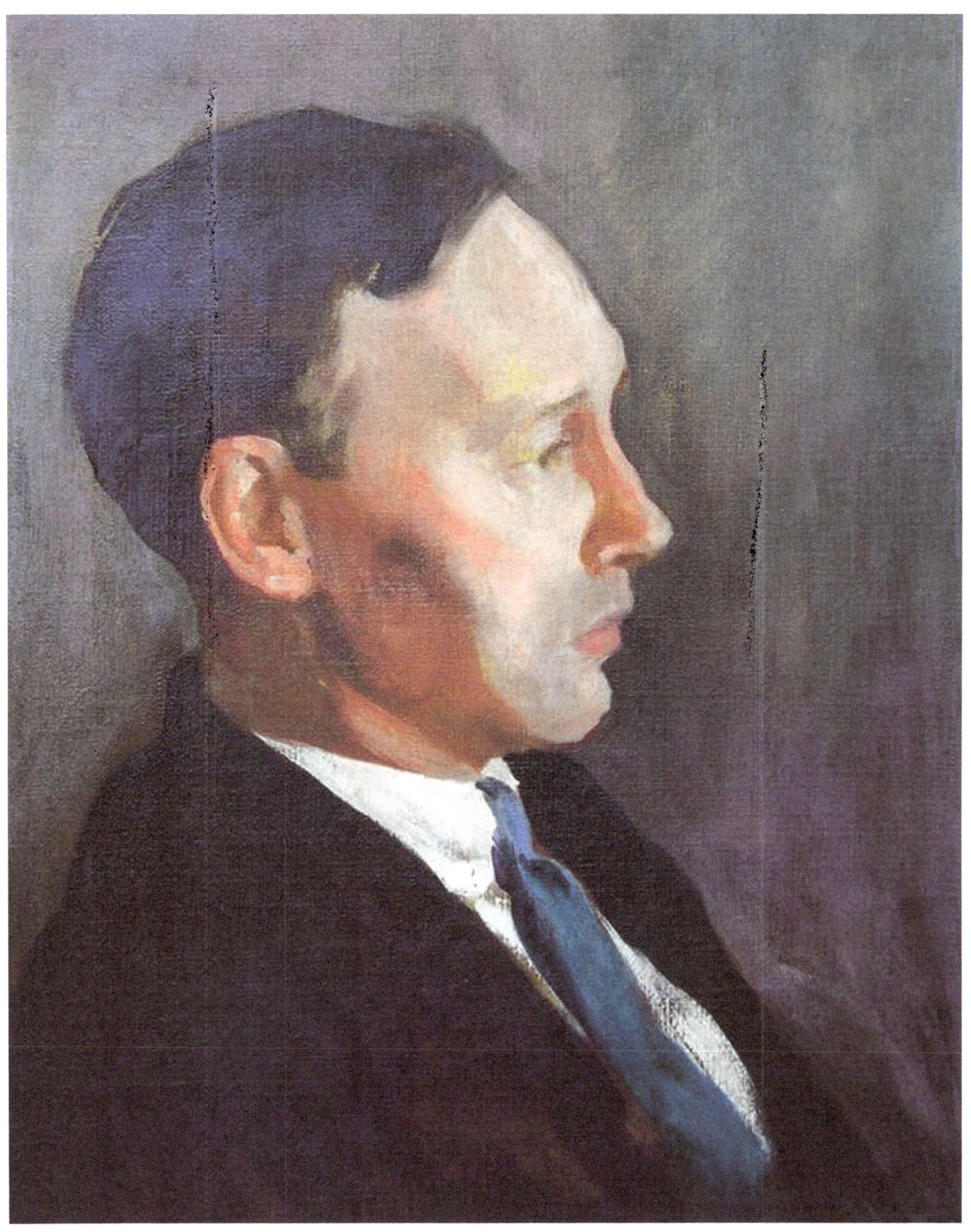

Franklin C. Dexter

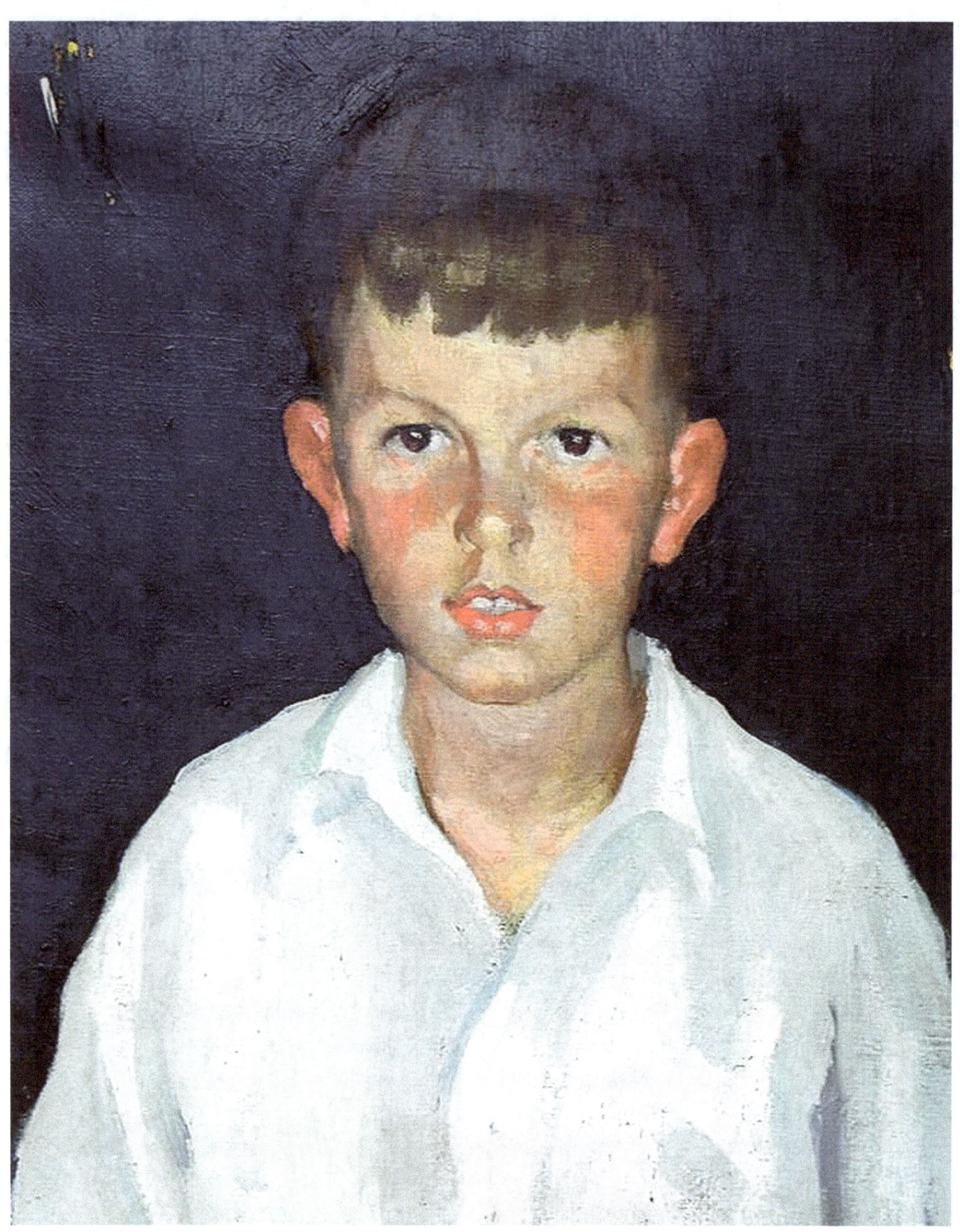

Franklin C. Dexter

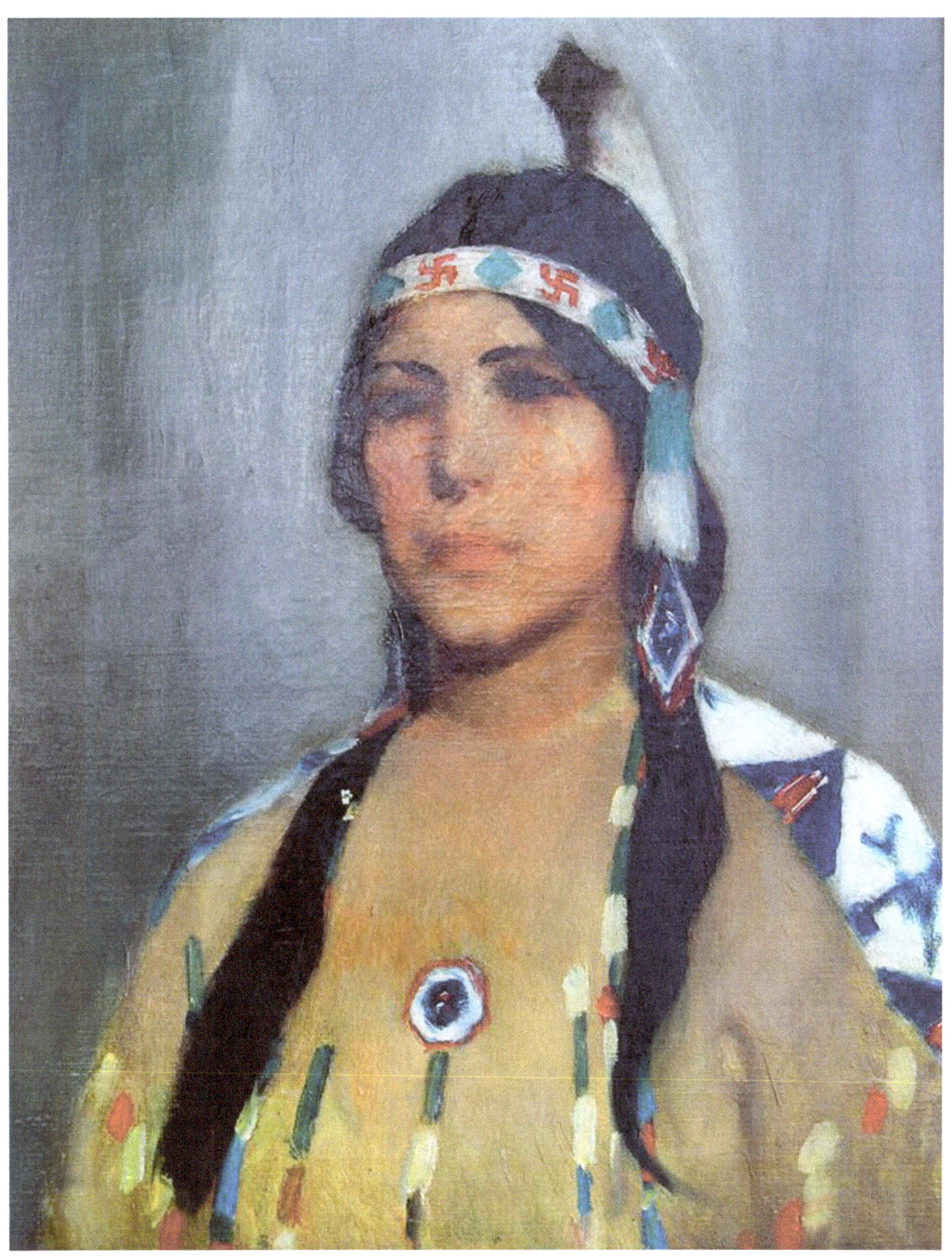

Unknown Model

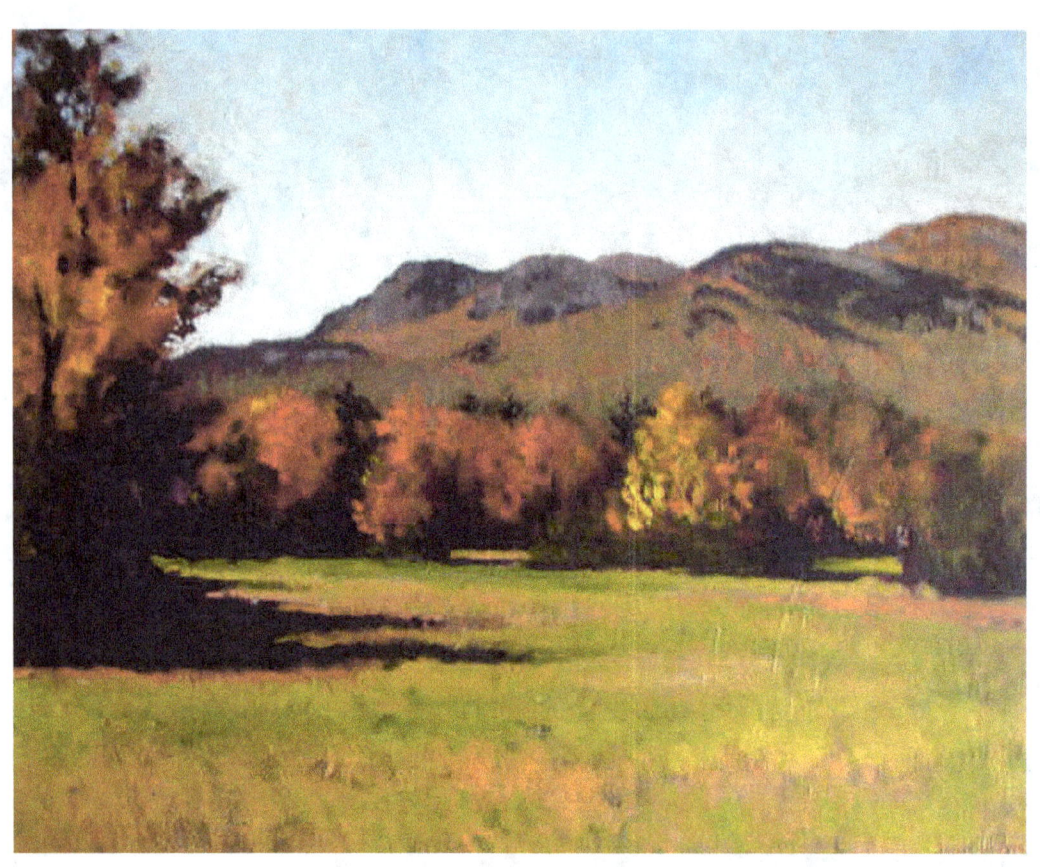

Tumbledown Mountain

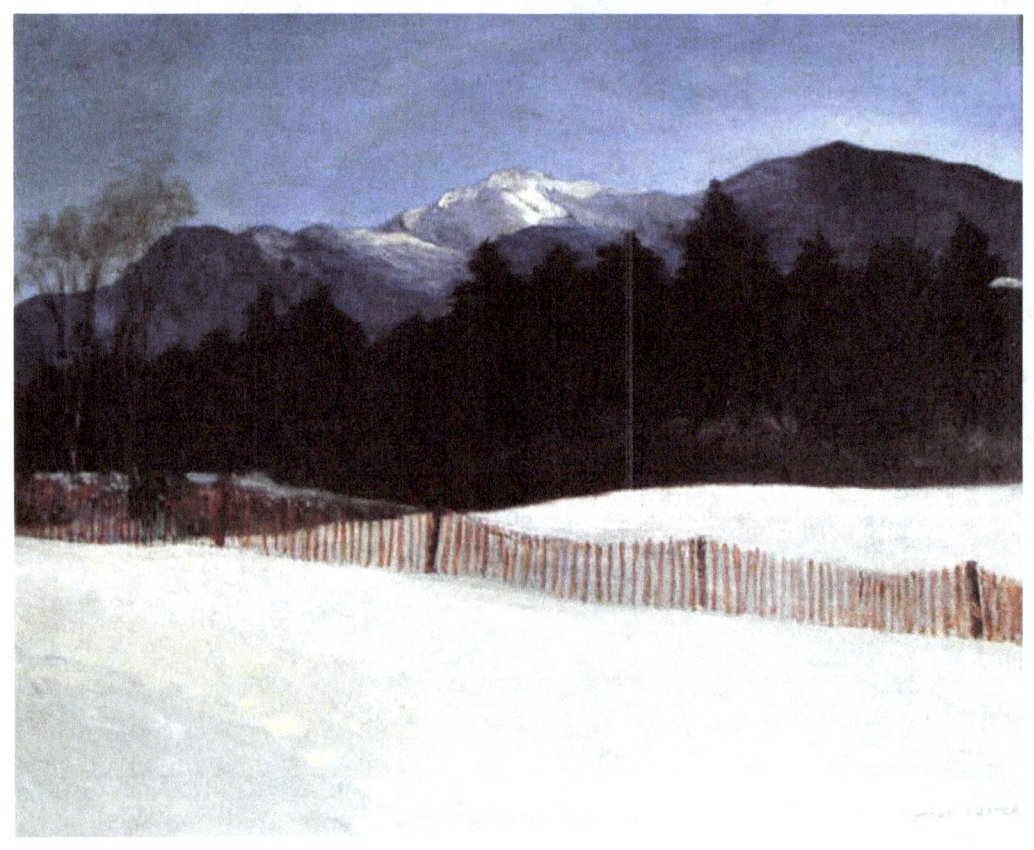

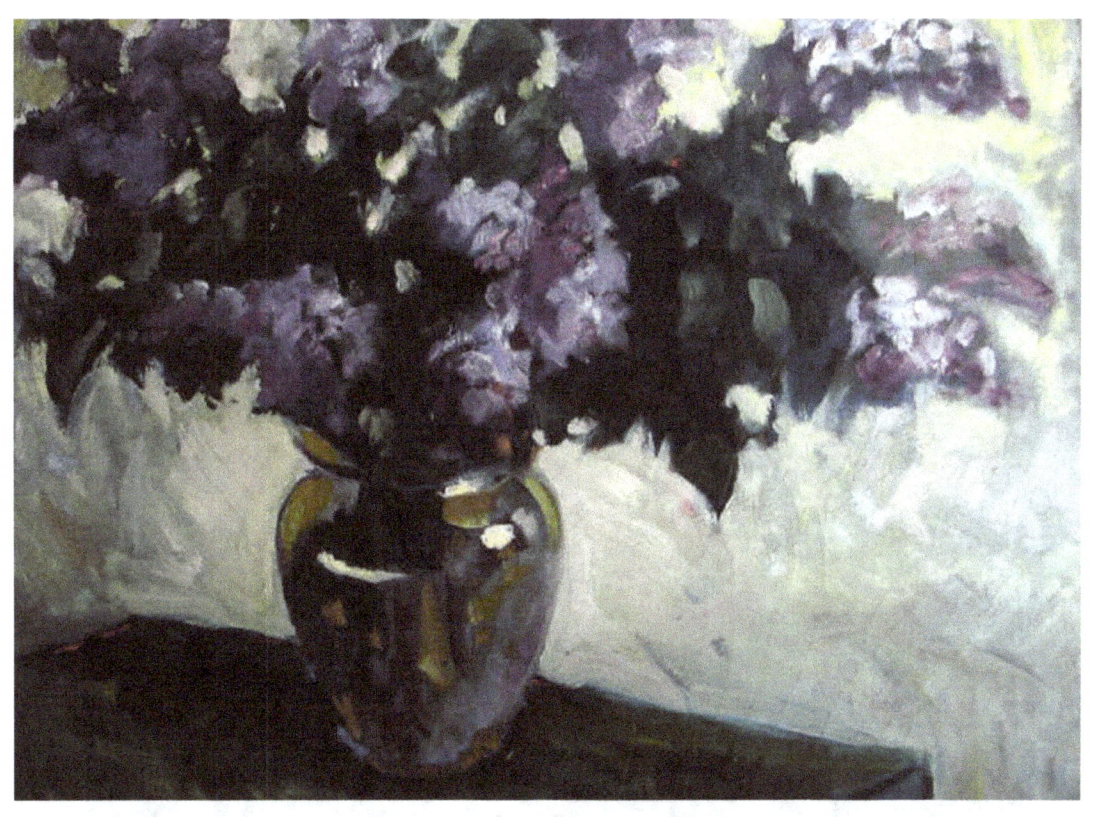

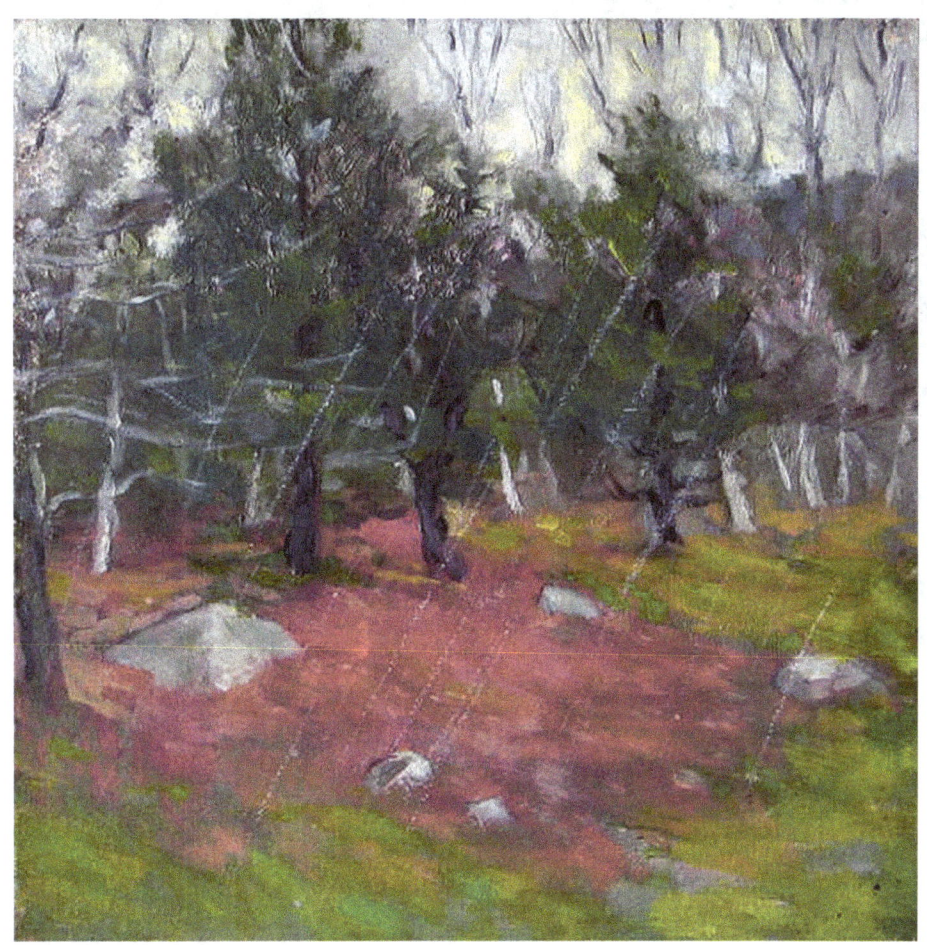

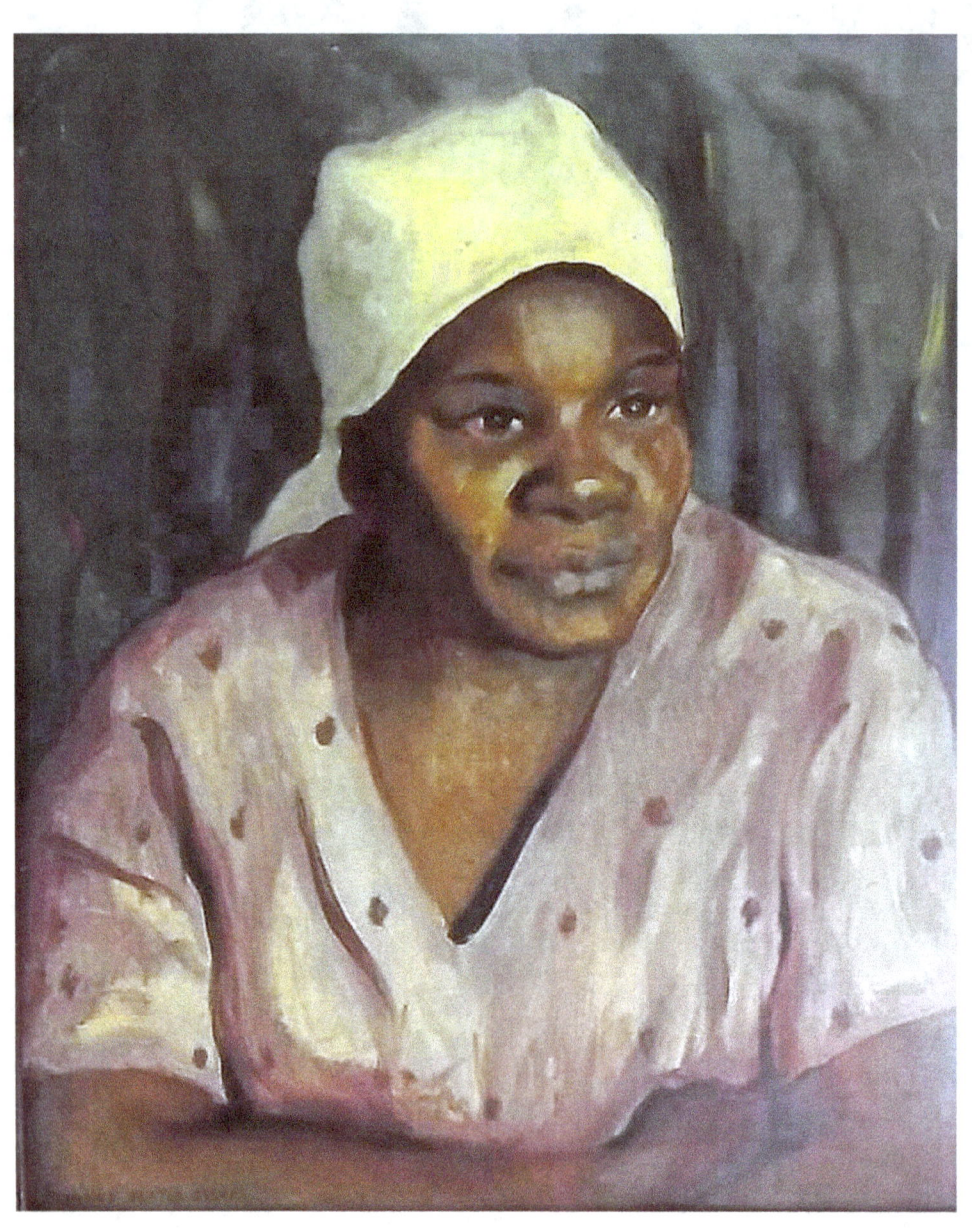

Unknown Model

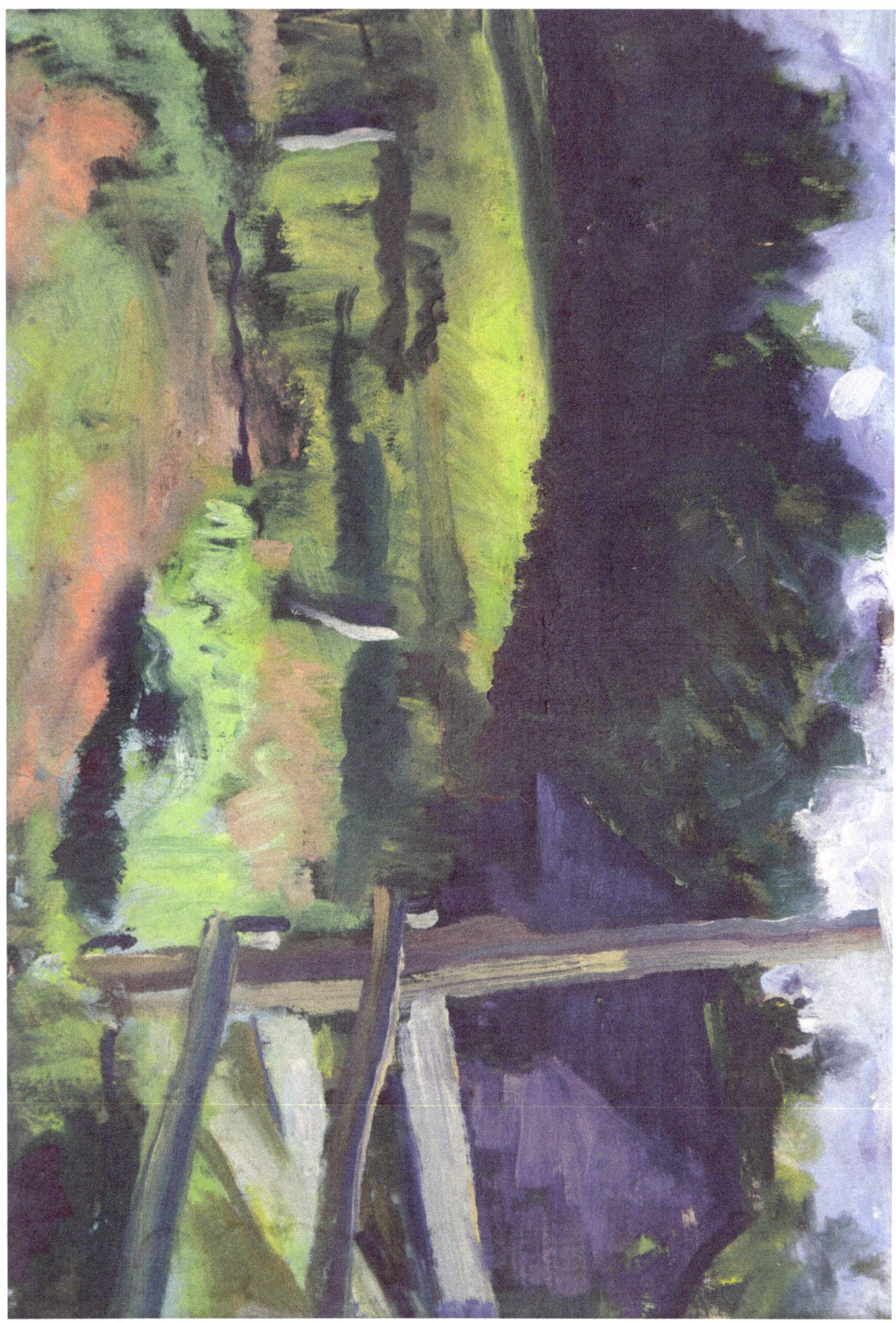

139

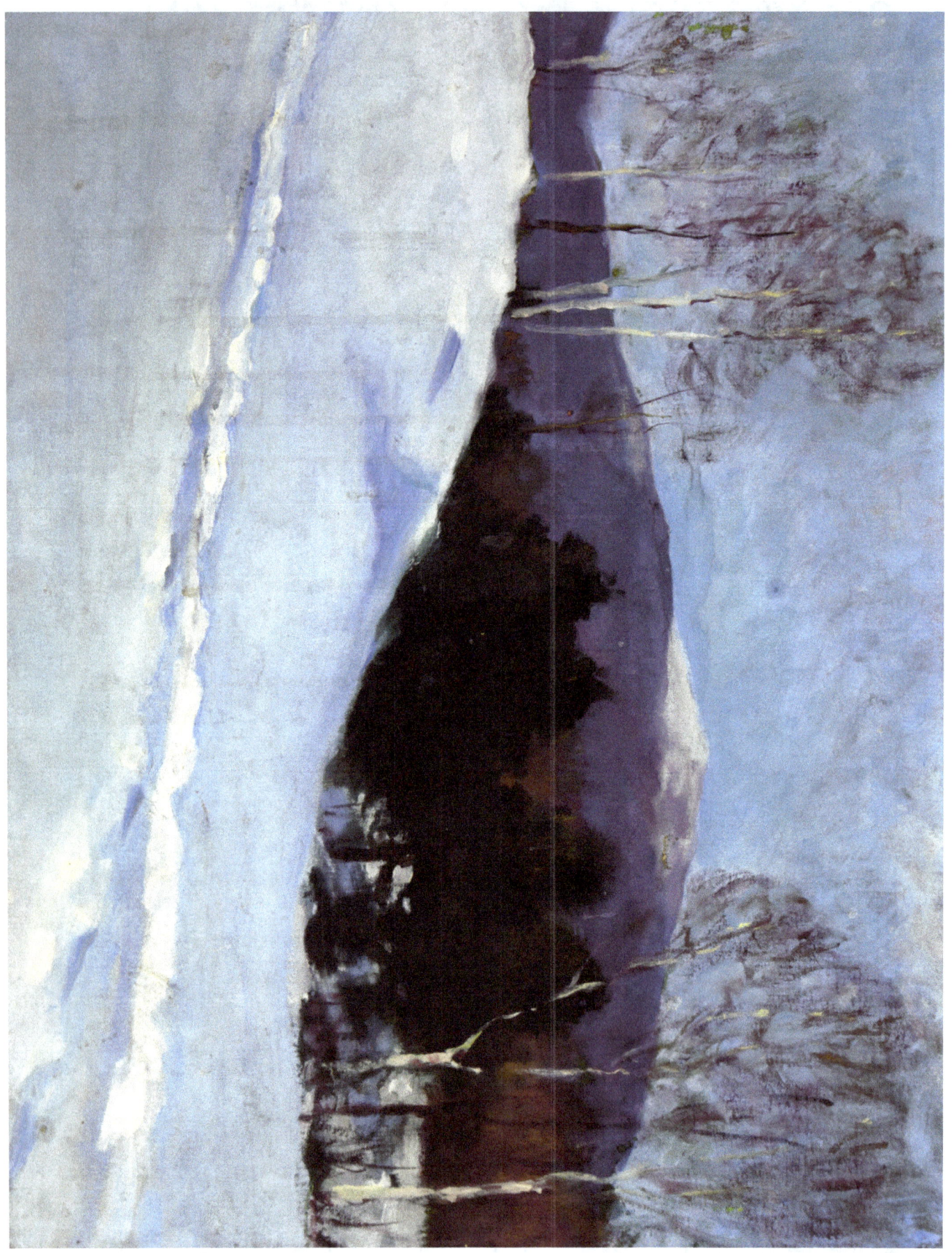

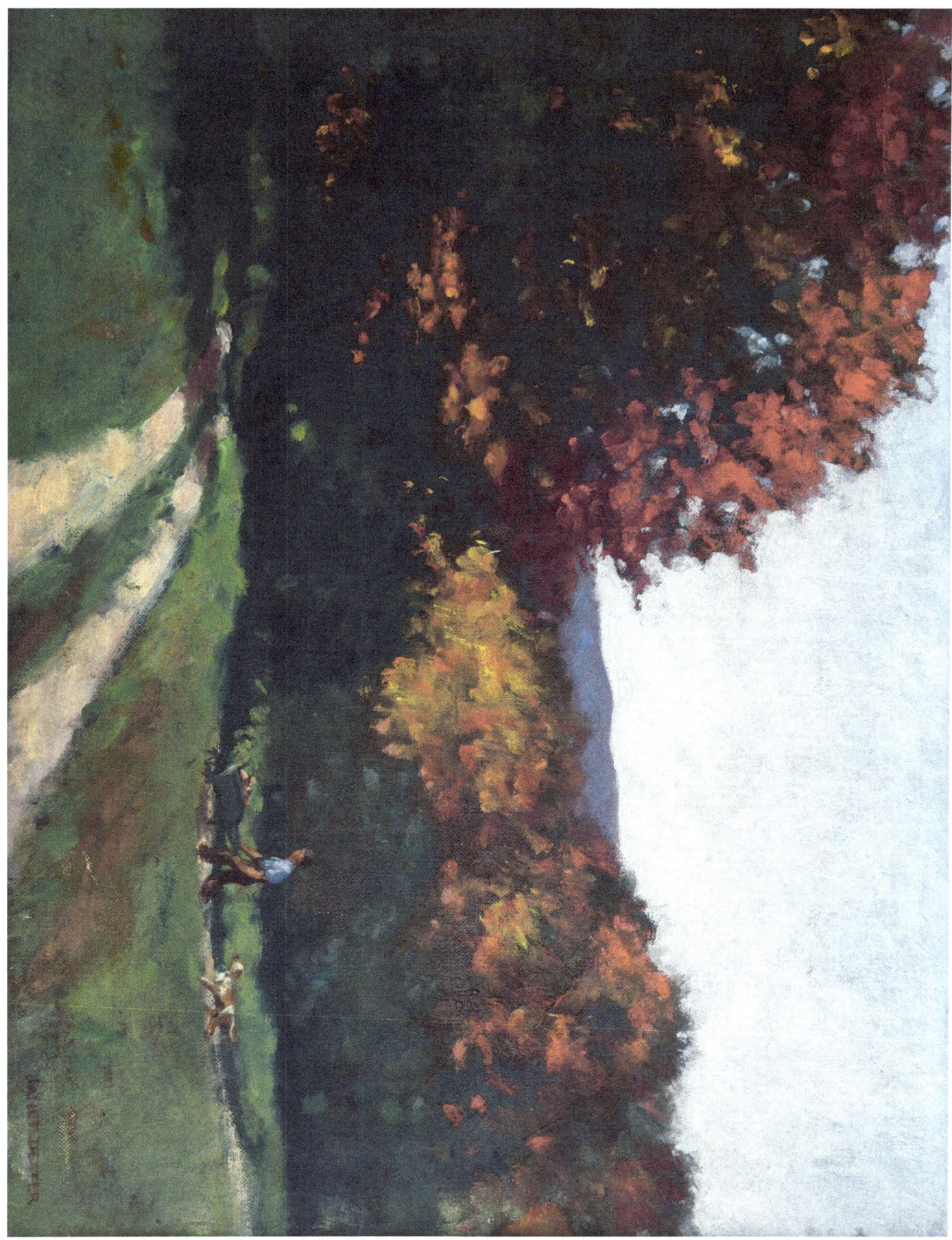

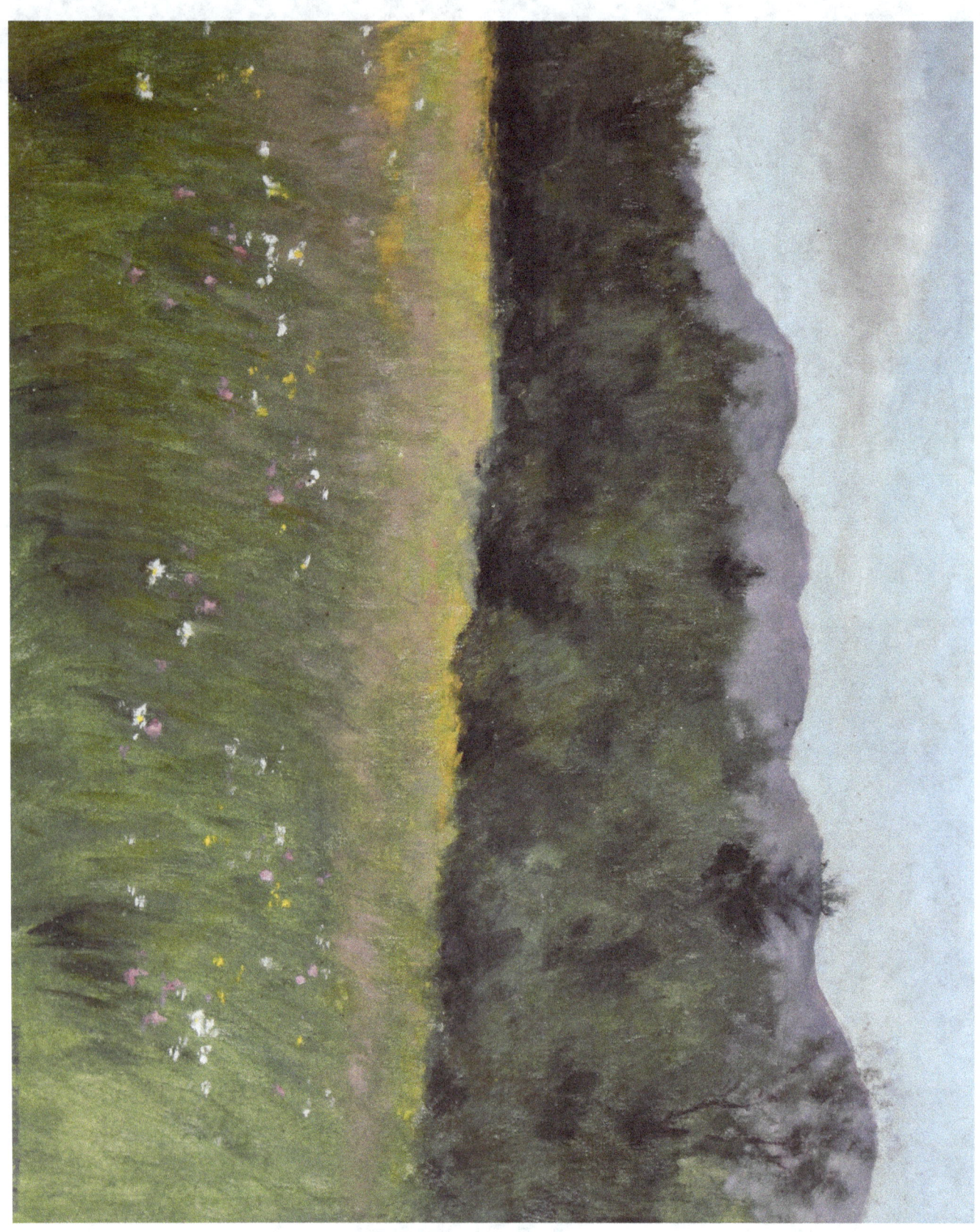

Tumbledown Mountain

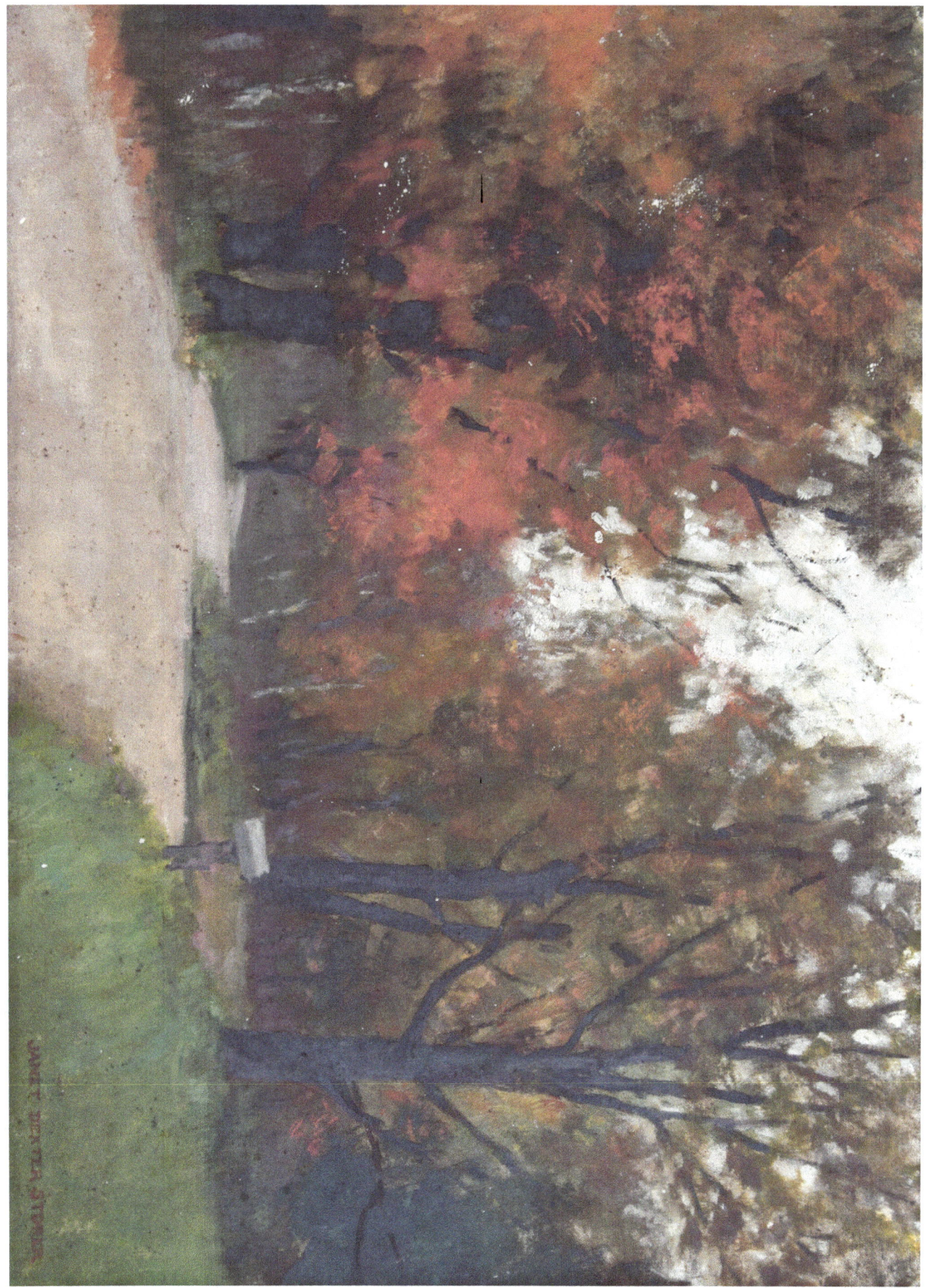

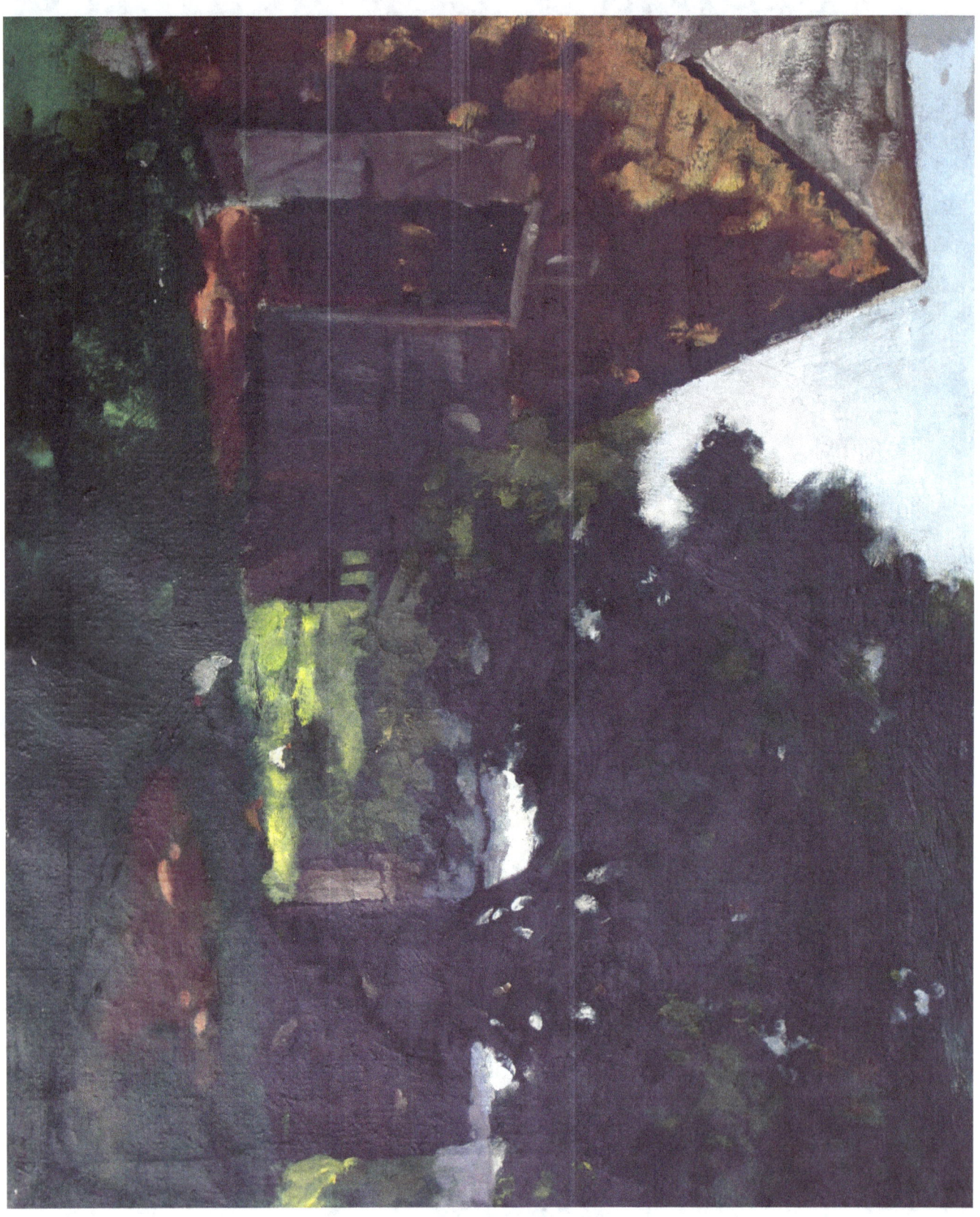

Storer Farm

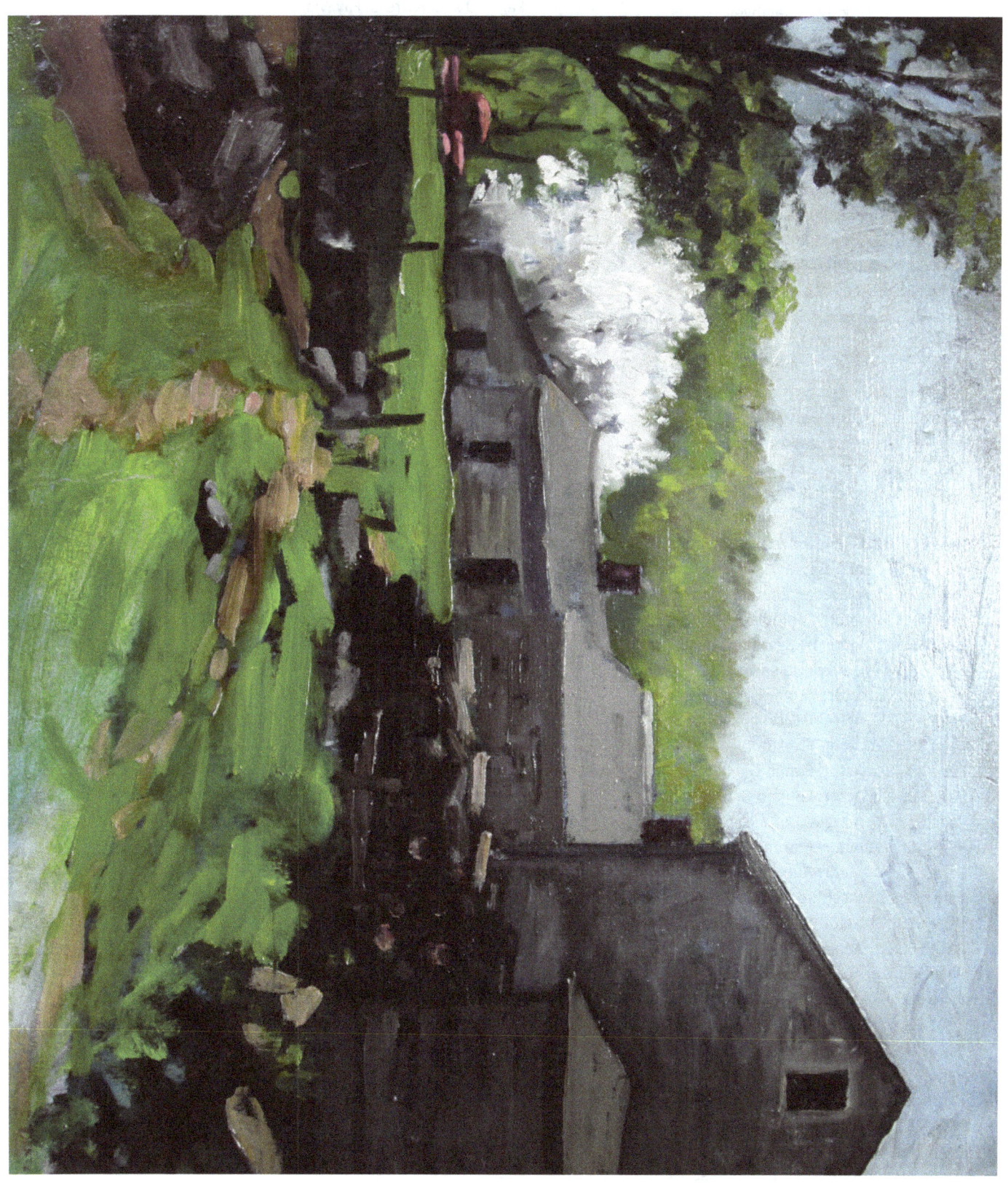

Storer Farm

Index of Portraits/ Artworks

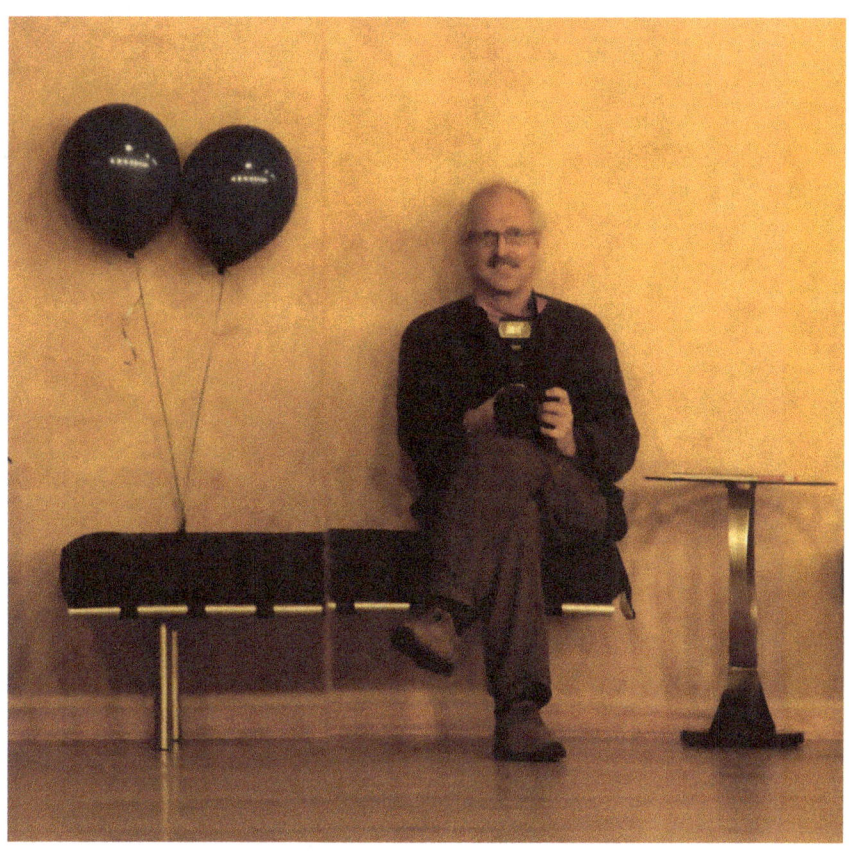

About The Author

Almost fifteen plus years ago Dennis Cleasby vacationed in Weld, Maine. He returned many years; playing music in the State Park, painting, and photographing. He fell in love with the land and people there. Mr. Cleasby lived in Nebraska before his current residence in New York. He found the people of Maine to be similar in spirit to his native Nebraska rural neighbors. It was serendipitous encounters with the Storer family that lead him to take note of the art hanging on their walls and listen to stories of life from the past. Years later the need to put this book together was a combination of admiring Janet Dexter Storer's art and amazement that she had passed through this world virtually unrecognized. Now is her time.

Mr. Cleasby holds two Masters Degrees from Long Island University; Fine Art and Master of Computer Sciences. He works as a photography teacher on Long Island, but his background includes three albums of originally composed music, two previously published books, radio and television guest spots, and a life of travel. He has lived in Costa Rica, Pakistan, and Panama. To date he has visited sixty-seven foreign countries, and counting. In 1989 he was awarded a scholarship to the Art Students League by the Pastel Society of America. (Like Janet Dexter Storer he attended this prestigious art school.)

To find more information and see the authors photography, and art, and listen to his music visit www.denniscleasby.com. Email: dennis@denniscleasby.com or cleasby@optonline.net

www.ingramcontent.com/pod-product-compliance
Lightning Source LLC
Chambersburg PA
CBHW080916170526
45158CB00008B/2134